The Mexican Border Cities

The Mexican Border Cities

Landscape Anatomy and Place Personality

Daniel D. Arreola and James R. Curtis

The University of Arizona Press

Tucson & London

Second printing 1993

THE UNIVERSITY OF ARIZONA PRESS

Copyright © 1993
The Arizona Board of Regents
All Rights Reserved

⊚ This book is printed on acid-free, archival-quality paper.
Manufactured in the U.S.A.

Library of Congress Cataloging-in-Publication Data
Arreola, Daniel D. (Daniel David), 1950–
    The Mexican border cities : landscape anatomy and place personality /
    Daniel D. Arreola, James R. Curtis.
        p.   cm.
    Includes bibliographical references and index.
    ISBN 0-8165-1287-6
    ISBN 0-8165-1441-0 (pbk.)
        1. Cities and towns—Mexico, North.   2. Urbanization—Mexico, North.   3. Mex-
ico, North—Geography.   4. Urban geography—Mexico, North. I. Curtis, James R.,
1947–   . II. Title. III. Title: Border cities.
HT127.7.A77   1993   92-22777
307.76′0972′1—dc20   CIP

British Library Cataloguing-in-Publication Data
A catalogue record for this book is available from the British Library.

For Kit, who inspired landscape sight and insight

Contents

Illustrations and Tables

FIGURES AND GRAPHS

MAPS

PHOTOGRAPHS

TABLES

Foreword

Personal experience and strong academic credentials make Daniel D. Arreola and James R. Curtis ideally suited to write this book. Arreola's first acquaintance with the borderlands was through his maternal grandfather, who worked in the copper mines of Arizona. While growing up in Los Angeles, Arreola visited Tijuana on numerous occasions and had opportunities to explore the city. He even had his first car reupholstered in Tijuana. Curtis's father was stationed on the border during World War I as a soldier in the U.S. Army Cavalry and traveled the region from Del Rio, Texas, to Fort Huachuca, Arizona. Raised in San Diego, California, in an ethnically mixed neighborhood, Curtis also became acquainted with Tijuana at an early age. Among his exploits were attending bullfights and sneaking into Mexico as an underaged "illegal alien" in the trunk of a friend's car.

    Academically, both authors also have had significant preparation for this project. Arreola lived in Veracruz and other parts of Mexico for extended periods while doing the research for his doctoral dissertation. By the early 1980s, he began to undertake field work in northern Mexico and along the border. Curtis chose Alviso, a Chicano *barrio* near San Jose, California, as the site for his dissertation, but he maintained an active interest in Mexico, visiting places such as Nuevo Laredo and Monterrey. Both authors have published extensively on geographical themes relating to the United States and Latin America. I find it remarkable that in their research for *The Mexican Border Cities*, Arreola and Curtis spent time in every one of the eighteen communities that they studied, conducting their work with little grant support. That is indicative of their dedication and passion for the project.

The Mexican Border Cities is essentially a study of the geographic-cultural personality of Mexico's urban centers that abut the boundary with the United States. Combining thorough documentary research with comprehensive field work, the authors render a highly illuminating portrayal of an area that has both fascinated and disturbed outsiders.

To Americans and Mexicans from the interiors of each nation, cities such as Matamoros, Nuevo Laredo, Ciudad Juárez, and Tijuana evoke images of gaudy tourist districts, unsavory bars and nightclubs, loud discotheques, tasteless curio shops, liquor stores, bargain dentists, and "hustlers" of many types. Such uncomplimentary features are standard fare on the border, of course, but *fronterizos* live in an environment that is infinitely more complicated. Arreola and Curtis go far beneath the surface to reveal complex communities of citizens whose lives revolve around different spheres of activity, including tourist, commercial, industrial, and residential districts.

Cognizant of the pivotal role of tourism in shaping the general image and traditional economy of the border cities, the authors discuss this industry with scholarly skill and objectivity. We learn about the system that has evolved over several generations, including the location of the tourist districts, their landscapes, and their peculiarities as "other-directed places." The analysis of the *zonas de tolerancia* ("red-light districts") is particularly interesting. Arreola and Curtis identify different types of zonas and discuss their unique characteristics. Nuevo Laredo's "Boys' Town" serves as a prime example of a famous compound zona known to many people in the United States and Mexico.

Similarities in spatial patterns and landscape character abound between the border cities and urban places in the interior of Mexico, and as the authors point out, it is therefore incorrect to assume that the border communities are not reflective of national norms. Just the same, proximity to the United States has engendered hybridization in some respects, notably in residential and industrial spatial patterns and physical appearance. For example, scores of affluent homes in various Mexican cities resemble American suburban styles. Many *maquiladoras,* or assembly plants, replicate structural forms found on the U.S. side.

Taking into account these external influences, the authors nonetheless insist that the frontier communities are Mexican to the core, and so they will remain far into the future. Viewed geographically, the border area is not a "third country," contrary to what many writers, journalists, and commentators have proclaimed. The physical distinctions between the two sides of the border are clear and dramatic, and the often-presumed tendency toward binational homogeneity finds little support in this study. Looking to the future, Arreola and Curtis anticipate that the expected free-trade agreement will enhance hybridization, but in their opinion, it will not alter the fundamental character of "Mexicanness" in these communities.

Such a conclusion will help allay the fears of many Mexicans that the border cities are awash in foreign influences and are suffering from "denationalization." That is a long-standing concern among officials from Mexico City, who have taken steps to prevent *agringamiento* (anglicization) and to strengthen national identity among *fronterizos*. Recent manifestations of such efforts are found in complexes created during the 1960s by the Programa Nacional Fronterizo (PRONAF), where museums and theaters extol the nation's heritage, and in statues of national heroes that line principal avenues in major border cities. These cultural centers and historical icons are reminders to *fronterizos* that the nation expects them to know, identify with, and be proud of their roots and the traditions and customs of the motherland.

Students of the border will find this a very useful study because of its focus on concrete features in the border environment supported by ample illustrations. It is deserving of a special place in the literature for its regional coverage, examining the border from Matamoros to Tijuana. Heretofore, urban studies of the Mexican borderlands have concentrated on individual cities, most notably Ciudad Juárez and Tijuana.

The findings in this book suggest the need for similar research on the U.S. side and comparative studies with other border regions. As transnational economic integration proceeds in the Americas and in Europe, more and more border communities are becoming prominent centers of trade, commerce, and industry. Hybridization is shaping physical and cultural environments in border zones as never before. Arreola and Curtis have provided an excellent model that can be applied by others seeking to enlarge our understanding of border phenomena.

Oscar J. Martínez

Preface

This book is about eighteen Mexican cities that line the international border where Mexico meets the United States. It is an attempt to understand the settlements as a type of urban form as well as a call for appreciation of the places as fundamentally Mexican towns, despite their proximity to and historic interaction with the United States. The border cities considered here currently range in size from small towns to major metropolises. Nevertheless, as we demonstrate through description and interpretation of the geographical anatomy and personality of these places, they share common elements of urban form and character, regardless of size. We believe, therefore, that the Mexican border cities form a distinctive urban subsystem within Mexico.

Although we have spent most of our lives in the region, this study was formally launched in January 1987 when we drove the length of the border to gather information for an invited contribution to a scholarly anthology dealing with cultural themes in the borderlands. This experience convinced us that there was a need to assess more fully the contemporary urban cultural geography of the Mexican border cities. Numerous field excursions together and independently followed over the ensuing years. We cannot emphasize how critical it has been, and will continue to be, to investigate these places in the field as well as the library. In many cases, as a result of follow-up field work, we found that the landscape was transforming faster than we could freeze it in our minds for study and analysis. This dynamic quality shows few signs of abating.

From its inception, this study was a joint effort. Together we read, edited, and shared ideas as well as research materials for the manuscript. The scope of the project, however, coupled with our own specialized interests, led to a division of labor: Curtis took primary responsibility for writing

Chapters Three, Four, and Five, while Arreola assumed principal author-ship for Chapters One, Two, Six, Seven, and Eight.

Formal presentations of research results from this work were delivered to the Conference of Latin Americanist Geographers and the North American Culture Society, both in 1989, as well as to the Association of Border-land Scholars in 1991 and the Association of American Geographers in 1992. We thank the North American Culture Society and the American Geographical Society for permission to reproduce published materials based upon this research. We also wish to acknowledge the courtesy of the Na-tional Archives in Washington, D.C., and the Pimeria Alta Historical Soci-ety in Nogales, Arizona, for permission to reproduce materials from their photographic collections. Geographers Charles R. Gildersleeve, Marvin W. Baker, Jr., and Peter R. Hoffman were kind enough to allow us to reproduce versions of their urban-structure models from their respective doctoral dissertations.

Several individuals and institutions were generous in sharing their knowledge about the border cities in the field and over the telephone, or in making accessible materials that were unavailable in our respective univer-sity libraries. We especially would like to acknowledge Jorge O. Gonzalez, former Curator of the Nuevo Santander Museum at Laredo Junior College; Yolanda Gonzalez, Special Collections Librarian, Arnulfo L. Oliveira Li-brary, Texas Southmost College in Brownsville; David Mycue, Curator of Archives and Collections, Hidalgo County Historical Museum in Edinburg; George R. Gause, Jr., Special Collections Librarian, University of Texas Pan American in Edinburg; the staffs of the Nettie Lee Benson Latin American Collection at the University of Texas at Austin, Special Collections Library at the University of Texas at El Paso, and most gratefully, those of the Inter-library Loan Services of the Sterling Evans Library at Texas A&M Univer-sity, Hayden Library at Arizona State University (A.S.U.), and Low Library at Oklahoma State University (O.S.U.).

Cartographic assistance was provided by the Geography Departments at Texas A&M University, Oklahoma State University, and Arizona State University. We thank Linda DeLeón at Texas A&M, who computer-drafted several early versions of our maps. Gayle Maxwell at O.S.U. and Barbara Trapido and her staff at A.S.U. each drafted maps and reproduced photo-graphic materials with spirit and efficiency. At The University of Arizona Press we are grateful to senior editor Joanne O'Hare, who saw merit in the project and gave support through the steps leading to publication and to Judith Allen, Marie Webner, and Omega Clay for editorial and production assistance.

We want particularly to thank our wives, "Las Dos Patricias," who supported this undertaking from the beginning and tolerated our frequent flights to the border. A special thanks also to Courtney and Kit Curtis, whose demands that Daddy deliver gifts from Mexico on his return encouraged even greater exploration of the tourist districts.

Finally, this work is dedicated to our mentor, Christopher ("Kit") L. Salter, who nurtured our early fascination with landscape study.

The Mexican Border Cities

1   Mexican Border-City Imperative

Like an idée fixe, the popular American perception of the Mexican border towns still conjures two persistent images. First, border towns are seen as tawdry yet convenient and accommodating tourist outlets, albeit for short-term visits. Second, they are viewed as small places, not really large enough to be considered cities. Although this view has become something of a cliché, much exploited by the mass media, it never was entirely accurate. Increasingly, it is more a product of fantasy than reality. Fueled by high rates of in-migration and economic growth, the border corridor of nearly 2,000 miles has emerged over the last three decades as one of the most urbanized regions in Mexico. Its largest cities are among the fastest growing in the Western Hemisphere. The six largest of these cities in rank order—Ciudad Juárez, Tijuana, Mexicali, Matamoros, Reynosa, and Nuevo Laredo—have populations that range from 800,000 down to 200,000, according to the preliminary results of the 1990 census. In 1950 their combined population was less than half a million. As a consequence of extraordinary growth, these communities have become dynamic urban places where a new structure and urban landscape have evolved. They exhibit aspects of Latin American as well as North American cities, but contain elements that are unique to the border as a place. Significantly, although almost all of these cities have grown, the degree of change varies considerably. It runs along a continuum from small, stable towns with more traditional urban forms and only a few thousand people to rapidly modernizing border metropolises with several hundred thousand inhabitants. This suggests that the border settlements are not today, and probably never were, as one-dimensional as they have been portrayed historically. Yet in spite of their diversity, the border cities from Matamoros to Tijuana have been shaped by similar forces. They share an

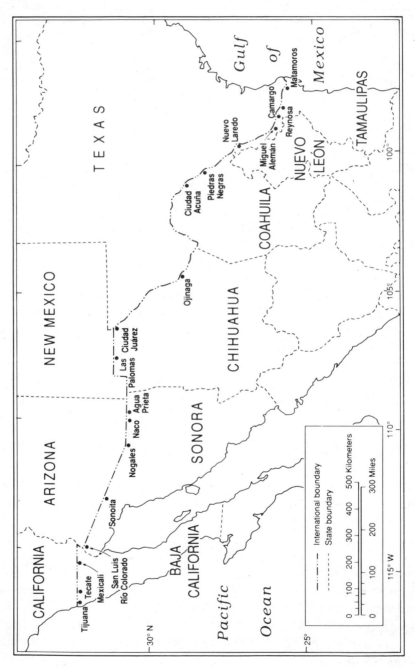

FIGURE 1.1 The Mexican border cities.

experience dissimilar to other regions of Mexico; it sets them apart and gives them a distinctive landscape anatomy and personality.

Whereas several important scholarly investigations of the border region have assessed conditions on both the Mexican and American sides (Nostrand 1970; Martínez 1977), our study considers only Mexican cities along the international boundary. We acknowledge that this is a dynamic zone of transborder exchange and interaction; people and products, ideas and information, and capital and technology move relatively freely across the boundary. The intent and scope of our analysis, however, make it unreasonable to examine and compare cities on both sides of the political divide. It is our contention that the Mexican border cities are less understood, and the pace and magnitude of their landscape changes are greater than those of their counterparts in the United States. With the exception of San Diego across from Tijuana, every Mexican border city today is larger than its American neighbor. Therefore, at this time it seems important to interpret the cultural landscapes of the Mexican border cities rather than those to the north.

We have purposely selected these eighteen border cities, named in order from east to west: Matamoros; Reynosa; Camargo; Miguel Alemán; Nuevo Laredo; Piedras Negras; Ciudad Acuña; Ojinaga; Ciudad Juárez; Las Palomas; Agua Prieta; Naco; Nogales; Sonoita; San Luis Río Colorado; Mexicali; Tecate; and Tijuana (see Fig. 1.1). We chose not to include other settlements, such as Sasabe, Boquillas, Villa Hidalgo, or Ciudad Díaz Ordaz, that are also on the Mexican boundary. The principal criteria used in selecting the eighteen settlements were twofold. First, these cities each share the borderline with a neighboring American community. Granted, some of the American counterparts, such as Tecate, California, across from Tecate, Baja California, or Lukeville, Arizona, adjacent to Sonoita, Sonora, are very small. Nevertheless, we believed it was important to examine border communities that have direct interaction with an American cohort. Because one of the claims raised in the professional literature about the Mexican border is the great dependence of Mexican settlements on the United States, we decided to use these criteria as a control to assess the influence of nearby American places on the anatomy and personality of Mexican border cities. This also eliminated relatively large places, such as Ensenada, Baja California, and Río Bravo, Tamaulipas, because technically they are located some distance from the borderline. A second reason we chose eighteen settlements—and not just the six or ten largest—was that we wanted to evaluate how selected elements of border urban geography compared across the hierarchy of places and over time. We believe that if the Mexican border cities are to be understood as a regional urban system, we need a basis for differentiating how the settlements are morphologically similar and different by population size as well as by time of settlement.

A second criterion that guided our investigation of the Mexican border cities was the need to elaborate on how these settlements are fundamentally Mexican urban places. This assertion is based not only on the obvious fact that the cities are sovereign municipalities of Mexico, but more importantly, on how their landscapes compare to cities away from the border. Thus, in several instances our interpretations of internal structure and landscape anatomy apply as well to traditional Mexican towns; we have not restricted our analyses to only those elements that may be unique or particular to border cities.

The cities we have chosen to examine range from settlements founded in the seventeenth through the twentieth centuries, and as already stated, vary significantly in size. For that reason, we thought it necessary to provide several case studies supplementing our broad interpretations and accentuating the diverse place personalities that characterize these communities. To complement our goal of describing the changing urban cultural landscapes of the border cities, we have presented case studies of Ciudad Juárez, Camargo, Matamoros, Tijuana, Reynosa, and Nogales; vignettes of several other places also are offered.

THE BORDER CITY IN THE BORDERLAND

Although there may be some ambiguity about how the border region is defined, there can be no argument with the notion that the area, however delimited, includes a borderline and borderland (Pederson 1990; Curtis 1991). The borderline is the result of political decisions based upon events and circumstances of the middle nineteenth century involving Mexico and the United States, and its particular history is still being chronicled and interpreted (Griswold del Castillo 1990; Metz 1989). The borderland, or borderlands preferably, is much more of an enigma (Stoddard 1975/1976: 5). The intellectual lineage of the area's definition likely derives from Bolton, who understood it in the context of the northern frontier of New Spain (Bannon 1974). The more recent term "United States–Mexico Borderlands" suggests a loosely defined geographic region or zone that straddles the borderline (Cumberland 1960; Stoddard et al. 1983; Reich 1984; Valk 1988; Lorey 1991). Typically, these borderlands encompass the political boundaries of four states on the U.S. side, Texas, New Mexico, Arizona, and California, as well as six Mexican states, Tamaulipas, Nuevo León, Coahuila,

Chihuahua, Sonora, and Baja California. Some also include Colorado and Baja California Sur.

Scholarly writings about this region have addressed its history of conflict (Martínez 1988) and especially its economic variation (Fernández 1977; Hansen 1981; Pick et al. 1987). Some have focused particularly on one or another subregion of the borderlands (Dunbier 1968; House 1982). That the borderlands represent a cultural configuration that may vary internally and extend well beyond the usual geographic limits has been explored (Nostrand 1983; Garreau 1981; Langley 1988), while the Mexican side of this divide, *El Norte,* has been considered distinctive from other areas of Mexico (León-Portilla 1972).

In area as well as by definition, the border is a separate resolution. It is usually depicted as a subset of the larger borderlands, yet holding tight to the borderline—what one sensationalized account called "a sixteen-hundred-mile pleasure strip" (Demaris 1970: 4). This bicultural zone, traversed and elegantly described in recent accounts, has been called "the common ground" and a "third country" between Mexico and the United States (Weisman 1986: xiii; Miller 1981: xii). Along this *frontera,* as the Mexicans call it, there is evidence of a cultural nationalism as well as a popular or vernacular culture specific to the zone (Ojeda 1983; Monsiváis 1978). Arguably, the nerve centers of this frontera culture are the settlements that have taken root and persisted here, some from colonial times but most of quite recent heritage.

When one looks for direction and explanation about the geography, history, and character of these Mexican border settlements as places or as a system, there is no single source to draw on despite the call for such work almost two decades ago (Gildersleeve 1975/1976: 19). The focus of previous effort, although limited, has been on the largest of these settlements, where information and materials are more available if not abundant (Price 1973a; Martínez 1978; Young 1986; Herzog 1990). The neglect shown the majority of these communities is perplexing as they are inherently interesting and regionally important places. Perhaps it is best explained by a perception that they are "illegitimate children" of a larger social system (Alvarez 1984: 120). A popular sentiment, for example, holds that the Mexican border communities are more "Americanized" because of their proximity to the United States; thus, they are not the *real* Mexico. We accept the idea that the Mexican border cities are regional variants of Mexico's urban system, but we reject the view that they are somehow atypical of Mexican cities in most fundamental ways. We contend that the Mexican border cities are first and foremost Mexican places, but places that have been tempered significantly by the strong hybridizing that results from interaction with the United States (Griffin and Ford 1976). However, many of these "gringo" influences—from fast-food restaurants to enclosed shopping malls to middle-class, auto-dependent suburbs with contemporary houses—are not restricted to the border. They are now found in larger cities throughout Mexico and much of the rest of Latin America.

LANDSCAPE ANATOMY AND PLACE PERSONALITY

If Mexican border cities are Mexican places modified by American influences, how can we differentiate these shaping forces? We propose to examine this dynamic from the perspectives of *urban morphology*, or city form, and the urban built environment, hence our emphasis on landscape anatomy. We believe that the cultural dimension in these cities cannot be adequately assessed except through historical and contemporary exploration of form and pattern. In fact, a recent critical study that compared American and Canadian cities found that cultural context, frequently neglected, was indeed a crucial factor in helping to explain urban differences (Goldberg and Mercer 1986: 1–8). We hold, therefore, that the landscape anatomy of the border cities provides clues to cultural differences between Mexico and the United States. Whereas urban geographers have most often interpreted cities as economic systems, we believe along with others that cities are equally cultural creations and need to be understood as such (Agnew et al. 1984: 8; Ley 1988: 98–105). Our contention is that urban landscape offers a convenient visual medium for interpreting the border cities as places, and critical analysis of landscape anatomy can be a vehicle for understanding place personality.

Most people regard the humanmade landscape as something to be looked at rather than thought about (Lewis 1979: 11). Moreover, we often associate the concept of landscape with the practice of landscaping, the decoration of gardens or building exteriors. To geographers, landscape is a medium, a cultural repository that can be read for clues about human preferences and the past (Rowntree and Conkey 1980: 461). What buried artifacts are to the archaeologist, built forms and expressions of the landscape are to the cultural geographer: diagnostic means for dating and evidence for interpretation about people and place. One geographer has even proclaimed that "ordinary places and landscapes are far more complex than anything encountered in an econometric model or a physicist's laboratory" (Relph 1984: 212). The buildings and forms of the landscape convey subtle yet important messages about cultural meaning—what one scholar has termed a form of "nonverbal communication" (Rapoport 1982).

Because our focus is on Mexican border cities, our bias is toward understanding the urban landscape rather than more rural, small-town anatomy (Stanislawski 1950). Similarly, because most of the settlements we have studied are products of the late nineteenth and twentieth centuries, our interpretations have been influenced by the character of modern urban landscapes (Relph 1987). We believe that the urban landscape can act as a mirror of the society as a whole, revealing signs and signatures that are held in common by a people. Our analysis will be concerned especially with those elements of urban landscape considered most diagnostic of cultural heritage: town plan, land-use pattern, and building fabric (Conzen 1978: 145).

Personality is a term generally reserved for reference to individuals or small groups, but on occasion, geographers have applied it to nations and even regions (France, Vidal de la Blache 1928; Britain, Fox 1932; Mexico, Sauer 1941; Ireland, Evans 1970; and the Algarve of Portugal, Stanislawski 1963; all cited in Dunbar 1974: 25–33). Places, like individuals, can be distinctive by themselves or as small collectives. Cities are specialized places, yet they too can project personality—the result of environment, history, and people interacting in a particular locale and situation (Sabelberg 1985; Venturi et al. 1977; Lewis 1976; Banham 1971). We believe that Mexican border cities, although individual and distinctive places in their own right, share a common general location, experience, and resulting personality that is visible in their landscapes and internal geographies. We conceptualize this in a landscape model of border cities. If the study of *urban morphogenesis*, defined as the creation and subsequent transformation of city form, is to be advanced in Latin America, then we need many more examples for comparative analysis (Vance 1990: 38; Sargent 1982: 221–234; Griffin and Ford 1980). We offer the landscape model for Mexican border cities as an additional tile to this incomplete regional, geographic mosaic.

ORGANIZATION

We present our observations and interpretations of the Mexican border cities systematically rather than regionally. Within each chapter, however, we have attempted to describe and analyze the topic on two scales: with the macro view, an overall examination of the border cities as a collective, and with the micro view, in complementary case studies or vignettes for towns that exemplify the chapter discussion.

Chapters Two and Three introduce the border cities historically and spatially. Our concern is to provide a context for understanding the range of border-city settlement over time and across geographic space. Although most of these towns were founded in the late nineteenth and early twentieth centuries, several are of colonial heritage. Examination of the founding conditions and subsequent growth phases for these cities reveals patterns of common experience yet differential growth. The cities are evaluated structurally to determine their collective morphologies. We describe a traditional and a modern context for the border cities and advance a generalized model that reflects the patterns of land use typical of most border communities. Case studies give focus to these larger topical issues by examining the founding and growth of Ciudad Juárez, the traditional urban structure of Camargo, and the modern city structure of Matamoros.

Chapters Four, Five, Six, and Seven explore border-city landscapes of tourist activity, commerce, residence, industry, and transit. Tourist districts may be the most recognized landscapes of the border, yet they are peculiar to these cities. They are not found in this arrangement anywhere else in Mexico. In Chapter Four, we describe tourist districts along the border, interpret their internal geographies, and discuss their landscape components. Special emphasis is given to the images of Mexico promoted by the iconography in these districts. An element of the traditional tourist district, the *zona,* or adult-entertainment enclave, is analyzed separately as a type of pariah landscape that has persisted in one form or another in many border cities. Tijuana, perhaps the most-visited border city, is examined as a case study of the historical development of a tourist district. Nuevo Laredo's zona is described in vignette as typical of one of the larger adult-entertainment compounds.

If the tourist districts are unique to border towns, the landscapes of commerce mirror the traditional and modern character found in many Mexican cities. In Chapter Five we analyze the inter- and intra-regional patterns of *el centro*—the heart of the traditional Mexican city, including plazas and retail land use. This district as found in border towns is compared with the central business districts in North American cities. Further, we assess the landscape of new automobile-oriented strips or spines that extend away from el centro, creating hybrid commercial spaces. These strips combine auto mobility with the recognizable signatures of the North American suburban landscape, such as convenience stores, fast-food eateries, and shopping malls. A case study of Reynosa discusses these spaces in the context of a large border city.

The landscape of residential space makes up the largest portion of the urban built environment. Houses are the greater part of this townscape fabric, and their arrangement and external features offer clues to building preferences and insights into cultural predilections. In Chapter Six we examine the range of contemporary housing in border cities, as well as traditional and modern dwelling types. The concept of *housescape* is used to interpret the "Mexicanness" of dwelling spaces. Characteristic features include the enclosure of personal properties as a building trait and the use of particular institutionalized and personal landscape signatures. A vignette of an upper-income residential district in Nuevo Laredo provides a place-specific example of one housescape type.

Outside of the tourist districts, the element of Mexican border cities most commonly recognizable to the average North American is probably the *maquiladora,* or "twin plant" as it is often incorrectly called. This industrial arrangement is only about three decades old along the border. Although we hear much about it through the news media, especially in regard to impending Mexico–U.S. trade relations, we have little sense of what it looks like or how it is situated in the border city. In Chapter Seven, we explore not only the geography of maquiladora industrial parks as a landscape signature but also describe the range of older industrial activities that historically have marked the border towns. Railroad corridors, yards, and bridge crossings particularly have persisted in more than half of the border cities studied. A third focus of this chapter is the assessment of the rapidly changing nature of transit across the border, both the routes and the varying volume of traffic into and out of the border cities. These conditions will likely affect future trade arrangements between Mexico and the United States. A case study of Nogales captures the range of these activities and landscapes as they have developed in a medium-sized border city.

Finally, we have chosen to use *norteamericano* (North American) to refer to persons from the United States and Canada as well as to their cities. Traditionally, geographers have grouped these nationalities together regionally, although it is recognized that they are distinct social and cultural systems. Our preference for North American is intended to distinguish American and Canadian from Mexican, the latter by convention being associated culturally with Latin America. Whereas some might feel that Anglo American is the appropriate counterpart to Latin American, in Mexico the practice has been to use norteamericano when referring to non-Mexicans from the United States and Canada. Therefore, we believe North American will best connote the distinction we wish to make.

Mexican government statistics, especially for population, have been taken from published census figures where available and have not been adjusted. Several scholars believe these populations to be seriously undercounted for the more recent reporting periods. Furthermore, inconsistencies exist in the reported populations of settlement units by type of settlement. Up to 1970, populations were reported in government sources by *localidad* (locality/place) or *ciudad* (city). In 1980 and 1990, however, populations were given by *municipio,* which usually includes a larger area than a locality/place or city and is somewhat analogous to U.S. counties. The peculiarities of these differences are discussed in Chapter Two.

Throughout the text, we have followed the convention of using Spanish-language spellings and accents as they appear in cited sources. For Mexican place names, we have followed the usage on topographic maps published by the Dirección General de Geografía. For Spanish place names in the United States, we have followed the U.S. Board on Geographic Names. For example, we use the English spelling and name Rio Grande, although in Mexico the official name is Río Bravo del Norte.

2 Founding and Growth of Border Cities

Despite the presence of colonial settlements, there was no border—and therefore, no true border towns—before 1848. During the second half of the nineteenth century, a series of small population nodes emerged along the border, and a few of these places became modest towns. In the hierarchy of Mexican cities, however, the border communities remained marginal. Between 1877 and 1900, no border town ranked among Mexico's twenty-five largest cities (Scott 1982: 38). Urbanization along the border has been largely a twentieth-century phenomenon.

In 1940, six border settlements were among Mexico's thirty-seven largest cities, but the two highest ranking, Ciudad Juárez and Matamoros, were only twenty-fifth and twenty-sixth, respectively (Scott 1982: 124). By 1970, three border cities—Ciudad Juárez, Mexicali, and Tijuana—ranked sixth, seventh, and eleventh respectively among Mexican cities (Wilkie 1984: 323). Urban growth has accelerated in the last three decades to the point that border cities are now among the fastest-growing places in Mexico.

The growth of border settlements in the nineteenth century was consistent with the pattern of urban development in Mexico set in motion during the Porfiriato, the political reign of Porfirio Díaz (1876–1910). This involved the development and export of mineral resources to foreign markets and construction of a railroad system to serve this industry. Along the border, mining especially spurred growth in Nogales, Agua Prieta, Ciudad Juárez, and Piedras Negras. Transportation development was a catalyst to growth in several border cities; Ciudad Juárez, Nuevo Laredo, Piedras Negras, and Nogales each became a railroad node before 1900 (Scott 1982: 29). In the twentieth century, agricultural development in northern Mexico benefited Mexicali, San Luis Río Colorado, Miguel Alemán and Matamoros, further stimulating regional and urban growth. In spite of these regional catalysts, twentieth-century border cities have grown mainly in response to local circumstances that are a function of their border location, tourism, and privileged manufacturing industries.

This chapter examines the founding and growth of border cities from Spanish colonial times to 1990. Although some towns were founded as long as 300 years ago, most of the Mexican border cities emerged in the nineteenth and twentieth centuries. Rapid growth has resulted largely from changes that began in the middle twentieth century. This growth was sustained chiefly by migrations, from the regional hearths of interior Mexico, which have historically sent migrants north. Since 1970, however, natural increase has replaced in-migration, or the movement from one part of Mexico to another, as the primary means of growth in almost all Mexican border cities. We will include a case study of Ciudad Juárez, which documents the population growth and geographic expansion of the oldest and largest Mexican border city, but whose pattern of growth is not unlike that of larger urban centers.

COLONIAL BEGINNINGS

Although most of the border cities were founded in the nineteenth and twentieth centuries, a handful of settlements were initiated during the Spanish colonial era. Six of these have persisted to the present and are considered in this study: Ciudad Juárez, Ojinaga, Sonoita, Matamoros, Camargo, and Reynosa. The earliest border settlements were part of New Spain's push to occupy and control its far northern frontier (Gerhard 1982). The Spanish system of colonizing the frontier involved three separate jurisdictional settlements: the mission, intended as a foothold of ecclesiastical conversion of Indians and kept under clerical authority; the *presidio,* which functioned under military supervision to guard against hostilities at strategic points along the frontier; and the *villa,* which was a civil settlement intended for colonists under the authority of an *ayuntamiento,* or municipal council (Bolton 1917; Moorhead 1975; Cardenas 1963). Along what is today the Mexican side of the border, the Spanish founded missions at Sonoita, Paso del Norte (present Ciudad Juárez), La Junta (present Ojinaga), San Juan Bautista (present Guerrero outside Piedras Negras), and San Juan de Los Esteros/Refugio (present Matamoros). The Spanish established presidios at Paso del Norte, La Junta, and San Juan Bautista/Presidio de Rio Grande, and they founded villas at Camargo, Reynosa, and Mier (Table 2.1). Because Mier does not border the international boundary today nor does it

TABLE 2.1 Mexican Border-Settlement Founding

	Date	Type
COLONIAL		
Paso del Norte (Ciudad Juárez)	1659	mission, presidio
San Juan Bautista-Presidio del Río Grande[a]	1699–1703	mission, presidio
San Juan de Los Esteros/ Refugio (Matamoros)	1700	mission
Sonoita	1701	mission
Camargo	1749	villa
Reynosa	1749	villa
Mier[a]	1753	villa
Presidio del Norte de La Junta de Los Ríos (Ojinaga)	1759–1773	mission, presidio
NINETEENTH CENTURY		
Laredo de Tamaulipas (Nuevo Laredo)	1848	border town
Tijuana	1848	border town
Piedras Negras	1849	military garrison
Las Vacas (Ciudad Acuña)	1877	military garrison
Nogales	1882	gateway
Agua Prieta	1899	gateway
TWENTIETH CENTURY		
Naco	1901	gateway
Mexicali	1903	agricultural colony
San Luis Río Colorado	1917	military garrison
Tecate	1918	gateway
Las Palomas	1921	gateway
San Pedro (Miguel Alemán)	1921	agricultural colony

SOURCE: Various as cited in text; adapted from Gildersleeve 1978.

[a]No longer a border city; see explanation in text.

face an American border town, it is not technically a border settlement for our purposes.

The mission Nuestra Señora de Guadalupe in present Ciudad Juárez was the earliest permanent settlement along what would become the border. Founded in 1659, the mission became a strategic settlement where the Rio Grande bends around the Franklin Mountains, creating a gateway to the upriver settlements of present New Mexico (Hughes 1914: 305). In 1683, the presidio Paso del Norte was built near the mission, reinforcing the importance of this settlement (Moorhead 1975: 21).

The middle Rio Grande frontier favored the location of additional missions and presidios besides those located at Paso del Norte. At the confluence of the Ríos Conchos and Grande near present Ojinaga, for example, the Spanish founded missions as early as 1683, but the sites were vulnerable until a presidio was built (Applegate and Hanselka 1974: 17–22). The first fortification known as Presidio del Norte de La Junta de Los Ríos was established at present Ojinaga in 1759. The presidio was moved in 1766 but returned to the junction of the rivers in 1773 (Moorhead 1975: 50). By the middle of the nineteenth century, Presidio del Norte had become a stopping point along the trade route between San Antonio, Texas, and Chihuahua. In 1867, the settlement name was changed to Ojinaga to honor Manuel Ojinaga, a former governor of Chihuahua who was executed by the French during their occupation of Mexico in 1865. When Southern Pacific completed its railroad from Los Angeles through El Paso to San Antonio in the 1880s, Ojinaga lost its position as the fulcrum of the Chihuahua Trail. Although the Kansas City, Mexico, and Orient Railroad linked Ojinaga to a larger trade area in 1930, it remained small with a population of less than 10,000 until 1970 (Applegate and Hanselka 1974: 44–47).

Along the mission frontier of present Sonora state, Jesuit missionaries founded a *visita*, or temporary mission, at Sonoita in 1694. Father Eusebio Kino established this site as a full mission in 1701, christening it San Marcelo de Sonoydag. The name was changed in 1736 to San Miguel de Sonoydag and later shortened to Sonoita (Kino 1913–1922: 133, 142–143; *Diccionario Porrua* 1964: vol. 2, 2012). Although situated along a small stream, Sonoita was isolated in the harsh volcanic outback of the Sonoran desert. Without access by paved road until 1925, Sonoita never became more than a mission and lower-order, mining-agricultural service center (Ives 1950: 1–12). Today, it is a highway junction town that services a small hinterland and is a tourist outlet for nearby Puerto Peñasco (see Chapter Four).

South of Piedras Negras, in present Coahuila, the village of Guerrero was the focus of a mission-presidio complex established along the Rio Grande. It was known as "the gateway to Spanish Texas" because its natural fords allowed for easy river crossing. The first mission, San Juan Bautista, was founded here in 1699, followed in 1703 by a fortified compound that became known as Presidio del Río Grande (Weddle 1968: 22; Eaton 1981: 1, 5). This settlement lost its strategic importance in the late eighteenth and early nineteenth centuries when transport and travel from Mexico into Texas shifted to towns that had been established downriver at Laredo and upstream at Piedras Negras.

Settlement at Matamoros, in present Tamaulipas, first occurred in 1700 with the small Spanish missionary site of San Juan de Los Esteros. By 1727 Franciscans referred to it as Congregación del Refugio (*Diccionario Porrua* 1964: vol. 2, 1282). After Mexico gained its independence, a group of settlers from Reynosa petitioned the governor in 1823 to elevate Refugio to a villa. The town was named Matamoros, in honor of Mariano Matamoros, a Mexican priest executed during the Mexican war for independence. The settlement became a strategic link between Tamaulipas (former Nuevo Santander) and Texas and served as a waterborne crossing on the Rio Grande (Scott 1966: 124, 129–130). A case study of Matamoros is in Chapter Three.

The roots of the Spanish municipality in Mexico lay in the free city-state, the civitas, established in Iberia during the earliest days of Roman occupation (Cardenas 1963: 3). Along the northern frontier, municipalities were organized according to various administrative titles, including *real de minas, lugar,* villa, ciudad, or *alcaldía mayor* (Cruz 1988: 13). Of the Mexican border cities considered in this study, two—Camargo and Reynosa—were founded as Spanish civil communities along the lower Rio Grande bordering present Texas. A third civil settlement, Mier, was founded in the area. These civil settlements and others were part of a larger colonization scheme of the province of Nuevo Santander organized by José de Escandón for the Spanish crown (Hill 1926). The Villa Santana de Camargo was established in 1749 near the confluence of the Río San Juan with the Rio Grande. The civil settlement of forty families from Nuevo León contained both a garrison and church, the latter under the authority of the Colegio de Zacatecas. Camargo was intended as a sheep-ranching center—some 13,000 head had been driven to the location—and as a distribution point for the salt trade because salines, or salt deposits, were situated across the Rio Grande (Scott 1966: 28–29). A second villa, Nuestra Señora de Guadalupe de Reynosa, also colonized by emigrants from Nuevo León, was located downriver from Camargo. The first site, known today as Reynosa Viejo, was upstream and across from the present village of Peñitas, Texas. Due to persistent flooding at the original site, Reynosa was moved to its present location in 1757 (Castañeda 1936–1958: vol. 3, 164). This location was close to grazing lands and situated strategically across the Rio Grande from the Sal del Rey, the largest saline along the frontier near present Raymondville, Texas (Hawkins 1947; Scott 1966: 29). Mier, the third villa, was located upriver from Camargo and just northwest of present Miguel Alemán. The town was incorporated in 1753, but the site had been occupied as a cattle ranch since 1734 and known as El Paso del Cántaro (Castañeda 1936–1958: vol. 3, 171–172).

NINETEENTH- AND TWENTIETH-CENTURY SETTLEMENTS

The twelve remaining border settlements considered in this study were founded in the nineteenth and twentieth centuries. Two resulted from the imposition of the border, three began as military garrisons, five were international gateways or transit points, and two were agricultural colonies (Table 2.1).

Both Tijuana and Nuevo Laredo owe their emergence as towns to the creation of the border in 1848. Nuevo Laredo, in present Tamaulipas, became the Mexican counterpart to the older Spanish colonial town of Laredo, founded in 1755 on the opposite bank of the Rio Grande in present Texas. Although the town was called both Laredo de Monterrey and Laredo de Tamaulipas during the nineteenth century, by the new century, it was known simply as Nuevo Laredo (Wilkinson 1975: 218; Prieto 1873: 330; García Cubas 1889–1891: vol. 3, 358; and Arguelles 1910: 126). Nuevo Laredo's early growth was especially dependent on Laredo, so social as well as economic connections between families in the two Laredos have persisted from colonial times. By the late nineteenth century, however, when railroads linked *Los Dos* (the two) Laredos to hinterlands as distant as Chicago and Mexico City, Nuevo Laredo began to emerge as a major town in its own right (Villarreal Peña 1986: 15–17). Today it is a transportation hub for traffic into northeastern and east-central Mexico (see Chapter Seven).

Fifteen hundred miles west on the Pacific coast, the boundary created by the Treaty of Guadalupe Hidalgo transformed a *ranchería* of little distinction known as Tijuana into a border town (Herzog 1985a: 297). The town was located along the Tia Juana river valley, a landscape of marine terraces, steep canyons, gorges, and a narrow river floodplain in present Baja California. The site had not been considered strategic to earlier Spanish colonization, which had been focused on settling river valleys to the north and south, where Franciscans and Jesuits founded missions during the eighteenth century (Piñera Ramírez and Ortiz Figueroa, 1983: 284–292; Irigoyen 1943–1945: vol. 1). Like Nuevo Laredo, Tijuana became an instant town that capitalized on its peculiar position at the southwestern back door of the United States. Unlike Nuevo Laredo, however, Tijuana never became a major transit point connecting distant hinterlands. Rather, Tijuana was a modest village of little consequence until it became a tourist and resort mecca in the early twentieth century, and its population would not exceed that of Nuevo Laredo until 1950 (see Chapter Four).

Piedras Negras and Las Vacas (present Ciudad Acuña) were founded in 1849 and 1877, respectively, as military posts along the Rio Grande frontier in the state of Coahuila (Cuellar Valdes 1979: 131, 175). The United States had established Fort Duncan in 1849 at the site of present Eagle Pass, Texas, as a protective measure against Indian and bandit hostilities. This apparently prompted a Mexican settlement across the river that became Piedras Negras, so named for the coal deposits in the local vicinity (Scarborough 1968: 48, 60–61). In 1900, Piedras Negras was the third largest border city, behind Matamoros and Ciudad Juárez, because of its location next to the coal district of Allende, about thirty miles to the interior. In 1883, the Ferrocarril Internacional Mexicano linked Piedras Negras with Eagle Pass. The resulting prosperity for the Mexican town elevated it from a villa to a ciudad with a new name, Porfirio Díaz, in honor of the president of Mexico (Cuellar Valdes 1979: 182–185). The name presumably was changed back to Piedras Negras after the 1910 political uprising that toppled the dictatorial Díaz regime.

Upriver at the junction of the Arroyo de Las Vacas and the Rio Grande, Ciudad Acuña was organized in 1877 as a military garrison with supporting cattle ranches (Cuellar Valdes 1979: 175–176). The town faced the American settlement of Del Rio that was founded along the Texas bank of the Rio Grande where a prodigious flow from the San Felipe springs allowed the creation of an irrigation system and agricultural colony (Work Projects Administration 1986: 611). During the Mexican revolution in 1912, Las Vacas was renamed by governor Venustiano Carranza in honor of Manuel Acuña, a nineteenth-century Coahuilan poet. Thus, it became one of Mexico's few cities not named after a patriot or military hero (Weisman 1986: 55–57). Although linked by railroad during the 1930s, Ciudad

Acuña was not connected by paved road to the Mexican interior until 1950. As a result, isolation kept the town population low and oriented chiefly to Del Rio.

From the 1880s through the early 1900s, five border settlements—Nogales, Agua Prieta, Tecate, Naco, and Las Palomas—were founded as gateways or transit points connecting to nearly simultaneously founded border settlements along the U.S. side of the line. Nogales, Sonora, and Nogales, Arizona—known together as *ambos* (both, or the two combined) Nogales—were founded in 1882 with the meeting of railroads from Guaymas and Kansas City. The towns grew symbiotically, sharing water supplies, firefighting services, and merchants (Ready 1980: 6, 10; Flores Garcia 1987). Chapter Seven includes a case study of Nogales.

Agua Prieta, Sonora, across from present Douglas, Arizona, was known to travelers as a water stop as early as 1848 (Officer 1987: 210). A small settlement grew up just south of the international border near the Agua Prieta springs when construction of the Ferrocarril de Nacozari began in 1899 (Sandomingo 1951: 56). The modern town grew chiefly after Douglas was organized as a copper-smelting town in 1900. As late as 1902, Agua Prieta had only eight or ten houses built of adobe with tin roofs. By 1903, there were about 50 houses in the vicinity. In that year, the town was designed and surveyed by Tomás Fregoso and A. Mendoza to incorporate the *fondo legal* (municipality) under Mexican law (Hadley 1987: 31). Agua Prieta commanded the western end of the Guadalupe Pass that linked Chihuahua to Sonora over the Sierra Madre Occidental. The border town bustled by catering to traffic between the mining towns of Janos in Chihuahua, Nacozari in Sonora, and Bisbee in Arizona (Dumke 1948: 283, 289). Nevertheless, like Ciudad Acuña, its isolation in the shadow of Ciudad Juárez to the east and Nogales to the west kept the town small until 1950.

Tecate, Baja California, founded in 1918, was a small ranching center along the border road that linked Tijuana and Mexicali. By 1919, it had become a stop on the Tijuana and Tecate Railway, part of the San Diego and Arizona railroad that linked the California port town with the Imperial Valley (Hofsommer 1986: 59). In 1921, Tecate became an official port of entry facing Tecate, California, but its mountainous site and relative isolation checked its early population growth until 1960 (Ramírez López 1983: 315–320; Price 1973b: 36; Goldbaum 1971: 21; Meade 1985).

Two additional settlements, Naco, Sonora, and Las Palomas, Chihuahua, were established as border gateways between 1901 and 1921. Their remote locations also restricted community growth, and they remain small today, with less than 10,000 people each. Naco, apparently named after the

Indian word for the fruit of the desert, barrel cactus, was founded as a twin-town railroad junction connecting the Sonoran copper mines at Nacozari and Cananea to Bisbee, Arizona (Barnes 1960: 44; Myrick 1975: 194–195). In 1901, houses were moved to the site from the settlements of Puerto Mulas and La Morita on the U.S. side near Bisbee (Sandomingo 1951: 43). Today, Naco, Sonora, and Naco, Arizona, are linked by a railroad and international port of entry, but each remains a small town on the periphery of larger settlements such as Agua Prieta and Bisbee.

Las Palomas started as a nineteenth-century cattle *hacienda* south of the town's present location, across from Columbus, New Mexico (García Cubas 1889–1891: vol. 4, 275). After the Mexican revolution, Las Palomas became an official port of entry around 1921. Soon thereafter, the Mexican government made it a casino-and-bar border town carved out of land from the American-owned Palomas Land and Cattle Company (Machado 1981: 33–34, 55–56). In 1977, the Mexican government changed the town's name to General Rodrigo Quevedo to honor a former governor of Chihuahua, but Las Palomas is still preferred today (Demaris 1970: 170; Weisman 1986: 104).

The remaining Mexican border settlements—Mexicali, San Luis Río Colorado, and Miguel Alemán—were founded in the twentieth century. Each emerged principally as a service center for an agricultural or ranching hinterland. Mexicali, Baja California, across from Calexico, California, had its origins in the California-Mexico Land and Cattle Company, the Mexican-chartered subsidiary of the Colorado River Land Company directed by Harrison Gray Otis of Los Angeles. Its lands were initially devoted to stock-raising, but at the turn of the century, irrigation systems were put in place to capitalize on the development scheme that had been successful north of the border in the Imperial Valley. Otis leased lands chiefly to Chinese farmers who formed cooperatives, developed land at their own expense, and planted and harvested cotton (Chamberlin 1951: 44–45; Herrera Carrillo 1976). Mexicali was organized in 1903 as the municipality to serve this regional economy and fittingly assumed a modern rather than traditional settlement plan (see Chapter Three). Early on, the town was controlled chiefly by Esteban Cantú, a local politico who licensed gambling and commercialized vice to raise capital for further urban investments (Kenamore 1917–1918: 25–28; Aguirre Bernal 1983: 347). The territorial capital was relocated in 1920 to Mexicali from Ensenada (Weisman 1986: 168). Today Mexicali is the only border settlement that is a state capital. In 1937, the Mexican government initiated a colonization scheme to encourage Mexicans to settle the valley area, because as late as 1930, Mexicali was one-third Chinese. Before 1950, the city was only connected by railroad to Baja and Southern California, its economic hinterland (Medina Robles 1970: 68, 99, 115).

San Luis Río Colorado, Sonora, is located on the eastern margin of the Colorado River delta where Sonora and Arizona meet Baja California and California. Although records indicate that people lived at the site as early as 1906, the settlement is said to have sprung up with San Luis, Arizona—its border counterpart—in 1915 when the Yuma Valley Railroad was extended south from its junction with the Southern Pacific Railroad along a levee built to contain the Colorado River (Myrick 1975: 433). In 1917, the official founding date, the governor of Sonora ordered soldiers to the site to establish a military garrison (Rogelio Alvarez 1988: 7216–7217; Verdugo Fimbres 1983). Later, San Luis Río Colorado became the center of government-sponsored agricultural developments carried out south and west of the town. Today San Luis Río Colorado is a major service center for this cotton- and sorghum-farming hinterland and is well connected by highway to nearby Mexicali.

Finally, Miguel Alemán, Tamaulipas, is one of the newer of the Mexican border cities. It was founded in 1921, although an earlier settlement called San Pedro was located at the site across the Rio Grande from Roma, Texas (Margulis and Tuirán 1986: 66–67). Miguel Alemán—the town name was changed to honor a former president of Mexico—became an agricultural service center north of the Marte R. Gómez Dam on the Río San Juan (*Diccionario Porrua* 1964: vol. 2, 1347). Mier, the earlier border town in the vicinity, was abruptly cut off from easy access to the border by the construction of Falcón Dam and Reservoir in 1953. This gave Miguel Alemán the advantage of location on the international boundary between Camargo to the south and Mier to the north (Byfield 1966). Today, Miguel Alemán is connected by Mexico Highway 54 to Monterrey, but it is one of the few border towns not linked by railroad.

TWENTIETH-CENTURY GROWTH PHASES AND
CHANGING DEMOGRAPHY

In 1910, Mexico was an agrarian society; nearly three-fourths of its people lived in villages with populations of 100 to 2,500 (Wilkie 1973: 99–100). By 1980, nearly three-fourths of its people lived in urban places with populations larger than 2,500. The rapid growth of Mexico's population in the late twentieth century is illustrated by the fact that the growth alone in national population between 1960 and 1970 exceeded the total population of Mexico in 1920 (Wilkie 1984: 333). Further, Mexico's population growth between 1970 and 1980 surpassed the total population of the country in 1940. The growth of Mexico's population in the latter half of this century has reached a total of eighty-five million. Mexico has become increasingly metropolitan with an urban growth rate currently in excess of 5 percent per year (Griffin and Crowley 1989: 294). In 1990, the eighteen border cities counted more than three and one-half million people, or 35 percent of the total population of the five northern border states (excluding Nuevo León) (Table 2.2).

Among the border settlements of this study, only Naco, Las Palomas, and Sonoita have populations of less than 10,000 and thus are small towns—although the Mexican government considers any place with more than 2,500 people to be a city. Most border communities in 1990 are classified as either simple (10,001–50,000 inhabitants) or complex (50,001–500,000 inhabitants) urban settlements. Just three, Ciudad Juárez, Tijuana, and Mexicali, would rank as metropolitan (greater than 500,000).

Table 2.2 gives population data for each of the eighteen border settlements. Although the data are incomplete and vary by source and by category (localidad, ciudad, municipio)—and there are most likely serious undercounts for particular periods, such as 1980—the numbers do suggest comparative growth phases by settlement size. For the largest cities, the first four decades of the century were characterized by high growth. For example, by 1940, both Ciudad Juárez and Nuevo Laredo had increased from four to six times their 1900 populations. Between 1920 and 1940, Matamoros nearly doubled its population while Mexicali and Reynosa more than doubled in size, and Tijuana grew more than tenfold. Medium-sized border cities grew modestly by comparison over the first four decades of the century. There was distinct stagnation and even decline for some of these towns between 1930–1940 (see Fig. 2.1).

The early part of this century was a period in which Mexican border settlements became dependent on tourist and entertainment economies sustained chiefly by North American patrons (Machado 1982: 349–361; Martínez 1988: 113–114). This period coincides with the U.S. Prohibition era (1918–1933) and follows closely an economic depression that devastated local border economies in the late nineteenth century. The so-called "culture of sin" that flourished in many border cities during this period was a combined product of North American investors fleeing moral reform in the United States and depressed conditions in border communities that led local politicos and businessmen to embrace *pariah* (socially outcast) economies (see Chapter Four). The results brought significant growth to most border

TABLE 2.2 Mexican Border-City Populations, 1900–1990

State/City	1900	1910	1921	1930	1940	1950	1960	1970	1980	1990
BAJA CALIFORNIA										
Tijuana	242	733	1,028	8,384	16,486	59,952	152,473	277,306	461,257	742,686
Tecate	127	—	493	566	—	—	7,074	14,738	30,540	51,946
Mexicali	—	462	6,782	14,842	18,775	65,749	179,539	263,498	510,664	602,390
SONORA										
San Luis Río Colorado	—	—	175	910	558	4,079	28,545	49,990	92,790	111,508
Sonoita	—	—	483	616	—	800[a]	1,925	2,463	—	9,691[b]
Nogales	2,738	3,177	13,475	14,061	13,866	24,478	37,657	52,108	68,076	107,119
Naco	519	—	1,267	2,132	—	—	2,864	3,580	4,441	4,636
Agua Prieta	—	656	3,236	4,674	4,106	10,471	15,339	20,754	34,380	39,045
CHIHUAHUA										
Las Palomas	128	—	192	342	—	—	1,134	2,129	—	16,565[b]
Ciudad Juárez	8,218	10,621	19,457	39,669	48,881	122,566	262,119	407,370	567,365	797,679
Ojinaga	1,709	—	836	1,536	—	—	8,252	12,757	26,421	23,947

COAHUILA										
Ciudad Acuña	667	933	2,423	5,350	5,607	11,372	20,048	30,276	41,948	56,750
Piedras Negras	7,888	8,518	14,233	15,878	15,663	27,581	44,992	41,033	80,290	98,177
TAMAULIPAS										
Nuevo Laredo	6,548	8,143	14,998	21,636	23,872	57,668	92,627	148,867	203,286	217,912
Miguel Alemán	185[c]	—	143[c]	323[c]	—	—	6,535	11,259	19,600	21,127
Camargo	2,194	—	1,478	1,799	—	—	4,008	5,953	16,014	15,029
Reynosa	1,915	1,475	2,107	4,840	9,412	34,087	74,140	137,383	211,412	281,618
Matamoros	8,347	7,390	9,215	9,733	15,699	45,846	92,327	137,749	238,840	303,392
TOTAL							1,031,598	1,619,213	2,607,324	3,501,217
Growth						—	—	587,615	988,111	893,893
% Change						—	—	57	61	34

SOURCES: *Censo General 1901* (localidad); *Censo General 1918* (localidad); *Censo General 1926* (localidad); *Censo General 1933* (localidad); Unikel 1976; *Cuadro 1-A1 1940, 1950* (ciudad); *Censo General 1963* (ciudad); *Censo General 1973* (ciudad); *Censo General 1983* (municipio); *Censo General 1990* (municipio).

[a] Ives 1950:7.

[b] Populations are given for municipios of Plutarco Calles and Ascensión, respectively.

[c] Town of San Pedro.

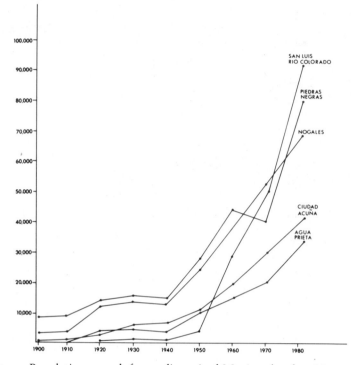

FIGURE 2.1 Population growth for medium-sized Mexican border cities, 1900–
1980. Sources: Unikel 1976, Cuadro I–A1; *Censo General* 1983.

settlements. Exceptions such as Nogales, Piedras Negras, and Agua Prieta, medium-sized cities that lost population between 1930–1940, were service centers for regional mining economies. The depressed nature of that industry during the 1930s is reflected in population decline.

A second growth phase in the border cities followed the economic depression of the 1930s and coincided with a U.S. military buildup during the 1940s and 1950s. Ten of the cities studied, including five of the six largest, are situated within driving distance of less than one hour to several hours from U.S. military installations (see Fig. 2.2). These facilities provided clientele for a rejuvenated entertainment and tourist economy in border cities after the Second World War (Martínez 1988: 115; Curtis and Arreola 1989). Additionally, during the 1950s, Mexicans from the interior came north seeking economic opportunity such as agricultural labor in the American Southwest. As a consequence, the border cities began to act as staging areas for further migration, adding significantly to their transforming populations. By 1960, the largest cities of Ciudad Juárez, Mexicali, Tijuana, Nuevo Laredo, Reynosa, and Matamoros had grown to between three and ten times their 1940 populations, while medium-sized cities had doubled and tripled (Table 2.2). As during the Prohibition era, border-city economies again became tied to North American tourist activity. However, other local factors such as petroleum industrial development at Reynosa, agricul-

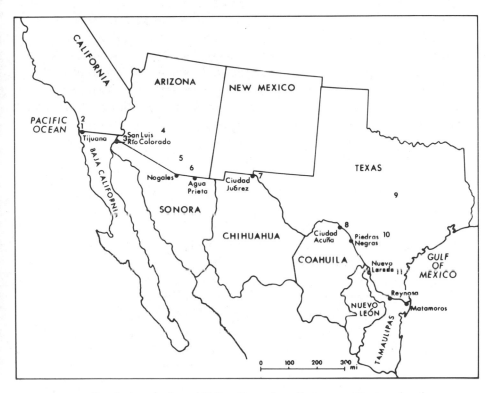

FIGURE 2.2 Proximity of selected U.S. military installations to Mexican border cities:

1. U.S. Naval Station—San Diego
2. Camp Pendleton Marine Corps Base—Oceanside
3. U.S. Marine Corps Air Station—Yuma
4. Luke Air Force Base—Phoenix
5. Davis Monthan Air Force Base—Tucson
6. Fort Huachuca—Sierra Vista
7. Fort Bliss Military Reservation—El Paso
8. Laughlin Air Force Base—Del Rio
9. Fort Hood—Killeen
10. Lackland, Kelly, Brooks, Randolph Air Force Bases and Fort Sam Houston—San Antonio
11. Naval Air Station—Corpus Christi.

tural expansion at San Luis Río Colorado, and highway construction promoted by the national government all across the borderland region contributed to this urban growth (see Chapter Seven).

A third phase of border-city growth was initiated in 1961 when the
Mexican national government created, by order of President Adolfo López
Mateos, the Programa Nacional Fronterizo (PRONAF) (National Border Program) (Chávez 1961). PRONAF was intended to change the "unseemly" image of border towns through public beautification projects, thereby creating
Las Puertas a México (the gateways to Mexico). Incentives were set up for
improvements in tourist services, including hotels, sports complexes, parks,
theaters, museums, and handicraft shops (Dillman 1970: 487, 501–502).
An outgrowth of PRONAF was the Border Industrialization Program (BIP) of
1965 that resulted in a free-zone industrial corridor where American firms
could take advantage of inexpensive Mexican labor. Border cities could
thereby act as magnets for employment and growth. Americans have come
to know this as the maquiladora industry (Dillman 1976: 138–150) (see
Chapter Seven). Both PRONAF and BIP were major catalysts to continued
urban growth along the border, catapulting population levels two to three
times the 1960 levels in the largest cities and stimulating continued growth
in medium-sized cities as well. (In part, the change in the population size of
border cities between 1970 and 1980 as given in Table 2.2 is a function of
the change in the size of the reporting areal unit, from ciudad to municipio.)

In the four decades between 1940 and 1980, the reasons for population growth in the Mexican border cities changed fundamentally. From
1940 to 1950, in-migration exceeded natural increase as the principal means
to population growth in eleven cities surveyed (see Fig. 2.3). In eight of those
cities, migration was two times greater than natural increase in contributing
to population growth. Significantly, these included the six largest border
cities—Ciudad Juárez, Tijuana, Mexicali, Matamoros, Reynosa and Nuevo
Laredo—and two medium-sized cities, San Luis Río Colorado, and Agua
Prieta. As discussed above, this pattern coincided with the border cities'
second growth phase. This was stimulated largely by the Second World War
military buildup along the U.S. borderland, rejuvenation of the border cities'
tourist economies, and the migrant staging function that some border cities
began to achieve. Each of these conditions helped to attract migrants to the
border (Dillman 1983b: 238).

In 1950, municipios that included Tijuana, Mexicali, Ciudad Juárez,
Nuevo Laredo, Reynosa, and Matamoros counted 15–30 percent of their
populations born in other political entities in the border states (Beegle et al.
1960: Figure 23). Nevertheless, between 1950 and 1960, only four border

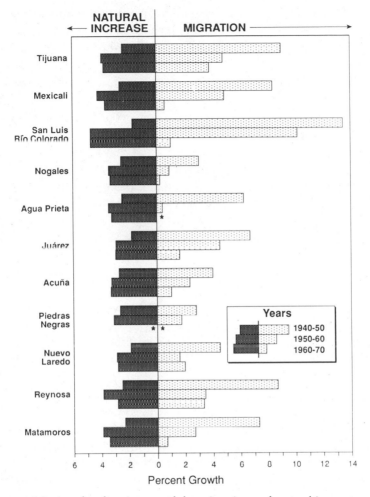

FIGURE 2.3 Mexican border-city growth by migration and natural increase, 1940–1970. Piedras Negras lost population 1960–1970 because out-migration exceeded natural increase. Agua Prieta had negative out-migration 1960–1970, but this was offset by natural increase. Source: Unikel 1976: Cuadro 1–A3.

cities grew chiefly by migration: Tijuana, Mexicali, San Luis Río Colorado, and Ciudad Juárez. This westward tilt in migrant flow mirrors, in part, the migration of Mexican Americans from Texas to California, where economic development spurred a perception of greater opportunity in the decade 1950–1960 (Grebler et al. 1970: 109–111; Muller and Espenshade 1985:

37–54). The continued migration streams to the western Mexican border cities, while all others grew principally by natural increase, suggest a correlation of migration shift south as well as north of the border (Alvarez 1966: 471–496).

Since early in the twentieth century, Mexican migrants to the United States have consistently come from a handful of specific states. While the Texas border has tended to receive immigrants from Mexico's northeastern states, including San Luis Potosí, California has tended to draw its migrants from nearby northern and western states such as Sonora, Chihuahua, and Jalisco (Gamio 1930: 13–29; Cardoso 1980: 18–37). Recent studies of illegal migrant flows from Mexico show that these areas continue to provide significant numbers of immigrants (Jones 1982: 83–84).

Data collected from the 1980 Mexican federal census documented that the migrants to the Mexican border cities follow similar source and migration channels. Although most migrants appear to come from in-state destinations, Figures 2.4, 2.5, and 2.6 show that out-of-state migrants to eastern border destinations such as Matamoros, Reynosa, and Nuevo Laredo arrive chiefly from the nearby states of Nuevo León, San Luis Potosí, and Coahuila. Figures 2.7, 2.8, and 2.9 reveal that western border cities such as Tijuana, Mexicali, and San Luis Río Colorado are fed principally by out-of-state migrants from Jalisco, the Federal District, Sonora, Baja California, Sinaloa, and Michoacán. Between these poles, the interior border settlements such as Ciudad Juárez, Ciudad Acuña, and Piedras Negras appear to draw out-of-state migrants primarily from Durango, Nuevo León, and Zacatecas (see Figs. 2.10, 2.11, 2.12). Thus, both regional proximity as well as historical precedence appear to influence the movement of migrants from the interior to the border cities. There appears to be a regional bias that varies among eastern, western, and central border-town destinations.

By 1970, however, only two Mexican border cities, Reynosa and Tijuana, had grown more by migration than by natural increase in the previous decade, although only slightly more so in the case of Tijuana (see Fig. 2.3). Reynosa's continued growth from migration is a function of its specialized oil-refining economy and helps explain why Veracruz (also an oil state) contributes so disproportionately to the city's out-of-state migration stream (see Fig. 2.5). In Tijuana, the dynamic Southern California economy as well as social ties continue to pull migrants to this major metropolis (Herzog 1990: 135–187). Also during the decade 1960–70, Piedras Negras actually lost population because out-migration exceeded natural increase. Further, recent studies suggest that out-migration played a small part in population change in Mexicali, Ciudad Juárez, Matamoros,

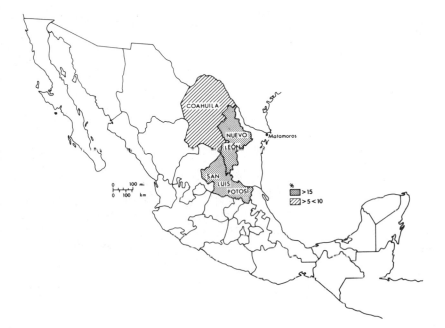

FIGURE 2.4 Origins of migrants to Matamoros, 1980. Source: *Censo General* 1983.

FIGURE 2.5 Origins of migrants to Reynosa, 1980. Source: *Censo General* 1983.

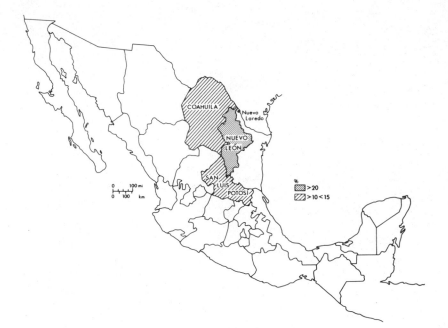

FIGURE 2.6 Origins of migrants to Nuevo Laredo, 1980. Source: *Censo General* 1983.

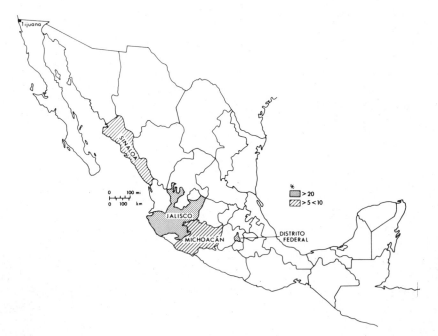

FIGURE 2.7 Origins of migrants to Tijuana, 1980. Source: *Censo General* 1983.

FIGURE 2.8 Origins of migrants to Mexicali, 1980. Source: *Censo General* 1983.

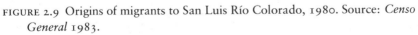

FIGURE 2.9 Origins of migrants to San Luis Río Colorado, 1980. Source: *Censo General* 1983.

FIGURE 2.10 Origins of migrants to Ciudad Juárez, 1980. Source: *Censo General* 1983.

FIGURE 2.11 Origins of migrants to Ciudad Acuña, 1980. Source: *Censo General* 1983.

FIGURE 2.12 Origins of migrants to Piedras Negras, 1980. Source: *Censo General* 1983.

and Reynosa between 1970 and 1980. Overall, however, its effect was offset by natural increase for the largest border cities (Margulis and Tuirán 1984: 415–416).

Thus, by 1980, population growth for most border cities was occurring through natural increase rather than migration. (At this writing, migration data for the 1980–1990 decade were unavailable.) The projections for future border-city growth are problematic, in part, because they are tied to expectations for continued economic development. Some anticipate that a North American Free Trade Agreement involving Mexico, Canada, and the United States will promote even greater growth along the border. However, one study suggests that the border cities might experience a slowdown in the near future compared with the sharp rises of the immediate past (Margulis and Tuirán 1986: 115–118, 312–313). As migration to the cities slows and as out-migration to other destinations both in the United States and in Mexico continues, overall population growth might be significantly moderated. Preliminary evidence from the 1990 Mexican census suggests that the rate of population growth in border cities has subsided somewhat, despite the continued increase in numbers of people (Table 2.2). The ways in which growth phases and changing demography are expressed on the landscape of a specific border city will give geographic pattern to these figures.

AREA AND POPULATION GROWTH FOR CIUDAD JUÁREZ

Founded as Paso del Norte in 1659, this Mexican border settlement was officially recognized as a city in 1888, and its name was changed to Ciudad Juárez in honor of Benito Juárez. Two monuments, one in the urban core and one at the outskirts along the Pan American Highway, commemorate the former Mexican president. The 1980 census counted some 663,000 residents, yet by 1990, the city was reported to have nearly 800,000 inhabitants. This makes it the largest settlement on the border and the sixth largest urban center in Mexico (Table 2.2; Griffin and Crowley 1989: 295).

During the Spanish colonial period, Paso del Norte was a classic gateway settlement. It linked the ranching and farming areas of the upper Rio Grande in present New Mexico with the mining and administrative areas of northern and central Mexico to the south via Chihuahua. Not a particularly prosperous settlement, Paso del Norte was, nevertheless, strategically positioned so that it benefited from travel and trade along this axis, and it was able to sustain agriculture with irrigation from the Rio Grande.

The Urrutia map of 1766 (see Fig. 2.13), drafted as part of an eighteenth-century inspection of the northern frontier, illustrates the position of the mission and presidio that were the core of the colonial settlement (Gerald 1966). Situated on slightly elevated land less than one mile south of the Rio Grande, the community overlooked a floodplain of irrigated fields. By 1800, it had an outlying population that extended down the valley nearly twenty-one miles (Cruz 1988: 50; Schmidt and Lloyd 1986: 28). With the creation of the international border in 1848, Paso del Norte continued its role as a gateway settlement, serving trade and travel across the new boundary. Its population dipped slightly by midcentury but regained momentum in the 1880s with the arrival of railroads from four directions. Three railroads converged upon El Paso, Texas, and one from Mexico arrived at Ciudad Juárez, creating a crossroads on the American side of the Rio Grande that would ultimately affect the growth of Ciudad Juárez (Martínez 1978: 21).

Ciudad Juárez grew significantly as a pivot for railroad commerce, allowing the import and export of varied agricultural and livestock products. With this growth, the skeletal framework of the modern city began to

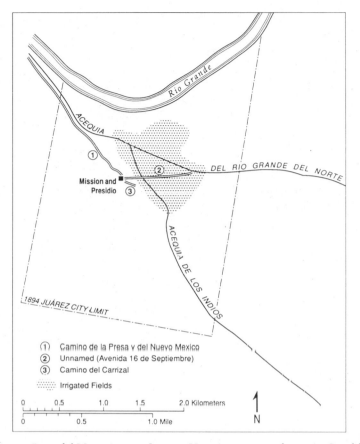

FIGURE 2.13 Paso del Norte, 1766. Source: Urrutia 1766, as shown in Gerald 1966.

emerge. An 1894 map (see Fig. 2.14) reveals the original colonial core of irregular streets and the road and settlement extensions east from this site following irrigation canals (*acequias*). The railroad, Ferrocarril Central, divided the old city and connected Ciudad Juárez to rail lines across the river in El Paso by way of a separate bridge. A loop with turnaround at the train station illustrates the route of the first streetcar service connecting Ciudad Juárez to El Paso via two separate bridges. These bridges would include automobile access by the 1920s. A platted subdivision to the west of the town center appeared as the first attempt to develop public lands. It would serve as a model for much of the urban expansion that followed in the twentieth century (Valencia 1969: 59).

By 1895, the city had spread over nearly 163 acres, a tenfold increase

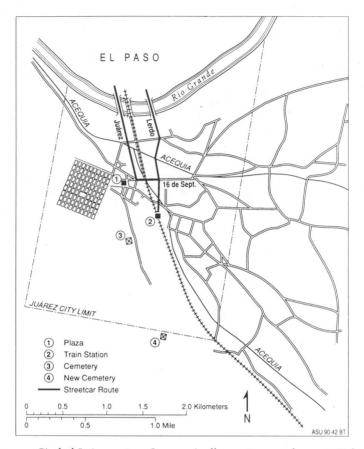

FIGURE 2.14 Ciudad Juárez, 1894. Source: Arellano 1894, as shown in Valencia
1969.

from 1760. By 1919, Ciudad Juárez had expanded west of the railroad
corridor in typical grid-pattern fashion with rectangular blocks oriented
slightly northeast to the Rio Grande. Between 1894 and 1919, the new city
blocks were divided into six lots of less than 750 square yards each. With
no restrictions on land use, property owners frequently sold portions of
their lots to relatives and friends. Individual lots quickly became fragmented, resulting in high residential densities (Valencia 1969: 64–69). Also
in 1919, a fourth bridge to accommodate rail traffic between the city and
El Paso was constructed. Further, a second rail line joined the city from the
south to create a junction of two railroads at the station located south of
present Avenida 16 de Septiembre.

The population of Ciudad Juárez increased nearly fourfold between 1910 and 1940. This was a result of Prohibition and a military service–oriented economy in adjacent American states as well as a result of a local manufacturing base (Martínez 1978: 57–77). This growth initially did not result in an increase in the city's area. Urban growth during the 1920s through the 1940s was largely an in-filling process west and east of the plaza, el centro, and the railroad corridor, especially along Avenidas 16 de Septiembre and Vicente Guerrero (Schmidt and Lloyd 1986: 36). In 1950 almost all residents of the city lived within a one-mile radius of the central plaza. By 1960, the built-up city reached approximately two miles in radius from the center, and by 1980, some three miles from this focus (see Fig. 2.15).

The population of Ciudad Juárez has grown most in the last three decades—more than a sixfold increase from almost 123,000 in 1960 to

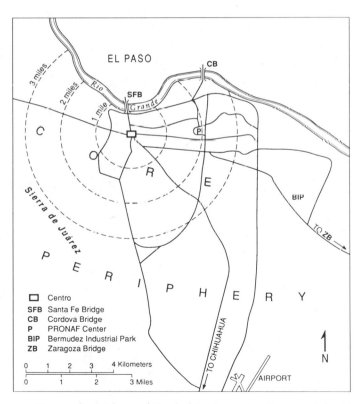

FIGURE 2.15 Core and periphery of Ciudad Juárez, 1983. Sources: Schmidt and Lloyd 1986; based on Valencia 1969.

nearly 800,000 in 1990. It has been reported that between one-third and one-half of the migrants to the city have come from within the state of Chihuahua, with smaller percentages coming from nearby Durango, Zacatecas, and Coahuila (Zoomers 1986: 61). While the PRONAF and BIP developments of the 1960s certainly exerted a migration pull, population growth in the city by 1970 was principally from natural increase, not migration (Margulis and Tuirán 1984: 415). According to a recent household survey, 52 percent of the population is eighteen years of age or younger. This suggests that natural increase will continue to contribute most to population growth in Ciudad Juárez, especially if birth rates remain high. Current population projections for the year 2000 range from 1.3 to 2.4 million (Schmidt and Lloyd 1986: 39, 42).

This recent population growth has transformed the dimensions of the city, pushing urban landscapes into previously fringe zones. Whereas in 1910 the city occupied 1,177 acres, in 1980 it spread over 21,750 acres. During every year since 1986, Ciudad Juárez has added as much as 300 acres (Cabral 1991). Growth on the periphery has occurred primarily west up the lower flanks of the Sierra de Juárez, south along the railroad and Pan American Highway (Mexico Highway 45) corridor to Chihuahua, and east into previously cultivated land. Today, agricultural land can be found inside the city limit, especially southeast along the river. The expansion west and southwest is primarily in residential areas, organized in a one- to three-mile radius from the central plaza and populated by squatters who have invaded public lands since 1960 (Ugalde 1974: 10–15; Valencia 1969: 86–105). The growth east and southeast is similarly one to three miles from the center but is mostly middle- to upper-income, residential development (Lloyd 1986: 51).

This growth has led to the construction of two additional bridges (see Fig. 2.15). The first, the so-called Cordova Bridge, connects Avenida de Las Americas to El Paso on the east of its central business district. It provides easy access to Ciudad Juárez's PRONAF tourist center, located just beyond the crossing. The second bridge, Zaragoza, is downriver from Las Americas crossing. It gives greater access to Ciudad Juárez's expanding east side and provides the maquiladoras at the Río Bravo Industrial Park with a separate crossing to El Paso.

The city enacted its first zoning ordinance in 1984 and its first subdivision regulations in 1988. Because unplanned, peripheral shantytown development accounts for three-fifths of the city's land area, a comprehensive municipal plan was approved in 1990. The plan's broad guidelines called for new residential growth to be steered south along the Pan American

Highway and for informal land development on the hilly westside to be halted (Cabral 1991: 22).

The impact of accelerating population growth spread over the traditional framework of streets and spaces in the border cities has created a particular pattern of cityscape. In Chapter Three we examine the elements and character of urban structure that form the geographic anatomy of these places.

3 Urban Structure

An astute observer of the urban landscape once wrote: "No true chaos is in the urban scene, but only patterns and clues waiting to be organized" (Clay 1980: 11). True as that statement may be, the contemporary Mexican border town may indeed appear rather chaotic to most North Americans who are accustomed to relatively well-ordered cities. Yet in spite of a sense of disorder created by a bewildering mosaic of urban forms and functions, Mexican border cities have a pattern of internal organization based on morphological characteristics and functional relationships. An understanding of urban structure, which includes the configuration of the city as well as the various land uses and activity spaces within it, is important. This structure not only affects the city's capacity for economic development and movement of goods and people, but also impacts its social milieu. A city's morphology and spatial arrangement play a major role in shaping its character. The sense of a city, its prevailing image, even its livability, are greatly influenced by its physical layout or structure. The Mexican border cities are no exceptions.

The character of the Mexican border cities is changing—in most cases, profoundly so. This is due in no small measure to the dynamic quality of their structure, which is shaped by and responds continually to a host of factors. These factors include the physical environment, population size, number and level of economic activities, socioeconomic conditions, technology, interurban relations, and cultural values and ideology (Yujnovsky 1975: 197–199). Because of the intent of this study, the influence of culture and ideology is particularly relevant. In both material and organizational ways, the Mexican border towns reflect, symbolize, and affirm the culture from which they sprang. Although differences certainly exist, these cities—especially those of comparable size—are remarkably similar in layout, land-use patterns, appearance, and in their *genius loci,* the spirit or essence of a place. The Mexican border cities also share similar population densities and social ecologies, if not population sizes and area. Variations beyond those influenced by size are primarily a consequence of site, situation, and the pattern of economic development. These elements of structural common-ality are the products of an ongoing historical process that continues to scrawl a distinctive urban signature across the built environment of *la frontera.*

Having examined previously the initial catalysts for settlement and population growth, this chapter focuses on two broad historical phases in the structural evolution of Mexican border cities: the traditional, based on Spanish colonial town plans and influences from the nineteenth and early twentieth centuries; and the modern, a consequence of post-1940s growth and technology as well as contemporary public programs and policies. Our goal is not only to provide an overview of the structural evolution of border cities but also to offer a framework for our interpretation of landscape char-acteristics of various areas within these cities. This quest for synthesis is not without its hazards, however, as urban structure is difficult to portray for even an individual city. For settlements that range, as the border cities do, along a continuum from compact towns to sprawling metropolises, from places of less than 10,000 people to cities approaching 800,000, production of a composite picture is exceedingly problematic. To offset the inherent shortcomings of this macro approach, we include case studies of Camargo and Matamoros, Tamaulipas, in the sections on traditional and modern structure, respectively.

TRADITIONAL STRUCTURE

The modernity that now characterizes most of the Mexican border cities is deceptive as it masks the importance and persistence of traditional urban forms and forces. Indeed, as the cultural landscape reveals, the patrimonial roots of the colonial and nineteenth-century urban legacy run deep. Al-though just six of the border towns considered in this study were founded during the Spanish colonial period—Paso del Norte (i.e., Ciudad Juárez), San Juan de los Esteros–Refugio (i.e., Matamoros), Sonoita, Camargo, Reynosa, and Presidio del Norte de La Junta de Los Ríos (i.e., Ojinaga)—the settlements established thereafter mirror in varying degrees the conven-tions of town planning handed down during that era. In almost all of the border cities, many of the organizing principles, if not the specific traditional forms, persist to this day. Descriptions of the "classic" Spanish colonial town have been restated and amplified in numerous studies (Beyer 1967; Hardoy 1972; Houston 1968; Portes and Walton 1976: 19–21; Sargent 1982: 221–225; Stanislawski 1947; Violich 1944: 28–31). However, review of these urban antecedents is important because they formed the structural foundation of several contemporary border cities.

Spanish colonial administration prescribed strict rules to govern the founding of towns in the Americas, including settlements in northern Mexico (Cardenas 1963). Under the rule of Philip II, by the late sixteenth century these so-called Laws of the Indies had become codified and guided by various *instrucciones* (directives) from the government to ensure regularity in the morphology of settlements (Crouch and Mundigo 1977; Nuttall 1922). These ordinances, which one scholar suggests are less ordinances per se than "a compilation of the accumulated standards and procedures" (Violich 1987: 79), created a centralized, rectangular urban form. Streets were oriented in cardinal directions and laid out in a gridiron lattice with the main north-south, east-west thoroughfares radiating outward from a *plaza mayor,* or central plaza (Crouch et al. 1982: 6–19; Foster 1960: 34–49; Stanislawski 1947).

The plaza was the principal public space as well as the functional and symbolic heart of the town. It was the hub of commerce, the theater of public rituals, and the focus of recreational activities. Flanking it were the two dominant colonial institutions, the church and offices of government. A majority of the commercial outlets were concentrated around it, and the *mercado central,* or main public market, was not far away. A "proper" Spanish colonial town also had small secondary plazas, sometimes called *placitas* or *alamedas,* though the latter term refers more formally to a park than a plaza. Some commercial establishments, especially lower-order notions and grocery stores, were scattered throughout the residential areas. The more offensive land uses, such as slaughterhouses, tanneries, fisheries, and the cemetery were relegated to the town's edges.

The distinction between the core and the periphery was even more dramatic in the pattern of residential settlement. Because the main plaza was the center of urban life and thus the most desirable place to be, it exerted a strong influence on the social geography of the community. Although land ownership was a tangible symbol of wealth and social standing, status was also assigned to town residents based on the distance of their homes from the central plaza. Residences close to the plaza were occupied by people of the highest stratum, such as government officials, prosperous merchants, master craftsmen, and ecclesiastics. Increasing residential distance from the plaza entailed relatively higher costs for mobility and generally meant decreasing status and a lower economic position. There also was a racial dimension to this residential pattern. It began with segregation of Indians into disorganized clusters of shabby dwellings on the outskirts of town (cercados) and accelerated with the rapid emergence of mestizo populations (Socolow and Johnson 1981: 33–37).

Because of the racial and socioeconomic reasons underlying segmentation of residential space coupled with the rigidity of colonial society, the barrios (neighborhoods) developed a strong sense of identity as they became separate and distinct from each other. They tended to be more competitive than cooperative in their relations (Beyer 1967: 304–306). In some settlements, each barrio specialized in a particular function or craft (Stea and Wood 1971: 103). It has been argued, however, that at the micro level these spatial patterns were less obvious because poorer relatives, servants, and slaves often lived in the homes of the elite (Lowder 1986: 78).

Although social and spatial segregation existed in the colonial town, its compactness and high population density, together with the inhabitants' reliance on walking, encouraged social interaction and face-to-face contacts. The abrupt break between town and country (in the case of Matamoros, the existence of a wall) symbolized that these settlements were not just marketing centers for a surrounding hinterland. They were microcosms of larger, complex cities that fostered an urban lifestyle and value system.

After Mexico won independence in 1821, the structure of border cities evolved throughout the remainder of the nineteenth century to reflect new city-shaping influences that supplemented and modified colonial designs. Two foremost influences were establishment of the international boundary at midcentury and improvements in transportation, especially the arrival of railroads in the 1880s. While el centro remained the focus of commercial activity, some decentralization occurred as secondary markets and shopping nodes emerged, followed by the formation of embryonic tourist districts near the border crossings (see Chapter Four). Within the city core, a transition began from mixed land uses to more specialized functions as competition for prime commercial space became more intense. This resulted in the clustering of retail and service businesses at the expense of residential and manufacturing activities. This process of land-use segregation and exclusion, which never has been as compelling south of the border as north, accelerated in the late nineteenth and early twentieth centuries with the creation of railroad-oriented industrial districts (see Chapter Seven). Characteristically located on the periphery of downtown near the border, especially in Ciudad Juárez, Nuevo Laredo, and Nogales, but also in Reynosa, Matamoros, and Mexicali, these new industrial spaces created corridors of growth and development. They also fragmented the city and became zones of *residential disamenity,* where living conditions were negatively influenced by proximity to industrial activities.

Compared to the commercial sector, changes in residential patterns were even more significant. One important catalyst was that the core increasingly lost its magnetism for the elite, who began to move into newer, larger, more fashionable homes out along the emerging thoroughfares, such as Ciudad Juárez's Calle Comercio, now renamed Avenida 16 de Septiembre. These were still convenient locations, within easy walking distance of the shops and attractions of the center, but far enough away to avoid the core's crowds and commercial character. This shift was facilitated by a gradual outward expansion of municipal services and utilities. The movement of the wealthy to these exclusive streets reflected on a micro scale an international trend that could be seen also on Baron von Haussmann's boulevards in Paris, the Ringstrassen of Vienna, and Mexico City's Paseo de la Reforma. These boulevards became synonymous with civility and cosmopolitanism, qualities that appealed as much to the wealthy in border towns as they did to those in larger, more sophisticated urban places. The concomitant of this move was that the housing abandoned by the elite filtered down to the middle class and sometimes to lower-income groups. Thus, the residential structure of the core became more diverse but dominated by middle-income populations.

Although associated with the postcolonial rise of commercial capitalism during the nineteenth century, many of these structural transformations did not appear, especially in the smaller border towns, until well into the twentieth century. In some places, they failed to materialize at all. Of course, several of the cities, most notably Mexicali, were not founded until the twentieth century. This delay was related partly to the nature of the border economy, but more fundamentally it was simply a matter of size. By the turn of the century, only four cities—Matamoros, Ciudad Juárez, Piedras Negras, and Nuevo Laredo—had populations larger than 5,000, and none exceeded 10,000. All four, incidentally, were served by railroads. Moreover, they remained compact places, spatially constricted by rudimentary, if any, public transportation. Although mule-drawn streetcars had appeared in Matamoros as early as 1873 and in Ciudad Juárez by 1881, they were slow, inefficient, and did little to alter the shape or landscapes of the two cities. Their impact was minimal even when the systems were electrified in 1902 in Ciudad Juárez and in 1924 in Matamoros (Price 1989: 6; Canseco Botello 1981). It was not until the introduction of bus service in the 1940s, and in some places later, that significant areal expansion occurred. By the advent of the modern period, which varied from place to place but was primarily a post–World War II phenomenon, the border cities comprised varying mixtures of colonial and post-colonial elements, many of which had evolved only recently.

PERSISTENCE OF TRADITIONAL ELEMENTS

While Mexican border cities have experienced an extraordinary metamorphosis during the twentieth century, especially over the last forty years, traditional forms, functions, and patterns of organization have endured. In general, the smaller the city the more prevalent they are, because structural change is largely a product of growth and economic development. Economic growth allows socioeconomic mobility that tends to be more fluid in larger cities and is reflected in a more substantial middle class and greater housing variety.

As a beginning observation, certain traditional elements of material culture have persisted. An inventory of historic properties, for example, would include buildings, especially churches and government structures, that date from the eighteenth and early nineteenth centuries. Many of these remain important landmarks. Regrettably, however, much of the material legacy has been lost, particularly in the larger, more prosperous cities. This is well documented in the *Catálogo Nacional de Monumentos Históricos* (1986). For the state of Tamaulipas, it lists only one structure—the Parroquia de Guadalupe on the central plaza—for the colonial city of Reynosa, whose population now exceeds 280,000. In contrast, the town of Camargo, with only about 15,000 people, requires 33 pages to list its historically important structures. Yet even where older buildings have been lost, many traditional styles and decorative idioms have been retained, if modified to suit contemporary needs and tastes (see Chapter Six).

In addition to historic properties and artifacts, the persistence of five other traditional elements should be mentioned, and two more warrant some elaboration. First, the main plazas remain symbolically and functionally important within the urban core, although rarely are they the paramount social centers they once were (see Chapter Five). In cities as old and large as Ciudad Juárez and young and small as Miguel Alemán, the plaza mayor is still a visual and social magnet. The major exception is Tijuana, where the central plaza (Plaza Zaragoza) failed as early as the 1920s to develop in the established manner (Herzog 1989: 111). The plaza's continued vitality is related in part to a critical shortage of open space and recreational amenities. It would be misleading, however, to suggest that these factors outweigh the enormous historical and emotional value of the plaza in the Mexican environment and psyche.

The second traditional element that has persisted is the relative compactness of the communities. This is especially evident in small to medium-sized cities, but it can also be seen in cities that have expanded several times as populations have grown, as low-cost public transportation has improved, and as automobile ownership has increased. These cities have higher population densities and less vacant land than do cities north of the border (Gildersleeve 1978). Moreover, the rural-urban fringe is much smaller—in several places nonexistent—as the break between town and country has remained abrupt.

A third element that has endured is the core-versus-periphery tradition. Despite widespread growth of suburbs for the elite and middle class, which has contributed to a diverse residential pattern, the ages-old inverse correlation between distance from the center and socioeconomic status is still evident in several cities. Even in a city as large and progressive as Tijuana, new elite housing continues to be built near the center where many of the city's most prestigious neighborhoods are located (Herzog 1989: 122). The margins of the border cities remain occupied primarily by the urban underclass. This is most pronounced in places such as Ciudad Juárez, Tijuana, Nuevo Laredo, and Reynosa that have large peripheral squatter settlements. In the case of Ciudad Juárez, however, one of the city's premier elite neighborhoods, the Campestre, is also located at the extreme periphery. Commercially, the dichotomy between the inner and outer city is even more sharply drawn. The traditional pedestrian-based, city-core commercial activities, including the old central markets, contrast with the new auto-oriented businesses along the major spines as well as the large shopping malls and industrial parks at the city's edge (see Chapters Five and Seven).

A fourth element that predates the modern era is that the barrios (e.g., the colonias and *fraccionamientos)* have remained distinct residential entities characterized by a sense of community. Whether rich or poor, most residents identify with and have a certain allegiance to their respective neighborhoods. In part, this is a consequence of relatively limited residential mobility. However, it is also related to motivations that range from the prestige associated with living in exclusive neighborhoods to a sense of belonging engendered by the many barrios composed largely of residents (often friends and relatives) who migrated to the border cities from the same regions or towns in Mexico's interior (Sherrill 1975; Ugalde 1974: 21–23).

The fifth traditional element is the persistence of small neighborhood stores and stands that offer lower-order goods and services. The most common are fruit and soft-drink stands and small grocery and notions stores, called *abarrotes* or *miscelaneas*. These individually owned and family-run establishments, especially prevalent in lower- and middle-income areas, usually face the street and are oriented toward serving the immediate community (Baker 1970: 276–278; Gildersleeve 1978: 288–289). Their persistence is a function of several factors: residents' limited mobility; the willingness of merchants (often children and housewives) to labor long hours for small profits; and community support and patronage not only for the convenience they provide but also for the important role they play as social institutions.

The gridiron street pattern is yet another traditional feature that continues to influence the spatial morphology of border cities. Without exception, every urban place along la frontera is laid out in this system, or more accurately, combined variations of this system, even where the environment would suggest the need for greater flexibility. One of the most indelible images of several border towns, including Tijuana, Nogales, and Ciudad Juárez along its western and southern margins, is that of roads that cut uncompromisingly straight up the face of steep-sided slopes; it seems a curious triumph of geometry over physical geography. Yet whether superimposed on hazardous and rugged terrain or on more accommodating topographical surfaces, this system fixes the city's skeletal outline and greatly impacts its transportation network. It should not be inferred, however, that streets in the various border towns are aligned in a single, tidy, efficient array. Even during the colonial period, Ciudad Juárez, for example, grew "untroubled by the royal ordinances" (Schmidt and Lloyd 1986: 35). As a consequence, its grid system in the older core did not develop in the prescribed, orderly fashion; it remains a maze of narrow, disjointed streets (see Chapter Two). Another exception is Tijuana, where the original city plan of 1889 incorporated a radial design and diagonal streets superimposed on the traditional grid format (Piñera Ramírez and Ortiz Figueroa 1983: 287) (see Fig. 3.1).

At present, especially in the larger cities, the road system could be characterized as consisting primarily of a complex series of nonintegrated grids. Some of these are oriented in cardinal directions while others are platted in relationship to various man-made features and natural phenomena, including rivers, railroads, principal thoroughfares, and the international boundary; still others have no external orientation (see Fig. 3.2). The resulting patchwork of grids and occasional irregular forms evolved from a lack of overall urban planning and uncoordinated development ef-

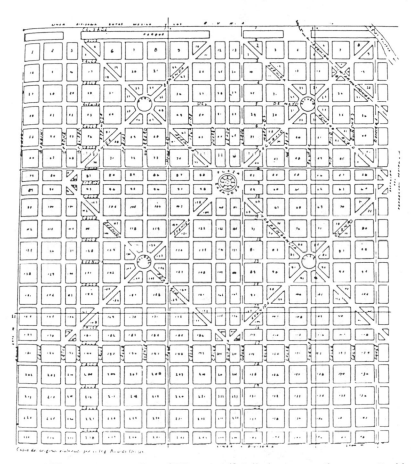

FIGURE 3.1 The 1889 town plan of Tijuana, officially known until 1929 as Pueblo
Zaragoza. Source: Ricardo Orozco 1889, as shown in Piñera Ramírez and
Ortiz Figueroa 1983.

forts between public and private sectors. It does not effectively tie the city
together but hampers the flow of goods and people and the delivery of utilities and services. The problem is exacerbated by the restricted number of
paved roads, which carry a vastly disproportionate volume of the traffic. As
one researcher concluded, they play "a pivotal role in defining the structure
and direction of urban expansion" (Hoffman 1983: 201–202). Although a
radial pattern is beginning to form in the major cities with the emergence of
large cross streets, the most significant paved traffic arteries continue to converge upon the central business districts and specifically the ports of entry.
They emphasize the existence of an international hinterland and the historic

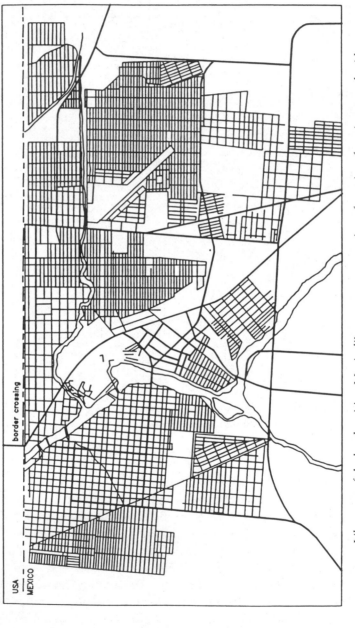

FIGURE 3.2 Like most of the border cities, Mexicali's street system consists of a series of nonintegrated grids.

and growing importance of transborder trade and travel (see Chapter Seven).

Finally, in keeping with traditional practices, the border cities have maintained comparatively compact and viable urban cores. For all but the largest cities, which in recent years have experienced considerable decentralization of commercial and institutional land uses into more peripheral areas, a centralized urban format has persisted. The centripetal pull of the city center reflects its continuing commercial and residential vitality. Although even in the smaller communities its role has been diminished, or at least augmented by the expansion of commercial enterprise out along the principal highways, the core remains the overwhelming focus of business, government, tourism, entertainment, and cultural activities. Consequently, it is the preeminent workplace and the nucleus of the public transportation system. In addition to providing employment and access to goods and services, the centralized structure persists for other reasons. Even with commercial and residential decentralization, for example, the continued clustering of many higher-order goods and services in the core is related to the limited purchasing power of the large lower-income sector. This raises the threshold population needed to support these functions to levels that can most efficiently and profitably be served by a central location (Baker 1970: 273). Historically, the provision of infrastructure and allied community services meant enhanced living conditions, thereby reinforcing the pull of the center (Herzog 1985a: 298; Lloyd 1986: 57–59).

The basic structure of the Mexican border city, especially the major metropolises, has been reshaped rapidly since the 1940s by the forces of modernization. In many smaller towns and in sections of the larger cities, however, modern influences are superimposed on an urban structure that remains fundamentally traditional, however tenuous its future may be. Camargo is such a place.

CAMARGO: TRADITIONAL STRUCTURE IN A MODERN CONTEXT

In none of the Mexican border cities has a traditional urban structure persisted longer, and perhaps in purer form, than in Camargo, Tamaulipas. Founded as a civil settlement in 1749 by José de Escandón, the Count of Sierra Gorda who had been commissioned by the Spanish crown to colonize the northern reaches of Nuevo Santander, Camargo is one of the oldest of the Mexican border towns (López Prieto 1975: 61; Garza Saenz 1980; Villarreal Peña 1986: 41–52). Yet, it is not a place that has been artificially frozen in time—a quaint museum village preserved for tourism. Rather, in a natural and unpretentious fashion, it has managed to accommodate modern influences without unduly sacrificing its traditional character or compromising its historical integrity.

Located about four miles south of Rio Grande City, Texas, this community of some 15,000 inhabitants is one of the few Mexican border towns that does not crowd the international boundary (see Fig. 3.3). It commands a site on the east bank of the entrenched Río San Juan at a point where the river bends sharply to the west before emptying into the Rio Grande about three miles downstream. The area is fertile and agriculturally productive, but the location historically has been prone to periodic floods. It is a relatively isolated place except for the proximity of its U.S. counterpart and its historic satellite village of Nuevo Camargo, or Villa Nueva as it is locally known, which is about two miles south of town on the west side of the river.

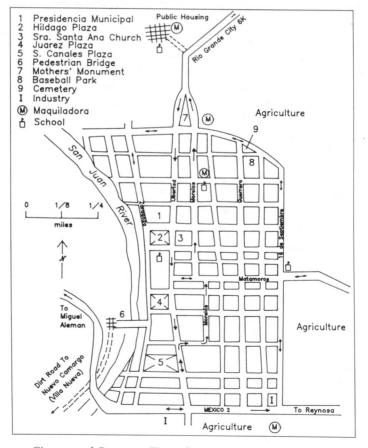

FIGURE 3.3 City map of Camargo, Tamaulipas.

The nearest Mexican cities of any consequence include Miguel Alemán, ten miles to the west, and Reynosa, some forty miles east, both accessible via Mexico Highway 2 that skirts Camargo's southern perimeter.

In keeping with conventional practices, Camargo is a compact, tightly bounded city with a clear break between the built-up area and the surrounding agricultural land, which is devoted primarily to the cultivation of maize on irrigated fields. The Río San Juan forms the western edge of town, Highway 2 the southern, and the northern and eastern limits are demarked by a two-way paved perimeter road, Avenida 16 de Septiembre. Outside this area of roughly one-half−by−one mile, there are two small residential developments located north and west of the town. There are also scattered old farmhouses and newer suburban-type homes, especially out along the eastern extension of Avenida Matamoros, which cuts through farmland for a couple of miles before intersecting Highway 2. The northern outlier, situated just west of the highway to Rio Grande City, is an area of modest dwellings built on unpaved roads; it includes a primary school, a small maquiladora operation, and a row of new public housing. The western exclave, which is a colonia of self-help housing inhabited by only a few families, is located immediately across the San Juan River and is linked to town via a pedestrian bridge erected several years ago to replace a primitive cart bridge. These two outlying areas have been long established and were not developed because of recent population growth. In this sense, they represent an older pattern of small exurbs that was typical of the traditional city.

The town is laid out in a grid pattern oriented in cardinal directions. The streets are narrow, in some places less than thirty feet wide, which led municipio officials to restrict the two principal north-south streets, Libertad and Morelos, to one way traffic. Most of the roads are paved, except for those in the newer and poorer residential areas of largely *in situ housing* (self-constructed and expanding) located in the extreme northwest and southwest sections of town between the river and Avenida Zaragoza.

Unlike the archetypal Spanish colonial town, the plaza mayor, Plaza Hidalgo, is not located in the center of the plat but rather is located on the town's extreme western edge near the river. In other respects, however, Plaza Hidalgo conforms to the classic model. One square block in size, it contains a bust of its namesake but focuses on a centrally placed wooden *kiosco* (gazebo, bandstand) with a large elevated platform that was built in 1898 in a Victorian style. The design of the plaza integrates paved and grassy areas, and the grounds are attractively landscaped with a fountain, ornamental benches, shade trees, tall palms, and rose bushes. Plaza Hidalgo remains the principal public space and social center of the community. In characteristic fashion, it is flanked on one side by government offices, in-cluding the Presidencia Municipal (City Hall), which are constructed in Spanish colonial style and date from the mid-nineteenth century. On an-other side of the plaza, representing the second half of the dual colonial anchors of state and church, stands the cathedral of Nuestra Señora de Santa Ana (see Fig. 3.4). Erected in the early 1750s, it is easily the oldest and most impressive structure in town, although it has been greatly modified over the years (*Catálogo Nacional de Monumentos Históricos* 1986: 136). Its single belfry is a prominent visual landmark, exceeded only by the town's water tower, on this flat floodplain. Due south of Plaza Hidalgo between Zaragoza and Libertad are two secondary plazas: Plaza Juárez, dedicated in 1913, is a small, intimate urban space; Plaza Canales has a more open, parklike setting. In a crowded city where land is at a premium, the value of these public places, now as in the past, cannot be overestimated.

Camargo's commercial structure likewise illustrates the persistence of many traditional features. The majority of commercial activities are concen-trated in the older city core, especially along Avenida Libertad between Plaza Hidalgo and Plaza Canales. This area consists predominantly of two-storey, wood-and-stucco, Spanish-style structures built flush to the side-walk. Many have wrought-iron balconies and tall, recessed wooden doors and windows with wooden shutters. Several of the structures date from the eighteenth century, but others were built in the last decade. Yet even here, true to the historic pattern, commercial outlets are mixed with residences.

Most of the establishments are small, family-run operations, and very little functional zonation has occurred, although several bars are clustered around Plaza Juárez. Atypical of the border cities, Camargo does not have a well-developed tourist trade. It is relatively distant from larger U.S. cities and military bases and is not on one of the major routes to the interior of the country. Consequently, there is no distinct tourist quarter. The few stores that carry curios, pottery, and related tourist items are located around Hidalgo and Juárez plazas as well as on the northern edge of town at a site adjacent to the highway to Rio Grande City.

Another commercial institution that is conspicuous by its absence is a mercado central, and there are no supermarkets. Evidently the main reason for this void is that residents of Camargo have taken to shopping for gro-ceries and food staples in Rio Grande City, especially at the large HEB gro-cery store, which is conveniently located at the first intersection north of the international bridge. Away from Camargo's older established commercial zone, a discontiguous chain of stores extends eastward along Avenida Matamoros, an incipient lower-order spine. In addition, widely scattered

FIGURE 3.4 The oldest structure in Camargo, the church of Nuestra Señora de Santa Ana, was erected in the 1750s but has been greatly modified.

throughout the residential areas are small grocery, notions, and meat stores as well as food and beverage stands and pushcarts. Clustered around the cemetery in the extreme northeastern section of town are several vendors of flowers and religious paraphernalia. Finally, there are a couple of highway-oriented retail establishments, including a PEMEX station, located along Highway 2.

The city's limited industrial activities are focused around the outer margins of the developed area. While the processing of grains remains an important if declining enterprise in this agricultural community, the manufacture of bricks has long been a local specialty. There are several *ladrilleras*, or brickyards, on the town's northern and southern peripheries. These traditional processing activities have been joined in recent years by four maquiladora plants. The plants reportedly employ about 380 workers collectively and specialize in contract sewing, jewelry assembly, and the production of patterns for foundries (Starr County Industrial Foundation 1990).

Camargo's residential structure conforms to the general framework of the traditional city, with the quality of housing generally declining from the core to the periphery as a reflection of social status. Yet the housing pattern is not one of extremes, and neighborhoods cannot be differentiated either spatially or socioeconomically based on appearance alone. Although Camargo is largely a community of middle-income residences, it has some elite housing that is concentrated primarily in the older, established residential area just east of Plaza Hidalgo. Many of these homes date from the late nineteenth and early twentieth centuries, but they have been relatively well maintained, and in some instances significantly renovated, as they have been passed on from one generation to another. Even in this neighborhood, however, large substantial homes are interspersed with small modest structures, and new homes are found adjacent to old residences.

A considerable amount of housing diversity exists within individual barrios throughout the city. Although housing differences among the various middle-income neighborhoods tend to be more subtle than profound, a distinction can be drawn between the barrios on the east side of town and those on the west. East of Avenida Zaragoza, an older residential area, most of the streets are paved and the houses, although mixed in age, style, and quality, tend to be better than those located west of Zaragoza; those are mostly in situ type houses and the roads are unpaved. Although a sign at the edge of town reads *7,000 habitantes* (inhabitants), the city's population has hovered between 15,000 and 16,000 over the past twenty years. While a shortage of housing still exists, a peripheral squatter settlement has not developed. Camargo remains much as it has been: a relatively isolated, small, stable agricultural community where a traditional urban structure survives, in large part because of these very attributes. Such conditions are increasingly rare along la frontera.

MODERN STRUCTURE

The complex forms and functions of contemporary Mexican border cities, especially the larger ones, can perhaps be interpreted best by assuming a more theoretical approach than we took in the preceding section. Models of urban structure are widely used and valuable analytical tools. They are particularly significant if synthesis and an understanding of the broad patterns of urban structure are research goals, notwithstanding their simplified, idealized representations of reality based on the analysis of highly selective data. Several models that generalize about the diversity of urban structure have been developed. As a theoretical construct, the applicability of a given model depends upon the purpose of the study; no single model of urban structure is considered to be analytically superior to all others or to be universally applicable.

Urban structure models of Third World cities have been divided into two main schools: the dynamic and the descriptive (Lowder 1986: 206–249). Models in the process-oriented dynamic school, including user initiatives, entrepreneurial initiatives, and state initiatives, seek to explain land-use patterns and the distribution of social groups within the city by treating land as a dependent variable and focusing on the identity and role of decision-makers in the allocation of space. The descriptive school consists of deductive models, such as those concerned with density gradients, social ecology, and physical morphology, which classify and compare urban form in relationship to land uses and population distributions. The most relevant to this study are the morphological models in the descriptive school. Often drawn on the isotopic plan and incorporating rings and sectors associated with the Chicago School of urban sociology, morphological models conceptualize the built environment of the city as well as its internal patterns of organization. Methodologically, they are most often based on direct observation, the classification and delimitation of land-use zones, and historical dating techniques. They rely on such data sources as land-use surveys, town plans, and architectural types (Lowder 1986: 208).

Scholarly opinions vary widely as to whether the evolving structure of the contemporary Mexican border city represents a unique case (Portes and Walton 1976: 163), is transitional between the classical Latin American city and the contemporary Anglo American city (Gildersleeve 1978: 238–239), or conforms to existing models of modern Latin American city structure (Sargent 1982: 227–228). The reasons for these differences reflect the inherent problems in modeling cities but also suggest that knowledge about the present internal structure of these cities is incomplete. Thus, meaningful conclusions about the pattern of their urban development are difficult to draw. Before examining the constructs of contemporary Mexican border-city morphology, it may be helpful to consider models of Latin American and Mexican urban structure as a context for comparison.

The Griffin-Ford Model of Latin American City Structure

Based on the few detailed land-use studies that have been conducted on Mexican border cities (Palmore et al. 1974; Gildersleeve 1978; Hoffman 1983; Lloyd 1986), the basic morphology of the larger communities is strongly congruent with the most widely accepted model of Latin American urban structure—the Griffin-Ford model (Griffin and Ford 1980). This comprehensive, if highly generalized, construct is based on empirical evidence from Bogotá, Colombia, and relevantly, from Tijuana. It is said to be applicable to the "large, dynamic urban centers of the region" (Griffin and Ford 1980: 399).

The basic framework of the model consists of concentric rings and radial sectors arranged in a distinctive configuration (see Fig. 3.5). Anchoring the model is a well-defined and thriving *central business district (CBD)*, which remains the city's core of prime employment, commercial activity, and entertainment. It contains a mix of modern structures and traditional landscape features. Emanating outward from the core and representing its linear extension along the city's most prestigious corridor is an affluent *commercial spine* that cuts across all subsequent urban zones. It features offices, upscale shops, restaurants, auto-oriented commercial outlets, theaters, and such amenities as parks and golf courses. Bordering this widening axis is an *elite residential sector* including suburban type developments, especially toward its outer end. In the remaining residential zones, housing quality and socioeconomic levels diminish with increasing distance from the central business district. The older elite zone nearest the plaza and surrounding core includes aging but often well-maintained residences that have filtered down to middle-income populations. The *zone of maturity* contains the best housing and public services outside of the new elite residential sector. Beyond this ring is the *zone of in situ accretion*, a transitional area where the housing is diverse and "in a constant state of ongoing construction" (Griffin and

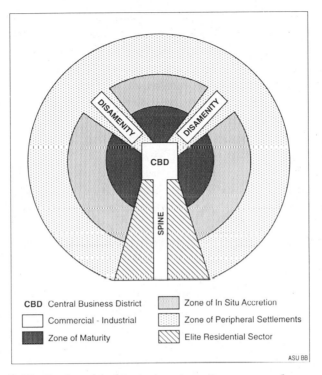

FIGURE 3.5 Griffin-Ford model of Latin American city structure. Source: Adapted from Griffin and Ford 1980. Reproduced with permission of the American Geographical Society.

Ford 1980: 409). It is populated by middle-income and aspiring lower-middle-income groups living in mixed occupancy. The outermost ring is the *zone of peripheral squatter settlements*, presumably including the lowest housing quality and fewest public services, the poorest populations and most recent migrants to the city. The model also incorporates *disamenity sectors*, which are marginal environments such as river beds and railroad corridors, that transect the concentric rings and contain high-density, poverty-stricken, persistent slums of largely self-help housing.

While the model offers a reasonable approximation of Latin American city structure, it has drawn its share of scholarly criticism. Some researchers have faulted its "imprecise parameters" and failure to differentiate between commercial and industrial land uses (Hoffman 1983: 70). Others have noted its need to incorporate a "stronger time element" (de Blij and Muller 1988: 325), while still others have opined that its authors appear to have been "over-influenced by the outward appearance of the cities' physical fabric" (Lowder 1986: 212). These shortcomings notwithstanding, the paradigm is useful in its broad conceptualization of city structure across the whole of Latin America. It offers an excellent starting point for comparing on a macro scale the internal structure of Mexican border cities with other urban centers found within the Latin American realm.

Mexican City Structure

As early as the 1930s, the transition from a traditional to a modern urban form within Mexico was noted in a study of Mérida, the capital of Yucatán state (Hansen 1934). A decade later, however, research in Oaxaca revealed the persistence of the classical plaza-centered structure; this was attributed to the city's relative isolation (Hayner 1944). By comparison, Mexico City's basic configuration was found to be shifting to the "zonal arrangement" similar to that found in larger U.S. cities (Hayner 1945: 304). By the 1950s, the breakdown of the traditional pattern was concluded to be far advanced also in Guadalajara; however, the emerging structure did not conform to the prevailing North American model (Dotson and Dotson 1954). Thus, these early studies revealed a differential rate of change from a traditional to a modern spatial configuration, but they also showed a lack of consensus regarding convergence toward the prevailing urban structure north of the Rio Grande. Contemporary studies conducted in Mexico City and Puebla are analytically more sophisticated than their predecessors and based primarily on the role of migration, industrialization, and socioeconomic mobility in the transformation of urban space. However, they have not resolved the latter issue or proposed a composite model that would allow comparative analysis of Mexican city structure (Brown 1972; Gormsen 1981; Popp 1985).

A notable exception to the single-city focus is Baker's (1970) study of land-use transition in twenty Mexican cities, including five border towns, which embodied a spatial-temporal model that can be used to analyze urban morphology in other Mexican cities. Following the lead of Caplow (1949) in his research on Guatemala City, Baker's model, derived from data gathered from field mapping of land-use patterns in the twenty sample cities and detailed land-use surveys conducted in three of the twenty, proposes a four-stage dynamic evolution of urban morphology: the preindustrial dating from the 1500s to 1850–1900; the early transitional from 1850–1900 to 1930–40; the late transitional from 1930–40 to present; and the industrial from 1960 to present. For the current discussion, it is germane to consider in this sequence of development only the final industrial state (see Fig. 3.6).

The model proposes commercial strips extending away from the cen-

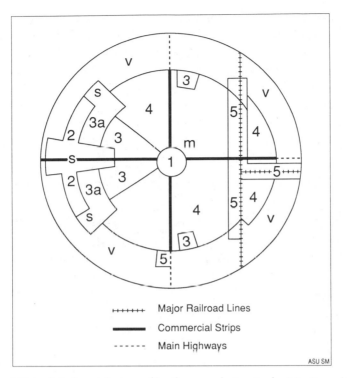

FIGURE 3.6 Baker's industrial stage of land-use evolution in the Mexican city.

1. central business district
2. upper-class residential
3. middle-class residential
3a. upper-middle-class residential
4. lower-class residential
5. industrial
m. public market
s. planned shopping center
v. vacant land

Source: Adapted from Baker 1970.

tral business district on main highways, with a planned shopping center on the strip that cuts through the upper- and middle-class residential areas. Shopping centers are also located on either side of the main highway in the arc of elite housing. Industrial land uses are found along the major railroad lines, at the outer edge of the city on main highways, and in a district beyond the built-up area. The residential pattern includes a wedge of middle-class housing that extends away from the central business district on one side; it grades progressively into areas of upper-middle- and finally upper-class housing. Surrounding much of the central business district, especially on the side where industrial activities are concentrated, is an extensive area of lower-class residences. This is interrupted only by two small middle-class developments located adjacent to main highways on the margins of the city.

In summary, Baker identifies five morphological traits that distinguish the modern industrial city from earlier stages on the preindustrial-industrial continuum:

1. the development of large upper-class and upper-middle-class planned subdivisions on the periphery of the city;
2. the growth of a ring of lower-class housing at the periphery of the central business district;
3. the growth of a ring of lower-middle-class housing beyond the central ring of lower-class dwellings;
4. the growth of highway-oriented suburban industry;
5. the growth of highway-user-oriented commercial strips. (Baker 1970: 293–294).

These findings led Baker to conclude that the Mexican city was likely to evolve away from the North American model in favor of a "dual city" structure. In this model, affluent residential neighborhoods, replete with their own commercial, educational, and cultural institutions, would emerge as separate enclaves from the rest of the city.

While there are obvious similarities as well as differences between this construct and the Griffin-Ford model, the two complement each other. When taken together, they are useful in understanding many of the morphological characteristics of the Mexican border cities. Yet, these models deal with the border communities only incidentally. Thus, they fail to convey possible structural elements and modifications that might be particular to the border region.

Models of Mexican Border-City Structure

In recognition of the peculiar set of structure-forming processes that have operated along the border, coupled with the region's relative isolation from the central axis of urban Mexico and the rest of Latin America, the border cities have been identified as "deviant cases" and classified as a distinct category of Latin American cities (Portes and Walton 1976: 163). Most of the research examining the internal structure of these cities, however, has been descriptive in approach and focused on a specific city. Among the exceptions are studies by Gildersleeve (1978) and Hoffman (1983), both of which were comparative and normative in their design and resulted in composite models of urban structure based on detailed land-use surveys (see Figs. 3.7, 3.8). The Mexican component of Gildersleeve's international border-city model was based on research in Ciudad Juárez, Nogales, and Agua Prieta. Hoffman's border-metropolis model was derived from research in Tijuana and Ciudad Juárez.

Although Hoffman's model (see Fig. 3.8) is graphically more revealing and sophisticated than Gildersleeve's (see Fig. 3.7), the substantive similarities between the two outweigh their differences. Moreover, obvious parallels exist between both of them and the Griffin-Ford and Baker models. The major points of disagreement are worth noting, however. They may reflect structural characteristics that are distinctive to border cities vis-à-vis other Latin American urban places as well as reflect differences among the border towns themselves.

The most evident discrepancy between these cities and others within Latin America is that their shapes are abruptly truncated along their northern edges by the international boundary. Notable exceptions include Camargo and the Sonoran junction town of Sonoita, across from Lukeville, Arizona. The magnetlike pull of the border has led one writer to describe Mexicali as flattened along its northern side "like a snail pressed against an aquarium wall" (Weisman 1986: 168). This comment could easily apply to nearly all other border cities as well. In the case of several so-called "twin cities," the boundary could be thought of as an artificial division between binational—functionally if not morphologically—urban complexes. However, the fact remains that the Mexican cities press against the border even where there are no immediate settlements of consequence on the other side, such as in San Luis Río Colorado, adjacent to tiny San Luis, Arizona. At Tecate, the Mexican residents refer to the American counterpart diminutively as "Tecatito" (little Tecate), but the Mexican city still presses hard against the international boundary. The attraction of the border is pervasive.

A second point of contention, and one that also might be unique to border communities, is the existence of specialized tourist districts within the urban cores and typically close to the ports of entry. Although neither Gildersleeve nor Hoffman identify such a district in their models, both document its existence in the texts of their studies and include it in the category of "miscellaneous business." Whereas the size and importance of these dis-

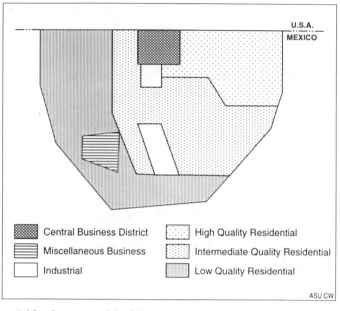

FIGURE 3.7 Gildersleeve's model of the Mexican border city. Source: Adapted from Gildersleeve 1978.

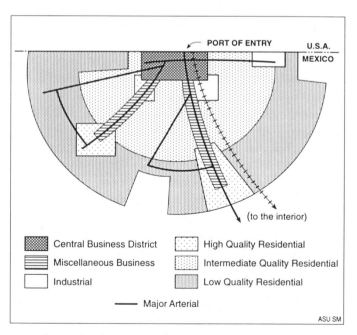

FIGURE 3.8 Hoffman's border-metropolis model. Source: Adapted from Hoffman 1983.

tricts may vary with a city's population and volume of tourist trade, their existence suggests again the impact of the border on the internal structure of these cities and on the regional economy.

A third distinction relates to the location of industrial zones. Whereas in the Griffin-Ford and Gildersleeve models industrial activities were found in or close to the central business district and spine, in the Baker and Hoffman constructs industry is found there as well as in outlying locations. It is associated with railroads, major highways, and in the case of the border-metropolis model, adjacent to the border, but it is removed from the central business district and located in low- to intermediate-quality residential areas. The latter signals the most recent changes in industrial location along the border, which have evolved largely from federal government programs that have fostered a proliferation of maquiladora industrial parks (see Chapter Seven). Thus, the attraction of the international boundary and its impact on the evolving spatial structure of these cities may well be increasing.

A fourth point of disagreement concerns the location of elite housing. The Griffin-Ford and Baker models are characterized by one contiguous elite residential area on both sides of a major commercial spine. In the Gildersleeve model, however, "upper-class" housing is concentrated along the border on one edge of the central business district, while in the Hoffman model, "high-quality" housing is found in central city areas and major arterial suburban locations. The differences in location of elite housing may be related partly to variations in city size as well as in formation and character of the spines. These points have been raised in research on secondary urban centers elsewhere in Latin America (Elbow 1983: 57–65), so they are probably not particular to the border region.

Finally, the models differ in the location and character of middle-income residential areas. The two border-city models show these areas occupying an intermediate position between the central business district and lower-income housing on the periphery. This is not unlike the Griffin-Ford model, although it differentiates between an older, higher-quality zone of maturity surrounding the central business district and a newer, more diverse outer zone of in situ accretion. By contrast, Baker has the largest middle-income area emanating outward from the central business district in sector fashion along the premier commercial strip; lower-income housing surrounds the rest of the central business district and extends to the edge of the built-up area.

Among the critical factors that may account for these differences is that most of the border cities are not very old in comparison to cities elsewhere in Mexico and the rest of Latin America, and they have experienced significant growth only in the post–World War II era (see Chapter Two). Because of their comparative youth, for example, a zone of maturity as defined by Griffin and Ford is almost nonexistent or so small as to be insignificant in the housing pattern of the border cities; the middle-income residential areas conform more typically to the zone of in situ accretion. The presence in Baker's model of lower-income populations residing in a large expanding ring around most of the central business district may also be attributable to the age of the border cities compared to other Mexican cities. Additionally, it may relate to housing shortages resulting from the rapid growth in recent decades of the border towns. This has favored the formation of spontaneous housing settlements for lower-income groups around the periphery, with the urban core dominated by middle-income populations. Of course, the classification of residential areas based upon appearance is subjective and in itself may account for some discrepancies among the various models, especially discrepancies involving the lower and middle "income," "quality," or "class" residential categories.

Given that size, location characteristics, and economic conditions vary among the border cities, it is unrealistic to assume that a typical city exists or that a single model of urban structure is regionally applicable. Of the two border-city models that have been considered, both have qualities to recommend them. In general, the larger cities seem to conform more to Hoffman's model, whereas the smaller cities appear more aligned with Gildersleeve's construct. Yet, although useful, both of these models are temporally static and restricted by their rather narrow classifications. Thus, they are not entirely suitable for the principal purpose of this study—the systematic comparison and interpretation of cultural landscape characteristics of the major functional areas within border cities. Based on field-mapping and selected land-use surveys conducted in the eighteen border communities included in this study, we propose a border-city landscape model that incorporates a dynamic, simple temporal element and an expanded land-use classification system that identifies features that have appeared only in recent years. This model graphically summarizes the most common structural elements and provides an organizational framework for the subsequent chapters dealing with the built environment of major functional areas within border cities (see Fig. 3.9).

The strongly sector-oriented model depicts two temporal-areal stages of urban development: the present and the traditional, separated by a broken line representing the extent of the built-up area at the beginning of the modern era, circa 1950. The model shows the temporal dimension through identification of "older" and "newer" land uses that have emerged during

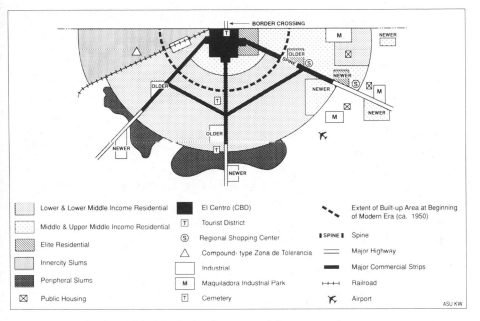

BORDER CROSSING

Legend					
Lower & Lower Middle Income Residential	El Centro (CBD)		Extent of Built-up Area at Beginning of Modern Era (ca. 1950)		
Middle & Upper Middle Income Residential	T	Tourist District		SPINE	Spine
Elite Residential	S	Regional Shopping Center			Major Highway
Innercity Slums	△	Compound- type Zona de Tolerancia			Major Commercial Strips
Peripheral Slums		Industrial		┼┼┼	Railroad
⊠ Public Housing	M	Maquiladora Industrial Park		✈	Airport
	T	Cemetery			ASU KW

FIGURE 3.9 Authors' border-city landscape model.

the modern period. In the model, the central business district surrounds a small tourist district; radiating away from it are interconnected major commercial strips, including a higher-order spine that supports regional shopping centers. Industrial activities, which have shifted progressively from inner- to outer-city locations, are found close to the railroad and main highways. In the case of maquiladoras, they are close to the international boundary and the airport. In general, residential quality decays with distance from the central business district, grading from primarily middle- and upper-middle-income areas to lower- and lower-middle-income neighborhoods; finally, at the edge of the city adjacent to main highways are comparatively small peripheral slums that are growing in an irregular pattern away from their points of origin. Exceptions to this pattern include innercity slums, which fan out from the central business district in a disamenity wedge between the railroad line and the border. On the opposite side of the city is a prestigious section separated from the rest of the community by the spine. The elite residential areas within it occupy limited space, are not connected to each other, and are pushing steadily toward the sector's outer margins. They are surrounded by newer middle- and upper-middle-income housing, which also is found in outlying suburban developments. Finally, situated near industrial areas, especially maquiladoras, are residential areas of public housing.

The border cities do exhibit certain structural characteristics that may be distinctive to the region, such as their peculiar configuration, tourist districts, maquiladora industrial parks, and a highly centralized arterial street network oriented toward the ports of entry. In spite of these distinctive qualities, it could be concluded from the discussion above that the modern structure of Mexican border cities is similar to that of urban places elsewhere in Mexico and the rest of Latin America, especially for cities of like size. Although undeniably influenced by the North American economy and culture, the border cities appear to be more congruent morphologically with contemporary urban centers of Latin America than Anglo America.

THE INTERNAL STRUCTURE OF MATAMOROS

Matamoros is one of the oldest border cities, tracing its origins to the founding of the village of Congregación del Refugio in the eighteenth century. Although it still retains strong vestiges of its early history, Matamoros has emerged in recent decades as a bustling and progressive city with a modern internal structure. As the largest city in Tamaulipas, Matamoros now far exceeds the population of the state's capital, Ciudad Victoria, located about 190 miles to the south. Typical of the growth pattern experienced by the other border metropolises, the city's population ballooned from just less than 10,000 in 1930 to 303,000 by 1990. In the early 1980s, the city's inhabitants were distributed among fifty-nine fraccionamientos. Only seventeen of these had a full complement of infrastructure, including water service, electricity, paved roads, and sewage systems, and they accounted for about 50,000 residents. The remaining 80 percent of the population lived in some 47 *colonias populares* with only partial utilities and municipal services (Canseco Botello 1981: 1). As elsewhere along the border, in spite of considerable economic growth and diversification, the city's extraordinary population boom has far outstripped its capacity to provide the desired urban services for even a majority of its townsfolk.

Both a border and a river town, Matamoros, named for a martyr of Mexico's independence, is situated near the mouth of the Rio Grande about twenty miles from the Gulf and opposite Brownsville, Texas. It is a flat site that is broken only by the levees along the river. Although poorly drained, it lacks the distinctive serpentine *resacas* (oxbow lakes) that enhance the natural environment on the Brownsville side of the river. Now as in the past, the city plays a regionally significant role as a crossroads and transportation hub, with major rail and highway linkages to the country's interior. It also functions as a critical central place for its surrounding, largely agricultural hinterland.

The city has a long and intriguing history as a trading and smuggling port for South Texas and Northeast Mexico. It achieved its maritime zenith during the American Civil War when Union forces blocked the port of Galveston, Texas, and Matamoros became the so-called "back door to the Confederacy." Through its satellite port of Bagdad, it exported large quantities of Confederate cotton to Europe and imported materials and supplies for the Southern cause (Daddysman 1984; Delaney 1955). Largely because of its port-related commerce, both legal and illicit, Matamoros attracted a relatively large and cosmopolitan population. During this time, the city counted some 14,000 residents, making it the most populated border settlement. Among its trading partners, it developed especially close economic and social ties with New Orleans, which enlivened its social geography and left its imprint on the cultural landscape and spirit of the place (Weisman 1986: 4). By the 1880s, however, the tiny port of Bagdad, which lacked protective barrier islands, had succumbed to tropical storms and the general inadequacies of its site. The economic malaise that resulted was offset partially with the arrival of the railroad at Matamoros later that same decade. Then during the early twentieth century, the introduction of irrigation set the stage for the cotton boom of the 1940s, which ushered in the modern period of growth and development.

If Matamoros' spatial configuration is now typical of the larger border cities, its early form was quite unusual: it was the only walled city along la frontera and one of the few in all of Mexico (see Fig. 3.10). The brick wall, built after 1865, stretched from one bend in the river to another, protecting the city on three sides; it was surmounted with nine named battlements or *fortínes* (small forts). This fortified enclosure rigidly defined the city's perimeter and constricted its expansion. The wall was dismantled early in this century, but the city did not expand much beyond the original area demarked by the wall until the 1940s cotton boom (Dillman 1968: 157). (The two *esteros* or salt marshes identified in Figure 3.10 have also disappeared.)

In 1890 the wall linked two legs of the river meander to form the base of a triangle, and the city's modified grid occupied the interior of this space. North-south streets were numbered one to nineteen, and east-west ones were named principally after Mexican patriots such as Morelos, Guerrero, Zaragoza, Teran, and Hidalgo. The main avenue leading to the center of town from the river crossing at the apex of the triangle was Calle Six, called Sexta today. A mule-drawn street railway stretched from the crossing along

FIGURE 3.10 Detail of 1890 street map of Matamoros. Source: Chatfield 1893.

Calle Six to Comercio on the northwest corner of the main plaza, Hidalgo.
This line returned to the ferry crossing via Calles Nine, Abasalo, and Seven.
In the suburbs between the river crossing and the center of the city, in classic
pre-industrial city form, were *jacales* (shacks). Thatched with reeds, broom
corn, and bamboo, jacales presumably housed the community's poorest residents. Throughout the central portion of the city, reaching east and west of
Calle Six for a mile, were cross streets lined with brick dwellings and interspersed with neighborhood plazas—Libertad, Zaragoza, and Allende on the
west of Calle Six and Independencia to the east. Along the blocks north of
and nearer the main plaza were "more pretentious homes, forming a continuous line of brick wall, flush with the sidewalk, from corner to corner"

(Chatfield 1893: 32). These residences were mostly single-storey buildings with flat roofs and shuttered or iron-grated windows. As one approached Plaza Hidalgo, structures became two storey with iron railings around second-floor balconies and large doors at ground level that gave access to enclosed patios (Domenech 1858: 253). Plaza Hidalgo, in typical fashion, was surrounded by well-kept streets and solid block-brick buildings. The plaza was (and still is) flanked on its west by the municipal palace and on its east by the parish church and customs house. To the north and south of the square along Calles Comercio and Morelos were private residences. Within its walls, Matamoros also contained a market, hospital, and cemetery. In this respect, nineteenth-century Matamoros mirrored a townscape more like the eastern Mexican cities of Veracruz and Puebla than any other border place (Arreola 1982).

At present, the urban area spreads for several miles from east to west and north to south (see Fig. 3.11). It is encroaching yearly upon former agricultural land and open space, creating a low-density city that is increas-

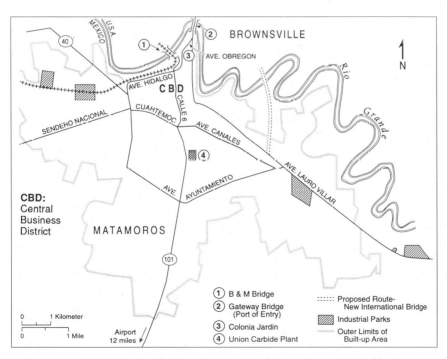

FIGURE 3.11 Current map of Matamoros, Tamaulipas. CBD = Central business district.

ingly dependent upon motor vehicles and that has become difficult to tie together. The street pattern consists of a maze of nonintegrated grids, with several major arterials cutting diagonally across the city, functioning both as traffic arteries and commercial strips. The spine, Calle Sexta, runs north and south through the heart of the city, then becomes Highway 101 and continues on to Ciudad Victoria.

While the city as a whole sprawls, the central business district remains relatively small and compact, roughly encompassing an eight-block square area that includes a mixed pattern of commercial and residential land uses. Its traditional plaza-centered core focuses on Plaza Hidalgo, which is flanked by the main cathedral and the Palacio Municipal, built in 1805. A few short blocks to the northwest is the mercado central, Juárez market. Now divided into old and new sections, it is one of the largest mercados on the border and an important tourist attraction. (A second public market, Treviño Zapata, is located in Colonia Industrial and caters to the local population.)

Another legacy of Matamoros' nineteenth-century, colonial-inspired design is that the streets in the central business district are exceedingly narrow. Although most were converted to one-way traffic to accommodate an estimated 40,000 vehicles in the early 1980s, and undoubtedly there are many more now, traffic congestion and parking problems are endemic (Paredes Manzano 1982: n.p.) (see Fig. 3.12). To enhance its retail appeal, several blocks near the main plaza have been closed to traffic, creating an open-air pedestrian mall that is lined with vendor stalls. North American tourists, however, are drawn primarily to the upscale shops and restaurants found along a kind of tourist "string" that extends from the Gateway Bridge border crossing along Avenida Obregón and Calle Quinta to Plaza Hidalgo. The older city exudes considerable architectural charm, with an abundance of Spanish and French colonial-style, stucco buildings with second-storey, wrought-iron balconies. It also has a distinctive subtropical feeling that is reminiscent of the Vieux Carré in New Orleans. Nevertheless, tourism remains relatively underdeveloped and el centro lacks the usual tourist district.

Over the last twenty years, largely as a consequence of the maquiladora phenomenon, industry in Matamoros has grown, diversified, and physically expanded across the city, particularly out along the major highways in new planned industrial parks. During the 1940s and 1950s, industrial activities were focused overwhelmingly on the processing and storage of agricultural commodities, especially cotton. Not only was industry highly specialized, it also was spatially concentrated. Most of the cotton gins, cot-

FIGURE 3.12 In downtown Matamoros, most of the streets are narrow and one-way. Many of the buildings date from the nineteenth century, reflecting Spanish and French colonial styles.

tonseed oil mills, and cotton-compressing plants, as well as the grain-processing and storage facilities, were clustered in the northwest section of the city near the railroad lines north of Sendero Nacional. By the early 1960s, industry was both overspecialized and overbuilt, with plant capacities exceeding the supply of raw materials (Dillman 1968: 161). With the demise of cotton culture in the 1960s, industry collapsed and an economic recession set in.

Industrial reorientation and growth began in 1968 with the establishment of the first maquiladora operation. By 1980, more than 15,000 workers, mostly women, were employed in these plants. They were located throughout the city but concentrated mainly in the northwest (Canseco Botello 1981: 6). In late 1990, there were reportedly ninety-four maquiladoras providing employment for approximately 38,000 workers within the city (*Twin Plant News* 1990: 84). Although the plants are involved in a wide range of products and services, automotive parts, electronics assembly, and contract sewing are especially significant (Brownsville Economic Development Council 1989). Here, as elsewhere in the border metropolises, the new industrial parks are increasingly built on the outer margins of the city, where they serve as growth poles and contribute to the expansion of the urban area.

Matamoros' residential structure, typical of larger border cities, includes a ring of mostly older, middle-income housing that surrounds the central business district, hemmed in between the river and Cuahtémoc Boulevard. Newer middle-income neighborhoods are found in the northeast near the principal elite area. They also appear in noncontiguous developments that have pushed progressively into the southern and eastern sections of the city, focusing for access on Calle Sexta and Avenida Lauro Villar. Lower-income colonias engulf and sometimes mix with these developments and extend generally toward the periphery of the city. Two older, lower-income areas, or what might be considered inner-city slums situated in disamenity zones, are located on the river's edge on the far east side and in the area west of the central business district and north of the railroad tracks surrounding the old industrial sector. Peripheral squatter settlements have emerged and grown, particularly on the southern and southwestern margins of the city. Public housing, such as the Buena Vista project on the south side, is found here as elsewhere in the larger cities in proximity to the new maquiladora industrial parks, although not all of the parks have public housing adjacent to them. Since shifting away from the vicinity of the plaza mayor during the late 1940s, the principal elite housing area has been Colonia Jardín, which emerged as a product of the prosperity associated with the post–World War II cotton boom. It has been called an "unlikely location," as it is squeezed in a narrow wedge of land created by a prominent river bend on the extreme northeast between the Gateway Bridge and the city core (Dillman 1968: 160). True to its name, the district is very lush and gardenlike, with homes that range from nice to palatial. Yet even here there are trucks lined up with engines running waiting to cross the border, and one finds an electrical assembly plant opposite the Mexican Consulate, all suggesting the incongruous, unpredictable nature of Mexican land-use patterns.

To disentangle Mexican border-city land-use patterns, we turn in the next four chapters to examination of the landscape districts within the cities: tourist, commercial, residential, and industrial. Perhaps the most widely celebrated image of the Mexican border city has been its tourist orientation. Chapter Four will probe this aspect of border-city anatomy and personality.

4 Tourist and Pariah Landscapes

It is probably fair to suggest that most North Americans consider the tourist districts in Mexican border cities to *be* the border cities. They are the only places that most tourists traditionally visit, and they are the places often depicted in the mass media about the border. The landscapes of these districts are among the most colorful, if contrived, of all those found in the Mexican urban scene. In its appearance as well as in its goods and services, the tourist district typically combines elements of a 1920s Hollywood version of "romantic old Mexico" with a kind of raunchy, military-oriented, honky-tonk drag associated with the 1940s and 1950s. It is an illusionary, anachronistic place where merchants cater to tourists' expectations by marketing a vision of Mexico that is a product of history, myth, reality, and fantasy. To cite an example that has become a cliché, one still sees tourists having their pictures taken with *serapes* thrown over their shoulders and wearing big *sombreros* with terms like BORRACHO (drunk) and JUST DIVORCED emblazed across them while perched atop wooden-wheeled carts with burros dyed to resemble zebras (see Fig. 4.1). Yet while these tourist areas are caricatures of both the border town and the country and could be criticized for perpetuating distorted images, in their own way they vividly express cultural and economic dynamics operating along the frontier. Although relatively small in size, tourist districts have played an important role in the economy, culture, and landscape of border towns.

There is a paradox to tourism in the Mexican border cities. On one hand, they are among the most popular tourist destinations within Mexico, attracting several times over the estimated six million tourists who visit the country's interior each year. Indeed, Tijuana claims to be the most-visited city in the world. By one account, in 1986, it attracted nineteen million

FIGURE 4.1 Tourists posing for the camera wearing *serapes* and *sombreros* in Nogales, Sonora.

tourists who contributed over $700 million to the local economy (Griffin and Crowley 1989: 334). Tourism has been and continues to be big business along the border. On the other hand, these cities are widely and often vehemently scorned as places to visit. To appreciate this contention, one need only consider how they have been depicted in tourist guidebooks. Characteristic of the genre, one travel writer summarily dismissed Nuevo Laredo as "a typical border town, with nothing of interest to see," while another cautioned that it "should not be viewed as representative of the Great Republic to the south" (Bashford 1954: 38; Terry 1935: 3). Coupled with the terms "dusty" and "nondescript," these observations have been applied countless times to nearly all of the border towns, if they have generated comment at all. Most of the border towns have been ignored altogether in popular literature about Mexico travel and tourism. Moreover, even when tourist "attractions" are identified, they typically are treated in an exaggerated and pejorative fashion; the focus is on stereotypical elements associated with the near-legendary reputation of these places as swinging "sin cities." Consider the comments of a travel writer who in the 1920s declared that "Tia Juana [sic] is a 'wide open' town, exclusively devoted to racing, gambling, and drinking" (Carpenter 1927: 12). Such sweeping, condescending statements about the border towns continue to be aired, as evidenced by a recent guide that concluded that "Juarez has so many bars that just counting them can make you tipsy. Most of them are rather unsavory, and even the savory ones can be dangerous" (Slater 1989: 525). It is paradoxical, then, that although Mexican border towns have a questionable popular image and historically have been derided as tourist destinations, they nonetheless have their appeal. This is confirmed by the millions of tourists who cross the border each year to visit border cities, or to phrase it more accurately, cross the border to visit *parts* of them—the tourist districts.

In this chapter, we consider not only the location and landscape character of the tourist districts but also examine the so-called *zonas de tolerancia* (zones of tolerance). These areas are devoted to prostitution and adult entertainment that traditionally have been part of the tourist quarter. In some border cities, the zonas, as they are usually called, are still found on the margins of the tourist areas. In other cities they have been either eliminated or intentionally relocated to inconspicuous sites or to the outskirts of the built-up area, where they typically are laid out in a compound-type enclosure. In spite of the historical significance of prostitution to the border economy and to the shaping of external perceptions about border towns, surprisingly little research has been conducted on the subject, especially related to its spatial dimensions. Examination of two leading bibliographic sources for the borderlands revealed that of nearly 13,000 citations, including articles, books, theses, and dissertations from a broad spectrum of academic disciplines, only four dealt with prostitution or zonas (Stoddard et al. 1983: 307–403; Valk 1988: 3–567). This paucity of research suggests that zonas have been treated as pariah places, or outcast landscapes of exclusion (Jackson 1985: 309). These pariah landscapes will be analyzed in terms of location characteristics, patterns of internal organization, and factors responsible for their origins and persistence. The zona in Nuevo Laredo will be examined as a vignette to illustrate this phenomenon, while Tijuana will serve as a case study to document the historical development of tourist districts.

SIZE OF THE TOURIST DISTRICTS

Given the long-standing economic importance of tourism in most border cities, it is somewhat surprising to find that the tourist districts are quite small. They range in size from less than a block in the small towns to a dozen or so blocks in the cities with the largest tourist trade, such as Ciudad

Juárez, Nuevo Laredo, and Tijuana. In most cases, they account for only a fraction of the city's area and are dwarfed by the surrounding commercial sector, in which they function culturally and economically as rather curious appendages.

Variations in tourist-district size reflect a city's total volume of foreign tourism. This is related in part to its population size, although there is not always a perfect correlation; several cities have disproportionately larger or smaller districts than their population might indicate. Moreover, the size of the tourist district seems to bear little relationship to the community's physical attractiveness or to its cultural, political, and economic significance. Rather, the district's size is influenced by a variety of internal and external considerations, especially location and historical precedence. Several examples can be cited to illustrate these points.

With a 1990 population of 602,000, Mexicali, the capital of Baja California, is the third largest of the Mexican border cities. It is a prosperous and modern city in the center of a thriving agricultural region with an interesting, if short, history. Its landscape includes the largest Chinatown along the border, La Chinesca, which is located in the heart of downtown and contains a number of good Chinese restaurants (*Los Angeles Times* 1990). The city also has a new and impressive government complex, a significant historical museum that occupies the old state palace, and excellent parks and recreational facilities. It has modern American-chain hotels along the major commercial spines and a superior bullring that features some of the best matadors in Mexico. It is home to the Mexicali Brewery, one of Mexico's largest. Coupled with these attractions, the city is readily accessible, located only minutes south of busy Interstate 8 across the border. In spite of these factors, Mexicali is, as correctly observed in a recent travel guide, "a city that doesn't cater to tourists. It is a government town . . . that simply doesn't have the pizazz that cities like Tijuana and Ciudad Juarez have" (Cahill 1987: 64). Consequently, the tourist district is comparatively small, extending south from the border for only a few short blocks, especially on Calle Melgar. Thus, like San Luis Río Colorado, Agua Prieta, and Piedras Negras, even good-sized cities with convenient access to the United States do not necessarily have correspondingly large tourist districts. The reasons for this vary from place to place. In the case of Mexicali, it has been a tourist backwater largely in the shadow of Tijuana since the days of Prohibition. Mexicali does not have a large U.S. counterpart to draw from—it is about fifty times larger in population than Calexico, its American border-town neighbor—nor is it near a significant American urban concentration. Perhaps more than any other Mexican border community, as one author has concluded, Mexicali "looks inward, rather than over its shoulder at North America" (Weisman 1986: 168).

To the west of Mexicali in Baja California is Tecate, a town of about 52,000. It is a picturesque, almost villagelike community nestled in a lovely valley surrounded by the granite-studded mountains of the Peninsular Range. A quiet, unpretentious sort of place, Tecate is laid out in a classical Spanish colonial style around the simple, understated Plaza Miguel Hidalgo, which remains the hub of the town. Although traditional in character, it has been able to accommodate modern forces of change. In fact, former Mexican president Gustavo Díaz Ordaz called it *la ventana mas limpia de México,* or Mexico's cleanest window (Price 1973b: 35). Although located less than forty miles from San Diego, the second largest city in California with a population exceeding one million people, tourism in Tecate is relatively insignificant. This is affirmed by its tiny tourist strip on Avenida Benito Juárez and in the marginal condition of the Centro Artesanal on the southern outskirts of town. The critical factor that undermines Tecate's tourist development is that the town is directly accessible from the United States only by a winding, rather treacherous mountain road.

Relative isolation imposed by limited accessibility also explains the modest size of tourist districts in several other communities, while in some places the subnormal size is related primarily to distance from U.S. population centers. One such example is Ojinaga, an attractive Chihuahuan city of 24,000. Located adjacent to remote Presidio, Texas, Ojinaga is more than 100 miles south of Interstate 10. The closest U.S. cities with populations exceeding 100,000 are El Paso and Midland-Odessa, Texas, both about 200 miles away and accessible only by indirect routes.

At the other end of the spectrum are a number of cities that have a larger tourist function than their population might suggest. In most cases they are situated in close proximity to large U.S. cities or recreational attractions, or are on well-traveled routes. Nogales, for example, with 107,000 inhabitants, has a large and well-developed tourist zone that extends for several blocks, especially along Avenida Obregón and Calle Elias. Located in a pass of historic significance, Nogales has long been the main port of entry to cities and resorts along the mainland side of the Gulf of California (Sea of Cortez) and the Pacific Coast. Its tourist district has been viable for several decades (Work Projects Administration 1940: 213–214) but has expanded considerably in recent years in response to the rapid growth of the Phoenix and Tucson metropolitan areas. These are conveniently linked to Nogales via Interstates 10 and 19 and are close enough for "day-tripping" excursions to the border.

Another town with a surprisingly large tourist trade considering its population size is the little Sonoran desert junction community of Sonoita, adjacent to tiny Lukeville, Arizona. Sonoita attracts tourists visiting the nearby Organ Pipe Cactus National Monument. Often these tourists stay at the park in their recreational vehicles for several days or even weeks and go across the border for supplies and entertainment. Sonoita also is the gateway to Puerto Peñasco (also known as Rocky Point), a popular beach town only sixty-five miles away on the northern Gulf of California; it is referred to in central Arizona as "Phoenix's Beach." Consequently, the town supports a bustling tourist strip that is lined with curio shops and liquor stores for about three blocks.

INTRACITY LOCATIONS OF TOURIST DISTRICTS

Within border cities, tourist districts are typically found along the streets adjacent to or within easy walking distance of the border crossings. These locations undoubtedly reflect the popular belief that border towns are dangerous places to visit, or at the very least unsafe places in which to drive. Some tourists, for example, are intimidated by the traffic and unfamiliar traffic signs and laws; they may fear the consequences of having an accident or of having their unattended vehicles stolen or vandalized. Others have heard stories of Mexican police issuing or threatening to issue traffic citations to foreigners for suspect or trumped-up violations in order to elicit a bribe. Stories of *la mordida,* the so-called "bite" that police and other government officials take in lieu of issuing fines for "violations" or for providing other "favors," are the stuff of legends along the border. Still others do not want to be burdened with the time and expense of purchasing Mexican auto insurance. Some may want to avoid the delays of waiting in line to clear U.S. Customs. Thus, for a variety of reasons, many tourists park their vehicles on the U.S. side and walk across the border. The location of tourist districts near or adjacent to the ports of entry are thus convenient for these ambulatory border-crossers. Such proximity to the United States may also temper the anxieties of many tourists, regardless of whether they arrive by vehicle or on foot, about venturing "too far" into these foreign cities. They may fear getting lost or encountering other unpleasantries or dangers, either real or imagined. For some tourists, these are indeed "landscapes of fear" (Tuan 1979).

There are, however, significant exceptions to this pattern. Camargo is separated from the river and the port of entry at Rio Grande City, Texas, by a swath of agricultural land. In Tijuana, the traditional tourist strip, Avenida Revolución, is located south of the Tijuana River channel about a mile from the border. While the distance and walking time to Revolución are not that great, the broad concrete river channel forms a perceptual barrier that discourages tourists from negotiating the walk; a fleet of Mexican taxis congregates at the border to ferry tourists into town. It was this situation that led in the late 1980s to the building of the Viva Tijuana shopping center, located on the north side of the river less than 500 feet from the border gate. The sprawling, open-air complex contains more than 800 parking spaces and is scheduled to accommodate some 220 stores. The first shops opened in late 1987, although the official dedication of the $18 million project was in November 1990. Interestingly, the design of the center and the architecture of the two-storey, pastel-colored, angular-shaped buildings with exterior stairs and balconies resemble a curious blend of San Diego's Seaport Village and Horton Plaza shopping center. Along with its borderside location, perhaps the center's design familiarity is reassuring to some tourists, even if it is out of context with its surroundings.

Another exception includes Matamoros, where Juárez market and the city center are linked to the international bridge by what might be labeled a tourist "string," a leader road into the tourist district. This road (Avenida Obregón) of tourist-oriented businesses includes the finest and most elegant shops and restaurants in the city mixed with other commercial and residential land uses. The string evolved, of course, to capitalize on the tourist traffic between the border and el centro; in the process, it probably helps reduce the psychological distance separating the two.

In Ciudad Juárez, a tourist circuit "loop" has emerged recently with the introduction of the El Paso–Juárez Trolley. Called the "Border Jumper," the bright red-and-green trolleys with rubber tires shuttle tourists from the El Paso Civic Center Plaza to eight scheduled stops along Ciudad Juárez's Avenida Lincoln, Paseo Triunfo de la Republica–Avenida 16 de Septiembre, and Avenida Juárez, then return to the Civic Center. Promotional brochures for the trolley stress that it is the "safe" and "easy" way to enjoy the city's major attractions. In this innovative way, selected locations beyond the traditional district have become accessible for tourists who are reluctant to drive across the border.

All of the larger and many of the smaller cities contain concentrated commercial nodes (clusters) located outside of the principal tourist districts that offer tourist-oriented goods and services. The most common of these include auto shops that specialize in upholstery and body work, pottery and tile businesses, liquor stores, and *casas de cambios* (money-exchange houses). These activities, which may also exist within the district, form clusters of competitive businesses that facilitate comparative shopping in a spatial strategy to increase the overall volume of trade. They are usually found in very accessible locations near the border crossings or on the outskirts of the commercial areas along the principal highways leading into and out of town. These locations are sought out not only for their accessibility and visibility but also for their space. Extra space is necessary for business clusters that specialize in the sale of heavy or cumbersome items, such as pottery and liquor, or that require on-site parking.

Additionally, in some of the cities, government-run commercial nodes display and sell crafts and artisan wares, often from the various regions throughout the country. Examples of these clusters are the Centro Cultural in Tijuana, the Centros Artesanal in Matamoros and Piedras Negras, the Mercado de la Amistad in Nuevo Laredo, and the PRONAF Center in Ciudad Juárez. Also in that city, a large, privately developed tourist node near the PRONAF complex called Pueblito Mexicano was under construction in 1992. One could even propose that the *plazas de toros* (bullrings) and *hipódromos* (horse racetracks) are tourist nodes, although these attractions probably cater more to Mexican nationals than to foreign tourists. Finally, the most prominent node is the cluster of sidewalk curio stalls at the border crossings, which have roving peddlers who hawk "last chance" souvenirs to motorists waiting in line to clear U.S. Customs (see Fig. 4.2).

TOURIST DISTRICT LANDSCAPES

The main tourist district in most border cities has traditionally focused on a single commercial street. Away from this strip there is a rapid decline in number of tourist-oriented businesses, especially those dealing in mass-appeal goods and services that require a high volume of foot traffic. Tourist functions typically extend for less than a block from the strip along the side streets, and in some places arcades, that intersect it at right angles, giving the district a linear configuration (see Fig. 4.3). In some of the larger cities such as Nuevo Laredo and Nogales where tourism has grown in recent years, the tourist district has expanded to the immediate adjacent streets that run parallel to the principal strip. In Ciudad Juárez and Tijuana, extension away from the traditional tourist strips of Avenida Juárez and Avenida Revolución, respectively, has occurred primarily along the newer major commercial spines, especially Avenida 16 de Septiembre in Ciudad Juárez

FIGURE 4.2 Curio stands, with roving peddlers, line the sidewalk at the busy Tijuana–San Ysidro border crossing.

FIGURE 4.3 The classic tourist strip in Ciudad Acuña, replete with bright, garish neon signs.

and Paseo de los Héroes and Agua Caliente Boulevard in Tijuana. Although this kind of archetypal border-town tourist strip is found only in the most popular of the districts, elements of it are mirrored elsewhere on a smaller scale.

The most notable exceptions to the dominant-strip pattern include Reynosa and Matamoros. In the former, tourism focuses on the so-called Zona Rosa district adjacent to the border crossing. As in Matamoros, tourist retail activities in Reynosa are spread over a street (Avenida Hidalgo) that has been closed to vehicular traffic, creating an open-air pedestrian walkway. In both places, however, tourist trade in these malls is not directed exclusively or perhaps even primarily to North Americans but seems to cater more to a Mexican clientele.

In addition to being small and spatially constricted, the edges of the tourist districts are often sharply defined by physical and psychological barriers. These can include abrupt changes in land uses, streetscaping, and signs—signs in English vanish. These changes, coupled with the linearity of the tourist districts, reduce the chances of tourists "getting lost" and wandering outside the districts. Most tourists seem content to stroll up and down the strip, and relatively few stray from the beaten path. As one young tourist gushed about Tijuana's Avenida Revolución, "This is almost like a mall" (*San Diego Union* 1989b: B6). Perhaps this insularity represents a sort of "field-of-care," or area where one feels secure, that may help reduce tourists' anxieties about visiting these places.

Within most tourist districts, especially larger ones, there is a discernible differentiation of retail activities. Mass-appeal and convenience establishments, including curio shops, apparel and jewelry stores, import outlets, liquor stores, bars, and restaurants, characteristically command the premier strip locations. Limited-appeal stores and specialty goods and services outlets—dental and medical offices, beauty salons, and bakeries that cater to tourists—tend to be located on side streets just off the strip, often near the border crossings. Moreover, in several cities, zones featuring risqué nightclub shows and prostitution are found on the margins of the tourist district. This will be discussed in more detail later in the chapter.

The districts are pedestrian-oriented places. This is convenient not only for the many tourists who walk across the border but also for those who drive across, park, and walk the strip. It is unusual for a tourist to drive from shop to shop or bar to bar within the quarter. By relinquishing the security and anonymity of their vehicles, tourists are forced to interact more personally with the people and environment around them. Because it is located on the margins of downtown and often is an important and busy commercial street in its own right, the strip may present a livelier, more intense scene than most tourists are accustomed to.

Along the crowded sidewalks of larger districts, street vendors operate out of makeshift stands or spread their wares out on blankets. Itinerant peddlers sell trinkets, candies, and assorted curios and apparel items. Indian women, sometimes referred to as "street Marias," sell artificial flowers and cheap jewelry, while their children hawk gum and cloth "friendship" bracelets—and generally panhandle tourists (*Los Angeles Times* 1987). They are joined by patrolling cops, cabbies, photographers, beggars, strolling musicians, and street entertainers. A line of shopkeepers beckon passersby to "come on in, take a look," and barkers in front of nightclubs inform passing males that it is "Showtime!" All of this activity, together with the colorful parade of tourists themselves, makes for a vibrant, almost carnival-like atmosphere that is akin to an amusement park for shoppers.

Yet as chaotic and unstructured as it may seem, the government attempts to control all street merchants, from food vendors to photographers to shoeshine-stand operators, through licensing and taxation (Price 1973a: 91–92). In recent years, however, unlicensed street vendors have proliferated, especially in larger cities such as Tijuana. This has upset competing merchants, who have petitioned authorities to remove unlicensed vendors from the tourist districts (*San Diego Union* 1991b: B3).

The architecture of the district is dominated by one- and two-storey buildings of Spanish and art deco, or streamline-moderne style, stucco or wooden construction, with flat or low-pitched tile roofs. These usually have few exterior embellishments but are often trimmed in bright colors and frequently display painted and neon signs. Because street frontage in prime locations is expensive, shop-fronts are comparatively narrow; this enhances the visual diversity at ground level. In the larger districts, side arcades, bazaars, and minimalls are common and becoming increasingly popular. Although some are rather extensive, they also feature small shops and artisan stalls. It is not unusual to find as many as twenty shops on one side of a block, most of the shops no more than twenty-four feet wide. Retail establishments are typically built flush with the sidewalk and usually open to the street in malllike fashion. To encourage browsing and to facilitate opportunities for shopkeepers to lure tourists inside verbally, many shops have open fronts instead of doors.

In addition to the curio shops, some of the larger districts have a few upscale department stores—Sara's Imports, Dorian's, and Le Drug Store in

Tijuana and Marti's in Nuevo Laredo—and expensive specialty and de-signer shops (*San Diego Union* 1987b). Most establishments, however, tend to be small, independent, often family-run operations. Although the districts have specialty shops, particularly for leather goods, jewelry, and imported items such as Paris perfumes, most of the curio shops carry essentially the same lines of products. Variations occur primarily by quality and price. Al-though it would be practically impossible to list the eclectic, even baffling, range of goods found in the typical curio shop, the most common groups of handicraft and related items include these: ceramics, glassware, leather goods, paper products, earthenware, wrought-iron works, carved wood, basketry, weaving, Mexican wearing apparel, and black velvet paintings. Here as elsewhere in the tourist world, T-shirts have become a mainstay.

The restaurants and bars in the district are not nearly as garish and kitschy as the curio shops, although one can find the occasional restaurant shaped like a giant sombrero or bar with jungle scenes and the likeness of King Kong painted on its facade. Not surprisingly, most restaurants in the district specialize in Mexican cuisine. It appears that many tourists consider dining at a Mexican eatery to be part of the desired tourist experience. How-ever, this culinary interest generally extends to patronizing only the most attractive, or at least cleanest-looking, establishments. Consequently, the pushcart food stands, which are common on the streets in the surrounding commercial and residential areas, are not very numerous in the tourist dis-trict. Where they do exist, they tend to be frequented mainly by the resident population. The stories of tourists getting sick from eating at these stands is part of the folklore about the border-town tourist experience.

In recent years, fast-food outlets have become increasingly popular and commonplace in the tourist districts as well as along the commercial spines. This growth has been spurred by a streamlined franchise registration process, part of the Mexican government's efforts to open its borders to international operations (*San Diego Union* 1991c: I1). Although major American hamburger chains have only begun to invade Mexican border cit-ies, fast-food chicken chains, especially Kentucky Fried Chicken (Colonel Sanders), Church's Fried Chicken, and El Pollo Loco have made significant inroads. Denny's has operated for several years in some of the larger cities. Furthermore, new Mexican hamburger, pizza, and ice-cream chains—Bur-ger Boy, La Fábula, Bing Helados—have emerged and are patterned closely after, if not clones of, their American counterparts (*San Diego Union* 1987a). They are patronized by both tourists and residents.

Especially since the creation in 1961 of the Programa Nacional Fron-terizo (PRONAF), which included the beautification of border cities as one of its principal objectives (Chávez 1961; Dillman 1970: 487–507), movement has been underway to "clean up" the tourist areas. This auspicious goal was undertaken to foster a more "wholesome" image of the country in general and the border cities in particular, and to broaden the traditional base of tourism. These clean-up and beautification programs have included both physical and functional changes within the districts. In Tijuana, for example, $4.2 million was spent on repaving Avenida Revolución; broadening its sidewalk to twenty-four feet; landscaping; and adding ornate sodium-vapor streetlamps, phone booths, street furniture, and trash cans (*San Diego Union* 1980). Beyond such streetscape improvements, other efforts initiated under the banner of clean-up campaigns have included building and staffing tourist information booths; increasing security and the number of English-speaking policemen; reducing police corruption and crime against tourists; creating public-arts projects; and constructing cultural centers, museums, parks, and government-run arts-and-crafts centers. In some cases, these tourist oriented projects have been located either at the periphery of the traditional tourist district or outside the district altogether.

These changes notwithstanding, the major focus of the clean-up efforts, indeed the cause célèbre, was to rid the districts of prostitution, or at least to spatially restrict where it would be tolerated. While the so-called *zonas de tolerancia* will be discussed later in the chapter, it is germane in this context to examine the impact of these programs on the nightlife currently within the core of the districts. Although exceptions exist, there are fewer bars and especially nightclubs in most of the cities than in the recent past. Moreover, current floor shows are neither as risqué as they once were nor as legend would have them (Griffin and Ford 1976: 435).

The establishments that remain represent the survivors of a culling process that has occurred over the last three decades. Bars and clubs have been eliminated that either were economically marginal or were incompatible with the need to appeal to—or at least not offend—a middle-class American clientele that included women. It is not unusual now to find a bar with a sign announcing itself a "Ladies Bar," meaning that women are welcome. A number of establishments have been spruced up, while others have been extensively renovated and redecorated into upscale, relatively expensive places, signaling the changes that have occurred in clientele. The latest additions to this landscape, at least in the largest districts, are new or renovated sidewalk cafes, "beer gardens" and especially roof-top terrace bars, and open-air balconies that overlook the strip where new, American-style discos have been built (*San Diego Tribune* 1986b; *Los Angeles Times* 1988b).

THE TOURIST DISTRICTS AS OTHER-DIRECTED PLACES

On the windows and exterior facades of commercial structures in almost all of the tourist districts are signs, tile mosaics, pictures, and other renderings that depict certain recurring themes. These symbols may provide important clues about the meaning of the tourist districts. The most common images seen are pottery, *serapes,* sombreros, and mounted bull horns, and the most common scenes portrayed are bullfights, mission-style churches, likenesses of Emiliano Zapata and Francisco "Pancho" Villa, and desert landscapes that include giant saguaro cacti and peasant men and boys *(campesinos)* wearing sandals and the traditional baggy, white cotton garb. The single most widespread image is probably of a campesino reclining against a saguaro with his knees drawn up to his chest and his sombrero tilted over his face while he takes a *siesta.* When a woman is portrayed, she typically has a high lady-of-Spain hairstyle and is wearing a frilly, low-cut, off-shoulder dress. Her head is thrown back gaily, and yes, she has dark "flashing" eyes and a rose in her mouth. These romanticized, stereotypical images perhaps symbolize a distinctive American way of thinking about Mexico, and as such may reflect the deep-seated cultural and historical forces that have shaped the landscapes associated with these districts as well as shed light on the attraction they hold for the average North American tourist. Indeed, one could argue that the cultural landscapes of these districts and the goods and services found there play on the preconceived images of what most North American tourists think Mexico *ought* to look like and what it *ought* to offer them for sale (see Fig. 4.4). In this sense, it has little to do with the Mexican people or culture and much to do with pleasing outsiders, especially American tourist-consumers.

Because of this external orientation, the tourist districts may be classified as "other-directed places" (Curtis and Arreola 1989). This term was coined by J. B. Jackson, one of the preeminent American landscape scholars, in a mid-1950s article that appeared originally in *Landscape* magazine. The article was entitled, "Other-directed Houses," and it was concerned with the then-emerging roadside architecture (Jackson 1970: 55–72). In the article, Jackson defines other-directed architecture as characterized by "conspicuous facades, exotic decoration and landscaping, a lavish use of lights and colors and signs" and meant for pleasure and popular mass entertainment (Jackson 1970: 68). Another scholar who has recently expanded upon the concept notes that "the total effect of such architecture is the creation of other-directed places which . . . declare themselves unequivocally to be 'Vacationland' or 'Consumerland' " (Relph 1976: 93). Some criticize these

FIGURE 4.4 This sign on a sidewalk in the *Zona Rosa* tourist district in Reynosa includes a *sombrero* and a *serape*, two of the most commonly invoked symbols of Mexico, and a listing of popular curios and tourist items.

touristscapes as being synthetic or even absurd and having a forced atmosphere of gaiety. However, Jackson writes, "Go in when you are looking for a good time and for an escape from the everyday, and at once the place seems steeped in magic" (Jackson 1970: 63). Viewed that way, the superficiality of these places does not in itself diminish the tourist experience and may even enhance it.

A great deal of research has suggested that most tourists enjoy, or at least are not put off by, contrived or unauthentic attractions, especially if they conform to preconceived notions (Cohen 1979; Curtis 1981; Curtis 1985; Eckbo 1969; Jackson 1962; MacCannell 1976; Pearce 1982). One distinguished scholar has gone so far as to conclude that tourists seldom like the authentic, preferring instead caricature that validates their own "provincial expectations" (Boorstin 1961: 100). There is evidently a certain ineffable satisfaction or wish-fulfillment that comes when a place lives up to preexisting images, even if it does so through contrivance. Although critics may assail such tourism, one important purpose served is that "contrived attractions also protect a locality from its visitors by focusing touristic activities temporally and geographically" (Jakle 1985: 23). These themes help explain not only the nature of tourist-district landscapes in border cities but also the characteristics and motivations of tourists who visit them.

In all likelihood, few tourists come to these cities for sight-seeing purposes, although "negative sight-seeing," or viewing disturbing scenes such as begging or poverty-ridden living conditions, may be a motivation for some. Rather, we contend, most tourists want to eat, drink, and purchase selective goods and services in an idealized "Mexicoland" that is somewhat insulated from the real world and danger but that evokes at least a veiled sense of excitement and foreign adventure. The romanticized imagery of pretty *señoritas* with roses in their mouths and peasant men taking a siesta in the desert sun and the associated iconography seems to support this position.

So, too, does the tawdry reputation of the honky-tonk border town, which continues to lure and fascinate. This might explain why the old Tijuana jail was remodeled and converted to a tourist attraction in the early 1970s. The Tijuana Convention and Tourist Bureau put up $60,000 of the cost, and the rest came from city funds (*San Diego Union* 1972). Through such renovation and clean-up efforts, the tourist districts have in many ways parodied themselves as they have offered an increasingly sanitized version of what they were, but not so sanitized a version that they have deflated tourists' expectations. To be successful, they must contain all that is usual and expected.

This desire for a mildly stimulating time in a "faraway" exotic land where tangible and mental souvenirs can be collected is not unlike the motivations that draw tourists by the millions to theme parks or even to Third World countries, especially those in the tropical realm (Britton 1979; Lea 1988; Matthews 1977). In essence, it represents a form of escape or "diversionary tourism." Some theorists have argued that such "escapes to fantasyland" are quests for individual survival and identity (Cohen and Taylor 1976), while others have suggested that they are a means of ego-enhancement (Dann 1977). A philosophy professor, Ruben Vizcaino, at the Autonomous University of Baja California shares these views. He has been quoted as saying that tourists come to Tijuana "looking for *their* identity.

They see themselves as supermen, leaders of the Free World, technological gods. They see Third World poverty—the skinny dogs, the people begging, the *indigenas* (Indians) kneeling before them—and they prove to themselves that *they* are great" (quoted in Martinez 1989: 20).

Regardless of whether or not one accepts this somewhat radical critique, the tourism-as-escape theme conforms to the compensatory leisure-behavior theory, which argues that people seek the opposite kinds of stimulation in their leisure environments to what they have at work (Pearce 1982: 20). This provides a context for interpreting the tourist-district landscapes as well as tourist motivations.

Since at least the Prohibition era (1918–1933) when large numbers of Americans first headed "down Mexico way," the vast majority of tourists have been "day visitors," or as they have been formally classified, "excursionists," who stay less than twenty-four hours. Although tourism statistics for these cities are notoriously unreliable, if available at all, conventional wisdom for the state of Baja California has it that only 15 to 20 percent of the tourists stay three or more nights. The figure is probably less in other Mexican border states (*San Diego Union* 1987a). In fact, by all reports, the average tourist stay in the border cities ranges from about six to eight hours in Ciudad Juárez and Tijuana to less than four hours in most of the other cities.

Based on available data, it appears that most tourists from the United States arrive from states immediately adjacent to the respective border cities. A 1985 study conducted by the Ministry of Tourism in Baja California found that 84 percent of foreign tourists in Baja were residents of California, 12 percent came from other U.S. states, 2 percent came from Europe, 1 percent came from Canada, and 1 percent came from elsewhere (Luis Valles 1985: 6; *San Diego Union* 1987a). Although it cannot be substantiated, it appears unlikely that those who arrive from more distant locations come to the border towns as their primary destinations. In the case of Tijuana, it is probably visited by non-California residents as a "side trip" from the tourist mecca of Southern California—Disneyland, which is less than three hours away. San Diego's principal attractions, the zoo and Sea World, are only half an hour from the port of entry at San Ysidro.

Complementing the short stay, the average tourist expenditure is relatively low and concentrated on only a few selected categories of goods and services. By most accounts, a tourist spends an average of twenty to thirty-five dollars per visit, depending on location. In Tijuana, per-capita spending of tourists reportedly increased from twenty-four dollars in 1986 to thirty-four dollars in 1987 (Luis Valles 1988: 8). As shown in Table 4.1 for Baja

TABLE 4.1   Tourist Expenditures in
Baja California, 1985

Category	Percent of Total
Restaurants	23
Bars	14
Curios	14
Liquors	11
Hotels/motels	9
Gasoline	8
Breads	7
Auto service	6
Entertainment	5
Other	3

SOURCE: Based on Luis Valles 1985: 6.

California in the mid-1980s, 62 percent of these expenditures were in four categories: restaurants, bars, curios, and liquor. Lodging, which is normally a high tourist cost, accounts for only 9 percent. It is followed by gasoline, breads, auto services, entertainment, and other miscellaneous expenditures.

In Tijuana, at least, there seems to be a significant difference in the pattern of expenditures between day and night. Reportedly, during the day about 70 percent of the tourist dollar is spent on curios, whereas during the evening about 90 percent is spent in bars and restaurants (Matthews 1987: 14). Elsewhere in the border cities, studies have documented that the most frequent service expenditures by U.S. tourists include entertainment, medical, dental, selected car repairs, and haircuts, while the most frequently purchased retail goods include liquor, food staples, prescription drugs, and "tourist items" (House 1982: 202).

It is interesting that although families and businessmen reportedly account for an increasingly larger percentage of the tourist trade, attempts to expand the range of tourist activities have apparently met with little success. The Centro Cultural (Cultural Center) in Tijuana provides a good example (see Fig. 4.5). Completed in 1983, the impressive and unusual complex is called La Bola because of its round shape. It is located within walking distance of the border in the fashionable Zona del Río district across the street from the new Plaza Río Tijuana shopping center. Designed

FIGURE 4.5 Tijuana's Centro Cultural, locally called *La Bola* because of its round shape.

by renowned architect Pedro Ramírez Vásquez, who also was responsible for the design of Mexico City's National Museum of Anthropology, the Cultural Center contains an anthropological museum, an omnitheater with a curving 180-degree screen, a performing arts center, an outdoor courtyard, gift shops, galleries, and a good restaurant and bar. It now draws over one million visitors annually. In the late 1980s, it hosted international jazz festivals and staged performances by such groups as the Bolshoi Ballet. Yet less than 15 percent of its visitors come from the United States (*San Diego Tribune* 1987). Likewise, the new U.S.-style shopping centers have failed to generate much interest among foreigners. What tourists want, one might conclude, is what always has motivated them to visit the border: a chance to frolic for a few hours in an "old" Mexico of their fancy. The lure is still escape to an imagined place.

This clearly seems to be the case for the fastest-growing group of tourists—young people aged eighteen to twenty-one. Especially since Texas raised its legal drinking age from eighteen to twenty-one in 1986, tourists in this age group have flocked to the border cities where the drinking age is eighteen, the liquor is relatively cheap, and the atmosphere is generally permissive (*Austin American-Statesman* 1989d). In California, where the drinking age is also twenty-one and the bars must close by 2 : 00 A.M., city officials in nearby Tijuana estimate that as many as 12,000 youths from north of the border, especially San Diego, visit on a typical weekend night (*San Diego Tribune* 1986b). This prompted one newspaper to report that Avenida Revolución "has evolved in recent years from a bastion of sleaze for U.S. servicemen and other pleasure-seekers to a kind of teeny-bopper fantasy-land" (*Los Angeles Times* 1988b). The young people are drawn at night primarily to trendy high-tech dance bars, which often have cover charges and even dress codes. One of the latest reported crazes is to drink Tequila Poppers. These are usually served complete with bibs by whistle-blowing barmen, some dressed like firemen or doctors, who pour the liquor and juice into the customer's mouth until they cannot drink any more (*San Diego Union* 1988).

One could argue that the tourist district has come full-circle: the more it changes, the more it remains the same. That, of course, is a cliché, but Mexican border cities have long been places of clichés and illusions. Consider again the burros painted with stripes. One of the photographers on Revolución in Tijuana once commented: "People believe they're striped to make them look like zebras, but it's because most of the burros are white, and depending on the light, they don't come out that well on the film" (*San Diego Tribune* 1982b: B1).

TIJUANA AND THE HISTORICAL DEVELOPMENT OF THE TOURIST DISTRICT

Although Tijuana's tourist district is the largest and most famous along la frontera, its evolution and the forces that shaped it illustrate the general historical pattern for the Mexican border cities collectively. It may also offer indications of the character and direction of future growth and change in the tourist district. Development of Tijuana's tourist quarter, as in most of the border cities, is essentially a twentieth-century phenomenon that can be divided into several distinct phases: an early period from about the turn of the century through the late teens; the Prohibition era; the Depression; the Second World War and its aftermath during the 1950s; and a modern phase beginning in the 1960s. Each of these phases in its own way reflects the extent to which Mexican border cities, and especially their tourist trade, are inextricably linked not only to the North American market economy but also to its social and political events. Nowhere is this more evident than in Tijuana, where proximity to Southern California has clearly influenced the creation and continued patronage of the tourist zone.

Prior to the beginning of Prohibition in the late teens, Tijuana was a fledgling, ramshackle town. It had a history of slow but gradual growth based on tourism that was financed and managed by Americans. This pattern persisted until the 1930s and the Depression. Although the city traces its origins to the granting of a *rancho* in the 1820s, it was not until 1889 that a section of the Argüello family's Rancho de Tijuana was subdivided and a town plan drawn up (Piñera Ramírez and Ortiz Figueroa 1983: 284– 292; Herzog 1989: 111–114). That was forty-one years after establishment of the international boundary, the catalyst for Tijuana's founding and subsequent growth, and fifteen years after the first customs house was erected near the port of entry. Tijuana was officially known as Zaragoza until 1929, although it was seldom called that on either side of the border. In 1890, the *pueblo* had a population of less than 250 who resided mainly in adobe huts strewn about the floodplain of the Tijuana River. Yet as small as the settlement was, the tourist strip had already developed. Indeed, principally along the incipient Avenida Olvera, a rather wide, unpaved street that would become Avenida Revolución in the early 1920s, there were a few stores and restaurants and several *cantinas*. These were mostly one-storey structures of wood-frame construction with false-fronts. The town also had a prize-fighting hall, a hotel with fifty-three rooms, and a bullring. A couple of miles to the south at the Agua Caliente springs stood the Tijuana Hot Springs Hotel, owned and operated by several San Diego physicians (Conklin 1967: 86; Summers 1974: 15). Twenty years later, in 1910, the population had grown to 733, most (568) of them men (Piñera Ramírez and Ortiz Figueroa 1983: 292). This growth resulted from increased tourism, spurred largely by the construction in 1907 of a railroad that linked San Diego to Tijuana. Up to 1915, however, development was stifled and the tourist trade declined precipitously. This was a result of the Mexican Revolution and a separatist revolt that had culminated in a battle in the streets of Tijuana between federal troops and the forces of the Mexican Liberal Party, led by socialist Ricardo Flores Magón (Martínez 1960: 474–484).

U.S.-Mexico relations were strained during World War I, as evidenced in 1917 by the requirement that persons entering Tijuana have a passport, by a reduction in hours of operation at the port of entry, and by a rule forbidding servicemen in uniform from crossing the border. Commencing in 1915, a resurgence in tourism began that would continue to build episodically through the Prohibition era. At the regional level it was sparked by "spill-over tourism" associated with the enormously successful San Diego–Panama Exposition at San Diego's Balboa Park. More fundamentally, however, it was related to the rising tide of moral reform that had begun to wash

FIGURE 4.6 An aerial view of Tijuana on June 20, 1924, then a city of less than
10,000 permanent residents but enjoying its so-called "golden era of tourism."
Photo courtesy of the National Archives.

across the United States after the turn of the century. This peaked with passage of the Volstead Act, which prohibited manufacture, sale, and transportation of alcoholic beverages.

From 1915 to the beginning of Prohibition, the race track, two casinos, and several clubs that had been built merely foreshadowed the kind
of tourist development that would emerge full-blown in the 1920s (see
Fig. 4.6). During that time, Tijuana's "golden era of tourism," the city capitalized on the demand for booze, gambling, sex, and other exotic diversions,
such as bullfights, boxing, and cockfighting, that were illegal or too expensive in the United States. Tijuana became a "haven for hedonism" in keeping
with the themes of excess and indulgence that came to characterize the Jazz
Age. In short, the boom was on. The image of Tijuana as a wide-open town
quickly took shape and persists to this day.

Although its population in 1920 was just over 1,000, on the Fourth of July that year an estimated 65,000 people and 12,650 automobiles jammed the town. The event illustrated dramatically the demand that existed for the lucrative "vice trade" and the profits that could be generated from it (Acevedo Cárdenas and Piñera Ramírez 1983: 436). This did not go unnoticed; growth occurred at a rapid pace thereafter. A reporter for the *New York Times* characterized the town in 1920 as "a recrudescence of a Bret Harte mining camp or a Wild West main street scene in the movies, with a dash of Coney Island thrown in . . . [where] new joy palaces are being shot up overnight" (Summers 1974: 36). By 1926, the town supported about seventy-five bars, mostly on Revolución, including a bar of more than 200 meters reputed to be the longest in the world (Pourade 1967: 83; Acevedo Cárdenas and Piñera Ramírez 1983: 437) (see Fig. 4.7). In addition to the ordinary saloons and "joy palaces," there were lavish casinos, resorts, and European-style cabarets. The most notable bordello was the Moulin Rouge, which had a miniature red windmill on its roof and became a Tijuana landmark of sorts. The main attraction, however, was the racetrack, which drew tens of thousands of visitors a week during the racing season. After strug-

FIGURE 4.7 On Tijuana's Avenida Revolución, circa late 1940s, a view of reputedly the world's longest bar. Photo of a postcard from the authors' private collections.

gling following its debut in 1915 and closing in 1919, the track reopened with fanfare in January 1920—ironically, the month the Eighteenth Amendment to the U.S. Constitution, creating Prohibition, went into effect. On opening day, boxer Jack Dempsey served as honorary race starter (Price 1973a: 53). In a nation gone dry and straight and in the absence of a Las Vegas, Tijuana emerged as a convenient yet foreign playground, tantalizingly beyond the prevailing morality and rule of law north of the border.

There was a decidedly glamorous dimension to Tijuana's tourist trade during the Roaring Twenties. The city lured the crème de la crème of Hollywood and the world of sports. Among the notable personalities who frequented it were baseball player Babe Ruth, comics Charlie Chaplin and Buster Keaton, cowboy star Tom Mix, satirist Will Rogers, actresses Jean Harlow, Gloria Swanson, and the "It Girl" Clara Bow, dancer and G.I. pin-up girl Rita Hayworth (née Rita Cansino), gangster Al Capone, and F. Scott Fitzgerald, the literary prince of the day (Acevedo Cárdenas and Piñera Ramírez 1983: 436; Price 1973a: 52). It was that kind of place, and its luster was enhanced in no small measure with the completion of the posh Agua Caliente Casino and Spa (see Fig. 4.8). Built in stages between 1926

FIGURE 4.8 The entrance to the posh Agua Caliente Casino and Spa, Tijuana's premier 1920s resort and tourist attraction. Photo of a postcard from the authors' private collections.

and 1930 on the site of the abandoned Tijuana Hot Springs Hotel a short distance south of the raucous downtown, Agua Caliente was a full-service entertainment complex. It included a first-class hotel and individual bungalows on lushly landscaped grounds as well as a casino, a golf course, and of course the racetrack. Hailed in advertisements as the "Deauville of America," a reference to an exclusive French resort and spa, the interior of the casino was a glittering baroque showpiece that included a salon where the moneyed elite played with solid gold coins instead of chips (Pourade 1967: 131; Price 1973a: 55). One scholar offers the following critical sociological interpretation of Agua Caliente in the context of that time and place: "The Casino de Agua Caliente mythically represents the physical and psychological space where a certain power group carried on its ultimate fun and games. Accordingly, Tijuana came to stand for a place liberated from moral pressures, a sort of wanton utopia where oriental maharajas and fugitives from Prohibition organized a network of luxury, complacency, and stupefaction at their own wealth and their cult of emotions. . . . Later they had to go to Havana when the agrarian reform and the oil expropriation came and the gambling houses were shut down" (Monsiváis 1978: 60–61).

In spite of its opulence and fame, the casino at Agua Caliente basked only briefly in the limelight, falling victim to the stock market crash, the repeal of Prohibition, the Depression, and a rising nationalistic morality within postrevolutionary Mexico.

When the casino closed in July of 1935—the last to do so in the city—it marked, as one researcher has observed, "not only the end of the era of widespread gambling in Tijuana, but an end to the domination of Americans over Tijuana's economic development" (Hoffman 1983: 103). In fact, since the founding of the town, but especially after 1915, American investors and entrepreneurs had established a near-monopoly over the city's liquor, racing, and gaming interests. Many of these "merchants of sin," as they have been labeled (Martínez 1988: 114), had relocated to Tijuana when their U.S. businesses closed because of the new morality and laws of Prohibition. Others were opportunists who realized the tremendous potential for profit and were willing to pursue new ventures. Not only was there an influx of foreign capital and management, but Americans also typically commanded most of the middle-echelon positions, such as bartenders, waiters, and dealers, in the casinos and nicer clubs. This situation prompted an altercation in 1923 in which about fifty Mexican workers stormed the Tivoli Bar and overturned gambling tables to protest the bar's practice of hiring Americans over Mexicans (Price 1973a: 55).

The investment of American resources in Tijuana illustrates how isolated the city was from the mainstream of Mexican society and government. It also reflects the open-door policy that had characterized the rule of President Porfirio Díaz from 1876 to the spring of 1911. As Díaz's presidency attests, American investment was not only tolerated; on occasion, it greatly enriched officials at the highest levels of the Mexican government. For example, General Abelardo Rodríguez, the governor of the northern district of Baja California during the 1920s, owned the Agua Caliente property and amassed a fortune from his involvement in the city's Prohibition-fueled economy (Acevedo Cárdenas and Piñera Ramírez 1983: 441; Demaris 1970: 117–118). Ultimately, General Rodríguez became interim president of the country from 1932 to 1934. By the mid-1930s, Tijuana, which in many respects had functioned as an extraterritorial American enclave, had reverted back to Mexican control.

The Depression brought the collapse of Tijuana's tourism-based economy. Although President Lázaro Cárdenas' decision in 1935 to close the nation's gambling houses and racetracks contributed to the decline, the situation was already grave. Indeed, the reopening of the track at Agua Caliente in 1937 under Mexican direction did little to improve the city's economic malaise; the rest of the Agua Caliente complex was converted to a technical school. Most of the clubs on Revolución closed or were torched in arson fires as owners desperately attempted to cut their losses by collecting on insurance policies. One by one, the businesses and commercial properties passed to Mexican ownership.

One indication of tourism's decline was the decreasing number of persons crossing the border at the San Ysidro port of entry. Whereas in fiscal 1931, the first year that such statistics were kept, more than 5,425,000 people crossed the border, it was not until 1946 that the five-million mark was again surpassed (Price 1973a: 57). Yet while Tijuana's economy languished, its population increased from 8,384 in 1930 to 16,486 in 1940. In part, this growth was stimulated by the creation in 1933 of a "free zone" encompassing the western border cities from Tijuana to Ciudad Juárez, which eliminated the payment of Mexican tariffs on goods imported from the United States. But the major reason was the settlement in Tijuana of repatriated Mexicans whose jobs in the United States had been terminated as a consequence of the Depression (Hoffman 1974).

The Second World War and the ensuing prosperity of the 1950s led to another tourist boom in Tijuana. This illustrated again how the city's fortunes have fluctuated in response to developments in the United States. During this period, the town's image as a "wicked" place was expanded upon as the character of tourism evolved to reflect the changes that had occurred since Prohibition in the ownership and clientele of tourist establishments. The initial stimulus for renewed tourism was the wartime rationing of commodities in the United States. Rationed commodities were readily available for sale in the markets and shops of Tijuana. San Diego residents and servicemen who were stationed there flocked across the border to purchase gasoline, tires, selected groceries, meat, dairy products, metal parts, and a wide variety of other consumer goods that were rationed or scarce (Price 1973a: 59).

Although the appeal of scarce goods was not an insignificant factor, the major factor in revitalizing Tijuana's tourist economy was the exploding demand for entertainment services. Thousands of unattached servicemen from military installations throughout Southern California were looking for a good time and erotic diversions. Tijuana, as it had during the 1920s, responded to the demands of the marketplace. Soon a new generation of curio shops, restaurants, beer joints, and clubs with explicit sex shows and prostitution appeared along Revolución. Unlike during Prohibition, there were few, if any, establishments that offered pretensions of class or catered to an elite crowd. The district took on a wild, bawdy, honky-tonk atmosphere to appeal to a younger, military-oriented male clientele. Some of the more notorious clubs, such as the Molino Rojo (Moulin Rouge), Chicago Club, Manhattan Club, and the Blue Fox, developed national and international reputations and became part of the city's lurid folklore (*San Diego Tribune* 1986a).

Although the casinos remained closed, gambling was revived in the form of horse and greyhound racing at the Agua Caliente track. In 1946, construction of the jai alai *frontón* (arena) on Revolución, which had begun and was abandoned during the lean years of the Depression, was completed and opened for legalized gambling. In addition, there was an escalating trade in narcotics, contraband, abortions, and "quickie" divorces. This was the period when Tijuana's "tourism of vice" reached its peak. Although it fulfilled a real economic need, it cast a shadow over the city that distorted its image and unfairly tainted its citizens in the process.

In 1956, the Governor of Baja California, Braulio Maldonado, vowed never to visit Tijuana during his term in office unless local authorities could rid the city of vice (Hoffman 1983: 103). This and similar statements from other government officials dramatized conditions in Tijuana and stimulated efforts to "clean up" the city. The Mexican government at all levels was understandably concerned about the negative image of border towns, perhaps especially Tijuana. It was once described by a muckraking writer as "the toughest, roughest, gaudiest, filthiest, loudest—the most larcenous, vicious, predacious—the wickedest bordertown of them all" (Demaris 1970: 18). Beyond being disdained for projecting a seedy image to tourists, border towns were also despised by some in Mexico City "as 'de-Mexicanized' beachheads of the country's peaceful conquest by the United States" (Riding 1985: 287). These sentiments led to the creation in 1961 of PRONAF and later to other federally administered projects, such as the Border Industrialization Program (BIP), aimed at enhancing the physical conditions and economic vitality of border communities. Tijuana has been a major beneficiary of these multifaceted efforts, and directly or indirectly, they have had an impact on tourism and the tourist landscape.

Over the last thirty years, the city's built environment has undergone a startling transformation as its population has ballooned from about 152,000 in 1960 to almost 800,000 in 1990. Although its economy has modernized and diversified, largely as a consequence of increased transborder commerce and the extraordinary growth of maquiladoras (see Chapter Seven), tourism remains critical to the economy. It has continued to grow in both volume and amount of revenue generated, especially since the massive devaluation of the peso in 1982. In addition to the previously mentioned improvements on Revolución and construction of the Cultural Center and Plaza Río Tijuana shopping center, other recent changes have contributed positively to tourism. One such change was the removal in the early 1970s of the squalid "Cartolandia" (cardboard city) shantytown, which was located in the bed of the Tijuana River near the border crossing and was considered a glaring eyesore (Herzog 1989: 128). New highways have been built and a second border crossing, on Otay Mesa near the airport and many maquiladora industrial parks, has helped alleviate some of the traffic problems that have long plagued the San Ysidro gate. The track and club facilities at Agua Caliente have been extensively renovated. There are new, upscale shops, restaurants, nightclubs, and hotels, including the luxurious Hotel Fiesta Americana with its eighteen storeys and gleaming mirrored tower. This hotel and its office-building twin of twenty-three storeys have become landmarks and symbols of contemporary Tijuana.

Yet, as much as tourism and the tourist landscape in Tijuana have changed, they have remained the same. In 1984, the U.S. Navy placed an evening curfew on the city, claiming that Tijuana police were accosting military personnel and extorting money (*San Diego Union* 1988); the curfew remains in effect. Tourists still flock primarily to Revolución, and although much of the strip has been cleaned up, it continues to play on the same symbols and imagery as in the past.

Indeed, at its northern margins, in an area known as La Zona Norte, the "old" Tijuana of Prohibition and the war years thrives in some forty bars and hotels where sex shows and prostitution flourish (*San Diego Union* 1989a; Owens 1982). Many of these establishments are named after the more famous (or infamous) clubs that once commanded prime locations on Revolución. It recently has been called "a haven for alcoholics, drug addicts, prostitutes and criminal fugitives from both Mexico and the U.S. But the average tourist, unless they zigged when they should have zagged, will never know it is there" (*San Diego Union* 1989a: B1). It is a place where the atmosphere, as one journalist put it, "alternates between alcohol-fueled gaiety and a veiled sense of menace" (*San Diego Union* 1989a: B1). La Zona Norte represents a small, somewhat isolated vestige of Tijuana's more sordid past, but it remains a vital part of the city and performs an important economic function (see Fig. 4.9). A tourism official in Tijuana once described the zone as "a very small area, very ugly, and we do not pave those roads because we do not want to promote those things. On the other hand, we are not working to drive those people out of business. We must keep one eye closed. They hire many people there and we are very short on working opportunities. The Zona Norte feeds many families" (quoted in Cahill 1975: 36).

FIGURE 4.9 Tijuana's La Zona Norte, a small, somewhat isolated vestige of the city's more sordid past on the northern end of Avenida Revolución.

Therein lies the dilemma. Ridding the city of prostitution and associated erotic amusements is seen as a meritorious goal. However, it is a difficult goal to achieve in a developing country because of the considerable financial returns that such activities provide both legally through taxes, official fees, and personal income as well as illicitly through various forms of corruption. Tijuana's strategy for dealing with this dilemma has been to spatially restrict prostitution to a zone on the margins of the tourist district. Although not the most common approach, this is one of three strategies that has been adopted by cities along the border.

ZONAS DE TOLERANCIA

Federal law in Mexico does not prohibit prostitution, although its extent and spatial characteristics vary widely from place to place, depending on tradition and local policies toward its existence. Where prostitution exists in urban Mexico, including the border cities, it is often concentrated in specially designated zones of tolerance, called zonas de tolerancia in Spanish (Curtis and Arreola 1991). Zonas, as they are known throughout the country, may be located either within the city itself or on the outskirts of the built-up area. They are a distinctive feature of the cultural landscape but have not been adequately investigated. The few published scholarly studies on contemporary aspects of prostitution in the border cities have been anthropological or sociological treatments based on research conducted during the 1960s and 1970s in either Tijuana or Ciudad Juárez (Guerrero 1968; Price 1973a; McNamara 1971; Roebuck and McNamara 1973). In all cases, they were not comparative, lacked a spatial component, and were devoid of concern for the character of place.

A simple spatial distinction can be drawn between cities with zonas and those without (see Fig. 4.10). The absence of a zona does not mean a city is free of prostitution; if one does exist, however, it is restricted to individual bars, hotels, and residences that are not clustered in a designated area. Similarly, even in cities with zonas, prostitution may be found elsewhere within the urban area. In the eighteen cities that were investigated, the following six did not have a zona: Tecate, Sonoita, Naco, Miguel Alemán, Camargo, and Matamoros. With the exception of Matamoros, all are relatively small towns, with populations ranging from about 10,000 in Sonoita and Naco to around 52,000 in Tecate. According to local authorities and published accounts, Matamoros, Miguel Alemán, Camargo, and Naco each had a zona in recent years; the other two cities may have as well (Cahill

FIGURE 4.10 A map of *zonas de tolerancia* in the Mexican border cities. Source: Adapted from Curtis and Arreola 1991. Reproduced with permission of the American Geographical Society.

1987: 111; Weisman 1986: 41). Obviously, zonas vary over time as well as space. Decisions to close or to relocate zonas reflect shifts in public opinion and social attitudes, changes in local and regional economies, and political considerations. Of course, reform efforts initiated since the early 1960s by the government to clean up border towns have provided a powerful stimulus for change, but they have not been more important than other factors, especially economic ones. Moreover, the fact that a zona has been shut down does not mean that it will remain closed indefinitely. The zona in Reynosa, for example, had been forcibly closed in the 1970s by the state with the election of a governor who had campaigned on an anti-prostitution plat-form, yet it reopened in the early 1980s and now is one of the two largest along the border (Weisman 1986: 41).

District Zonas

Zonas were identified in twelve of the eighteen cities. Based on location, organization, and landscape characteristics, they can be differentiated into district and compound types. The district zona is a designated area within the city with a cluster of commercial establishments, such as bars, night-clubs, restaurants, and hotels. Prostitution in the district is tolerated on a de facto if not a de jure basis by police and other authorities. Although many of these places cater to prostitution, there are no true brothels whose exclusive function is prostitution. Establishments within the zona also pro-vide music, dancing, floor shows, room accommodations, and food service. These attract customers who may not be interested in the services of a pros-titute. For this reason, zonas might best be thought of as adult entertainment and erotic amusement districts where prostitution is only one, albeit the most significant, of several attractions. Furthermore, zonas typically include bars and clubs where prostitution is not allowed, and other commercial and residential land uses are also found.

Five cities were classified as having district-type zonas, including Ti-juana, Mexicali, Nogales, Las Palomas, and Ciudad Juárez. Except for No-gales, where the zona is on a single street in a lower-middle-class neighbor-hood a dozen blocks or so from the city center, the districts within these cities are located in the older urban cores on the periphery of the traditional tourist strip, as in Tijuana. The size of the district zonas range from little more than a block in the small and impoverished Chihuahuan town of Las Palomas to ten or more blocks combined in Ciudad Juárez's dual districts; these are about a mile apart off Avenida Juárez, especially on Calle Mariscal. The districts' boundaries are either sharply defined as in Tijuana and No-gales, or vague and transitional as in Mexicali and Ciudad Juárez. Irma's, perhaps Ciudad Juárez's most famous club for prostitution, is located out-side of the two principal districts.

Historically, district zonas have been differentiated from each other and also internally by such factors as race, ethnicity, and socioeconomic considerations. At one time or another, most of the border cities had more than one district, which typically were separate Anglo or Mexican zonas. Some towns also had districts designated exclusively for blacks (Exner 1917: 209). Segregation by ethnicity and race as well as by income and social status likewise characterize individual districts, where certain "sectors" or single establishments cater to one group or another. Further distinctions can be drawn between businesses with on-premises versus off-premises prostitution, and also between heterosexual, homosexual, and transvestite establishments.

Contrary to popular belief, most clubs and prostitutes within these districts have long served primarily a Mexican clientele. In Tijuana, for instance, a survey revealed that of approximately 1,000 registered prostitutes in the city, 200 had a foreign clientele, 100 a mixed clientele, and 700 a Mexican clientele (Price 1973a: 94). In a study of prostitution in Ciudad Juárez, fifty-three bars were identified in the "American sector" and fifty in the "Mexican sector" (McNamara 1971: 5). While differentiation by income groups persists, the evidence suggests that segregation by race and ethnicity has declined in recent years as the number of Americans who frequent the zonas has plummeted and Mexicans have come to represent an even larger majority of zona patrons.

The district zonas are relics of an earlier era when prostitution and strip joints played a more important role in the tourist trade. These five districts are survivors of that period. In almost all cases, however, they have retracted in size and assumed the classic characteristics of a zone of discard, or skid row, having been badly neglected in terms of infrastructure and landscape improvements. Elsewhere, in cities that formerly had districts, the zonas were eliminated or relocated to more remote or less conspicuous sites.

Compound Zonas

Seven of the eighteen border cities have compound zonas: San Luis Río Colorado, Agua Prieta, Ojinaga, Ciudad Acuña, Piedras Negras, Nuevo Laredo, and Reynosa. In the English vernacular, especially along the Mexico-Texas border, compound zonas are frequently known as "boys' towns" (West 1973: 73, 109). Compounds are, or at least were originally, set off and isolated from other sections of the city, typically near disamenity zones. Agua Prieta's zona, for example, is shut off from its surrounding area by physical and land-use barriers that include a railroad on the west, an arroyo and cemetery on the north, and an industrial park and baseball field on the east; low-income residences are located on the south.

Although the zonas in Ojinaga and Ciudad Acuña are situated a couple of miles from those cities, and the zona in Piedras Negras is not connected to the built-up area, the remaining compounds have all been encroached upon. The compound in San Luis Río Colorado, for instance, once removed from the city's edge, has been surrounded by in situ and squatter housing. Nearly all of the compound zonas are accessible only by unpaved and typically unimproved roads.

The present-day compound zonas emerged during the 1950s and early 1960s, and perhaps before then in some locations. They developed as an alternative to the districts and in response to the mounting campaign to rid the cities of prostitution. The model for establishing spatially discrete zonas located outside the city proper likely dates to the early twentieth century and the U.S. military occupation of Chihuahua. During Pershing's Punitive Expedition in 1916, Chinese and Mexican entrepreneurs pursued the military, following their camps and offering women and liquor. The expedition settled at Colonia Dublán some fifty miles south of the border at Ciudad Juárez and remained there for seven months, during which time the vice vendors congregated around the camp (Sandos 1980: 625). The alarming number of men with venereal disease and the fear instilled in the local Mexican population by American soldiers on the prowl for women led a local bishop to advise Pershing to set up a "restricted district" on the southern limits of the camp (Braddy 1966: 21). A Mexican managed the restricted zone and only Mexican prostitutes were allowed. Pershing assigned a military physician as health inspector and fixed a flat fee of two dollars. The disease rate dropped. Although the solution was potentially controversial, it provoked little public outcry in the United States. In the words of Pershing, it "proved the best way to handle a difficult problem" (Vandiver 1977: vol. 2, 622). When Pershing's force moved farther south to El Valle in 1917, a restricted zone for prostitutes was once again established. This time it was organized by the Chinese, who had been involved in the vice trade in several border cities, especially Mexicali. Although compound zonas did not emerge until perhaps the 1950s, the rationale for their creation mirrored Pershing's earlier solution.

Nuevo Laredo's Boys' Town

Once hailed as "The Broadway of Boys' Towns," the zona in Nuevo Laredo is the largest and most famous along the border (West 1973: 109). Yet it is not unlike the other compound zonas in terms of location, layout, and appearance as well as in the motivations for its creation. In the 1950s, local officials decided that the old district zona of bars and clubs near the Palacio Federal was a black mark on the central city and projected the "wrong" image to tourists (Gonzalez 1989). Official discussions of moving the zona had actually surfaced as early as the 1930s (Benedicto 1956: 723). Consequently, under civic pressure, the zona was forced to move in 1964 to its present site on the southwest side of the city off Calle Anahuac, then a relatively remote location beyond the built-up area (see Fig. 4.11). Although the city has expanded and the site is no longer isolated, it is still a rather inconspicuous place. It is separated on the west from the main highway into town, Avenida México, and by a trucking area, railroad, and stockyards; low-income residences and a new industrial park are on other sides. Like other compounds, it clearly has been contained spatially by land-use barriers. On a 1979 map of Nuevo Laredo produced by a map company in Laredo, the zona is labeled a *Zona de Evasión,* or zone of escape (Asvestas 1979). Access to the zona via Calle Anahuac is hindered by a potholed road that is close to impassable during periods of even moderate rain; at its best, the road is something of an obstacle, but one that is frequently overcome. Completely encircling the zona and giving it a fortresslike appearance is a tall, dirty, white stucco wall with a single opening.

Inside the sprawling compound, which is several acres in size, the zona is laid out around an unpaved circumferential road and two parallel cross streets. Along these wide, chuckhole-pitted roads are more than thirty commercial establishments and several apartment-like residences as well as abandoned structures and vacant lots. In respect to its internal organization, six elements that collectively make up the zona can be identified: structures devoted to institutional activities; primary clubs; secondary clubs; "cribs" or "flats"; lower-order convenience goods and service establishments; and residences.

Institutional-type structures and spaces begin with the small gatehouse at the entrance. The gatehouse is manned by armed police who control access to the zona, maintain law and order within the compound, and may also collect nominal entry fees. Adjacent to the gatehouse and shaded by a small stand of pepper trees is the police post and jail. Next to it is the medical clinic where the zona prostitutes receive weekly gynecological checkups and biannual blood tests. Although prostitution is not illegal, prostitutes must register with the local government and submit to the required examinations. Across the street from the police post, not far from the gate, is another institutional space, the taxi stand. It appears that many zona workers and patrons, especially Anglos, use taxi service; for first-time visitors, Boys' Town can be difficult to find, particularly at night. Finally, there is a small public facility for long-distance and international telephone calls.

A second element in the zona's internal structure is the primary club—which includes the Papagayo, the Marabú, and the Tamyko. The Papagayo and Marabú, once called "as posh as anything in Mexico City," evoke a kind of 1950s Las Vegas–type style embellished with large neon signs (De-

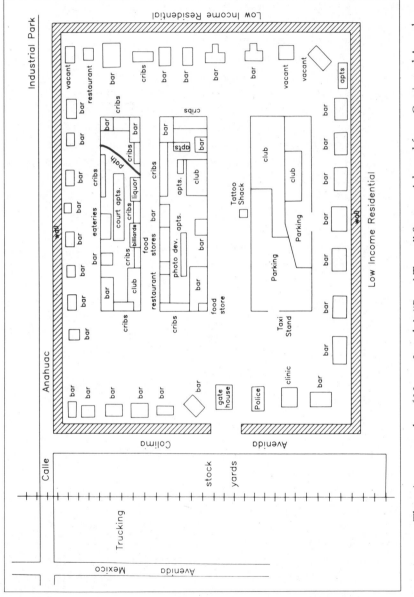

FIGURE 4.11 The microgeography of Nuevo Laredo's "Boys' Town." Source: Adapted from Curtis and Arreola 1991. Reproduced with permission of the American Geographical Society.

maris 1970: 3). Located near the gate, these primary clubs exude a sense of exclusivity by being fenced off from the surrounding clubs and providing their own security and parking attendants. Certainly the most interesting club architecturally is the Tamyko, which has a bright red, fifty-foot Japanese pagoda and an outside patio with fish ponds spanned by arched bridges; Japanese motifs and decorative influences are found throughout the club's buildings (see Fig. 4.12). In the summer of 1989, the street in front of

FIGURE 4.12 The Tamyko Club in Nuevo Laredo's "Boys' Town," architecturally the most unusual structure within the compound.

the Tamyko was paved—the first and only one paved within the compound. Primary clubs, which are complexes rather than single structures, feature on-premises prostitution and cater to Anglos or to higher-income, generally younger Mexicans.

Secondary clubs and bars are concentrated mainly around the zona's perimeter. They vary in size and range in appearance from relatively attractive to completely run-down. These establishments, on an individual basis, tend to be more specialized in function than primary clubs. Some have strip shows, others offer music and dancing, and still others are country-style Mexican bars for men that emphasize beer and tequila drinking. There also are two gay-transvestite clubs, The Dallas Cowboys and the Club Miramar. The secondary clubs may or may not have on-premises prostitution or provide rooms. In general, they appear to be frequented mainly by middle-aged Mexicans of lower- to middle-income status, but great variation occurs from club to club.

"Cribs," or "flats" as they are sometimes called, are long, one-storey structures that have been partitioned into small single rooms that open directly onto the street. This allows the women who work in the cribs to solicit trade directly from passing zona patrons. In Boys' Town's highly structured social system, the cribs represent the bottom of the order; the oldest and physically least-attractive prostitutes are relegated to these rows of dingy, austere rooms. Exhibiting a distance-decay pattern, the cribs are found in the most inferior locations within the compound, farthest removed from the gate and at least two of the three primary clubs. The cribs are frequented primarily by an older, poorer Mexican clientele.

In addition to the clubs and bars, the zona supports a variety of other businesses, including lower-order convenience goods and service establishments such as small restaurants, grocery stores, a liquor store, beauty shops, a pool hall, and even a tattoo shack. There also are "floating" activities, such as food, flower and curio vendors, photographers, and musicians. Residences compose the compound's final element. Many of the people who work in Boys' Town, not only the prostitutes and their children but also room maids, shopkeepers, and kitchen staff, live in the compound. They reside in rooms behind the clubs, in the cribs, or in residential apartments.

A sociologist who studied Nuevo Laredo's Boys' Town in the early 1970s described it as an isolated community offering services, including room and board, income opportunities, police protection, health facilities, a market place, beauty shops, restaurants, transportation, and entertainment centers, for those who worked there (Stevenson 1975: 154).

Functionally, little seems to have changed. Overall, however, the zona appears to have declined in patronage and suffered from neglect. The signs are manifest in abandoned buildings, vacant lots, and the generally deteriorated condition of the compound; it has the unmistakable look of having fallen on hard times. In the early 1970s, Boys' Town was reported to have had 38 bars and clubs and to have employed between 650 and 1,000 prostitutes as well as 200 "service" workers (Stevenson 1975: 27). There now are a little more than half that many establishments, and it seems likely that the number of zona workers has dropped by at least as much, if not more so. Yet in spite of its decline and rumors of an impending relocation, Boys' Town survives. On a typical Saturday night, it is a crowded, lively place. Although local and regional circumstances have contributed to this situation, the reasons for its persistence despite the decline in business are the same as those that have affected zonas in all the border cities.

Zona Persistence Despite Decline

It has been widely reported that prostitution in the Mexican border cities has lost its "magnetism" and has declined markedly since its heyday in the 1950s (Martínez 1988: 115). One author, for example, states that "there are two hundred registered prostitutes in Juárez today when twenty-five years ago there were seven thousand." Another concludes that "now it seems that those who come looking for prostitution are Blacks, Filipinos, Chicanos, and Mexicans" (Langley 1988: 37; Monsiváis 1978: 61). While these and similar claims are difficult to document, it seems clear that there are fewer prostitutes and that prostitution plays a far less significant role in the border economy than it did in the not-too-distant past. Among the reasons cited for this apparent decline are the emergence of "topless" and "bottomless" bars in the United States; the spread of pornography shops, massage parlors, and escort services; the availability of x-rated movies and videos; and increased sexual permissiveness. More recently, fear of AIDS has been mentioned. Thus, other than providing an "exotic" setting and perhaps cheaper prices, the zonas had little to offer that was perhaps not readily available in the United States. As one former nightclub owner in Tijuana who was driven out of business by U.S. competition remarked, "We lost our monopoly on immorality" (*Wall Street Journal* 1988: 1). The declining population and closure of some military installations and mining operations in the borderlands may also have contributed to this decrease.

It has also been suggested that an increase in job opportunities for young women in the Mexican border cities, especially in the maquiladora assembly plants, may have been a factor in the decline of prostitution (Langley 1988: 37). That notion was rejected during the summer of 1989 by a group of prostitutes in the city of Chihuahua who were protesting the closing of the zona in that community and threatened to strip in front of the government palace. A spokeswoman for the newly formed Chihuahua Prostitutes Union scoffed at the governor's suggestion that prostitutes seek factory jobs, saying, "Factories only pay 60,000 *pesos* ($23) a week, and we make that much or more in two hours" (*Daily Oklahoman* 1989: 2). Although maquiladoras have given women greater employment opportunities, a correlation with the decline in prostitution has yet to be established.

Explanations for the persistence of zonas range from the sweeping to the specific. One argument is that prostitution "thrives in places like border cities where language and cultural differences foster impersonality and contempt between the adjacent societies" (Price 1973a: 94). In a similar vein, it has been suggested that "vice is usually found in large doses in border areas and ports throughout the world, especially in regions visited by affluent tourists" (Martínez 1988: 11). These lines of reasoning are probably oversimplifications of complex, place-specific circumstances; they overlook countless examples that contradict such statements. Moreover, in the case of Mexico, prostitution has never been confined to the border region. It exists throughout the country, especially in the larger urban places. The persistence of prostitution and zonas seems to have less to do with location per se than with other considerations.

The simplest superficial explanation is that a continuing demand for prostitution exists, both by foreigners and by Mexican nationals; a continuing supply of prostitutes is available; and this demand can be met in the context of a favorable operating environment. The factors that contribute to this situation, however, are fundamentally social and economic. They include the fact that, through legal and illegal avenues, prostitution provides an important source of personal and institutional income. Even more significant perhaps is that prostitution within Mexico is not universally viewed with the same sense of moral indignation as it ostensibly is viewed in the United States.

Now as in the past, tourism and the tourist districts in the Mexican border cities are being influenced by forces and events that originate in the United States as well as within the country itself. Clearly the districts and industry continue to evolve in response to these internal and external factors. Yet while the changes they have experienced recently are significant, many are changes in degree, not kind. In many ways, one could conclude that the traditional patterns of tourist behavior and the present tourist land-scape are not unlike what they have been since the beginning of the century. Some may lament that, and others may not. The zonas persist because they fulfill needs, some social, some economic, of both buyers and merchants, visitors and visited. The cultural landscape reflects this dynamic.

5 Commercial Landscapes

Because the marketplace often responds to the forces of change faster than other segments of the urban scene, the commercial landscape first and perhaps best reflects the contemporary dynamism of the Mexican border cities. The new automobile-oriented spines, for example, with their modern chain outlets, minimalls, and large multifunctional shopping centers herald not only the diffusion of North American commercial design and marketing concepts but also the rise of a mobile and affluent Mexican middle class. Yet while some commercial areas signal formation of a new social order, others bear brick-and-mortar witness to the continuity of long-established cultural and economic practices. In the central business district, many Mexican and Spanish traditions persist in the pattern and imprint of commercial enterprise as well as in the character of public institutions and spaces. Of course, commercial areas are not only places of exchange but also of interaction. As such, they play a critical role in the social geography of the city. Although they are not major consumers of urban space, commercial landscapes exhibit a richness of diversity and exert great influence on the anatomy and personality of these cities.

Unlike urban places north of the border, where zoning laws and other legal restrictions institutionalize the segregation of land uses, in Mexican border cities the functional zonation of activity spaces is not so rigidly defined. Commercial activities are comparatively widespread. Indeed, it is unusual to find *any* section of the city without them, except possibly new elite residential developments. In spite of its nearly ubiquitous presence, however, commerce is most concentrated in the central business district and along the major urban arteries. Accordingly, this chapter examines first the contemporary central business district, excluding the previously discussed tourist districts, with particular focus on the central plaza as well as the commercial-retail area. Attention then shifts to the higher-order spines, including their use as sites for regional shopping centers and the placement of public monuments. To supplement the discussion of the spatial pattern and landscape character of these contrasting commercial zones, land-use patterns are analyzed in downtown Reynosa and along a two-mile stretch of that city's principal spine, Avenida Miguel Hidalgo.

EL CENTRO: CONTRASTS WITH THE NORTH AMERICAN
CENTRAL BUSINESS DISTRICT

The central business district, usually known as el centro but also called *el primer cuadro,* has experienced significant functional and demographic changes in the post–World War II boom. There has been a strong, and in most places accelerating, centrifugal drift of commerce and other former land uses in the central business district to more peripheral locations. Commercial activities have pushed out in sector-like wedges along the major roads that historically converged upon the core. Recently, commercial activities have leapfrogged to newly developed areas on the fringes of the expanding city.

Yet even in the sprawling and rapidly multinucleating border metropolises, the term el centro, the center, remains appropriate. As a symbol of the city and of urban identity, it continues to be endowed with emotional and institutional commitments. Even when its social cachet and land value have declined, it has retained a commercial vitality and sense of urban appeal. Thus, despite surging growth and the trend toward decentralization, el centro remains a key component—if not the fulcrum it once was—in the organization of city space. In comparison to the tourist districts, which are particular to the border cities, or to the new commercial strips, which are only variants of their North American counterparts, the cultural landscape of el centro is not unlike the centers of cities located in the interior of Mexico. Indeed, it is arguably the most "Mexican" of the commercial areas. Before analyzing specific elements of its composition and character, consider first several generalizations about el centro and how it may differ from central business districts in North America.

Located in the oldest quarter of the city, el centro was usually established when the community was little more than a town or village. Now, in all but the very smallest of the cities, it is dwarfed by the surrounding built-up area. In Ciudad Juárez and Tijuana, for example, the central business district in 1983 accounted for only 3.1 percent and 5.2 percent, respectfully, of the total urban land uses (Hoffman 1983: 212). Although modest in size, el centro is compact and intensely developed, with a high population density and little vacant land. It also is characterized by a low, rather uniform skyline because the availability of abundant and inexpensive land has favored horizontal expansion over the vertical intensification of commercial functions. In a panoramic view of the city, el centro is hardly a visually prominent district. The uninitiated eye may have difficulty even identifying it (see Fig. 5.1). Structures rarely exceed four or five storeys, and two-storey buildings are the norm. In more than a few communities, the belfry of the central cathedral still casts shadows over the surrounding secular structures. The skyscraper has not become the symbol of the modern border city that it has for cities of comparable size north of the border. In fact, the tallest building along the Mexican frontera is an office-hotel, twin tower with twenty-three storeys, located in Tijuana about two miles from the city's urban core.

In further contrast to North American central business districts, land-use patterns in el centro are more diverse and spatially more complex. Today as in the past, the city center contains a mixed assortment of residences, manufacturing establishments, and governmental, cultural, and commercial activities. This complicated, sometimes chaotic ensemble of land uses has

FIGURE 5.1 Typical of the Mexican border cities, the skyline of downtown Tijuana (as seen in January 1991 looking toward the northwest) is rather uniformly composed of modest, low-rise structures.

resulted from a lack of comprehensive planning coupled with a kind of laissez-faire aversion to zoning and government regulation in general. It is also the consequence of inertia and the power of tradition.

The case of housing in el centro is illustrative. The point could be argued that downtown residences have endured in part because of tradition and the lingering historic connotation of social prestige. Another contributing factor is that the notion of incompatible urban activities is not deeply ingrained in either the public or private mind. Although attitudes may be changing, mixed land uses are still not perceived as intolerable or even particularly worrisome. Yet another behavioral reason for the persistence of housing in el centro may be related, in the words of one researcher, to a form of "personalism and the premium placed on direct interaction with other people," in concert with "privacy needs which require relatively little solitude" (Robertson 1978: 112). This kind of sociological explanation suggests that certain Mexican character traits are urban-adaptive and may lend themselves to successful residence in a milieu that other culture groups might have difficulty adjusting to or might not find rewarding. Insightful expositions on the complex and often contradictory nature of the Mexican character, including public versus private behavior, are found in the works of others (Paz 1961; Riding 1985). Finally, when considered as a place, el centro often enjoys superior infrastructure and municipal services. Thus, it affords the practical benefits of proximity to center city employment, shopping, government services, cultural amenities, and transportation.

The latter reason underscores the continued value placed upon urban centrality in the border cities. Accessibility remains critical and the heavily used public transportation system invariably focuses on el centro. In 1980, most of the Mexican border states had fewer inhabitants per automobile than the sixteen-to-one ratio for the country as a whole. Baja California, with four-to-one inhabitants per car, varied significantly from the national average, signaling its strong acceptance of the automobile; the state of Chihuahua's ratio was eleven to one (*Instituto Nacional de Estadística, Geografía e Información* 1982, cited in Herzog 1990: 112). In Tijuana, Baja California's largest city, the comparatively close ratio of inhabitants per automobile has been attributed to incomes above the Mexican mean and the availability of used cars and auto parts in adjacent Southern California. Even so, the downtown and nearby river development zone continue to "dominate in terms of the distribution of commercial uses" (Herzog 1990: 111, 124). This essentially nuclear form has persisted in spite of the fact that the city now sprawls from the core toward the southeast for no less than nine miles.

The expansion and improvement of the highway network, however, have not kept pace with increases in car ownership. The cities are served mainly by two- and four-lane roads, which often are poorly maintained and in disrepair. There has been a paucity of freeway construction; only Tijuana and Ciudad Juárez have short strips of freeway, or *autopista*. While this impedes the flow of traffic in the city, its impact on the landscape of el centro may not be entirely negative. In contrast to U.S. cities, where freeways and high-speed thoroughfares often converge upon and ring the urban core— physically and perceptually isolating it from the surrounding community— the edges of el centro lack these imposing barriers. It remains relatively open and accessible as it integrates spatially with adjacent areas. (Of course, in most of the cities, el centro is truncated on the north by the border, and in several places, it is cut off on at least one side by railroads or physical features.) Yet because of its modest dimensions and limited space for vehicles, including narrow streets and relatively few public parking garages or surface lots, el centro is frequently choked by traffic and beset with serious parking problems. It was designed as a pedestrian place in pre-automobile times, and few concessions have been made to motorists in the modern period. These problems will probably intensify as "automobility" rises and intracity highway systems are improved. What this portends for el centro—beyond the possibility of hastening decentralization—is less certain. However, convergence toward the North American model of a central business district that occupies a small, highly specialized niche in the urban system is not a foregone conclusion. Different processes continue to be in effect vis-à-vis cities in the United States.

A critical factor in the sustained health of el centro is that it did not suffer the core abandonment that accompanied suburbanization in cities north of the border after World War II. In the United States, the flight of retail trade led to demographic changes that often involved an absolute loss of population and increasing concentration of the urban underclass in the core. These events transformed the central business district into a deteriorating space that quickly became a source of civic concern if not outright embarrassment. The large urban renewal and public works projects that followed compounded the dilemma. These projects included the massive razing of structures, the construction of freeways and off-ramps in and around the city center, and the building of multistorey and often poorly designed public housing projects. Once the epitome of urbanity, "downtown" became "the inner city," with its attendant images of economic poverty, social oppression, and physical neglect. More recent renovation, historic preservation efforts, and new developments in the central business

district demonstrate greater social sensitivity and awareness of the importance of good urban design. However, the measured success of these projects
suggests how difficult it has been to revive the North American central business district to even a modicum of its former stature (Frieden and Sagalyn
1989). By contrast, despite burgeoning growth and shifting urban priorities
that have favored development along major traffic corridors and peripheral
sites, el centro has been neither forsaken as a commercial-retail hub nor
relegated to second-class status as a cultural center. Its space limitations
notwithstanding, the conventional wisdom has been that el centro was the
heart of the city, and that if it was sound, the city itself was sound.

This is not to suggest that in all cases el centro still commands the
preeminent position in the urban system or that it has somehow managed
to avoid social and morphological decline. On the contrary, the mounting
forces of decentralization, especially the establishment of suburban shopping complexes and the relocation of government centers outside the traditional core, have diminished el centro's role, particularly in the large cities.
Yet even where this has happened, and unlike the situation in North
America, el centro remains a viable entity in the realigned commercial
hierarchy.

Blighted areas and structural deterioration are commonplace and
sometimes widespread, however. Inner-city slums and *vecindades* (i.e., tene-
ment-like, lower-income apartment housing, often built around a courtyard)
not only persist but in several cities may be growing. Moreover, although
roads within el centro are usually paved, they are often marred by potholes
and have inadequate drainage. Sidewalks frequently have large cracks, broken curbs, and potentially hazardous conditions such as open utility holes.
Nor, for that matter, is the streetscape of el centro particularly tidy or aes-
thetically pleasing. Trash and rubble are often allowed to accumulate and
there is a minimum of landscaping, street furniture, and associated amenities. These conditions are a product of aging and the effects of a traffic
load that far exceeds the area's carrying capacity. They also reflect a limited
budget for road maintenance and perhaps a different attitude toward public
space and litter than prevails in North America. These are not altogether
new conditions and do not necessarily signal the beginning of urban rigor
mortis. Rather, el centro is usually a dynamic quarter of the city where new
buildings are erected as old ones are demolished. Decay and revitalization
are ongoing, consequent processes.

The potential for redevelopment of el centro has increased considerably since the 1960s with the passage of laws that enhance the government's
ability to undertake renewal projects and through the creation of border

development programs. At the national level, government-sponsored urban renewal was greatly bolstered in 1976 with enactment of the federal General Law of Human Settlements *(Ley General de Asentamientos Humanos)*. It enabled the government to appropriate private property and then resell it to private parties; previously the government could acquire land only for direct public uses (Crowley 1987: 40). Many of these renewal efforts have focused on el centro. Regionally, multifaceted, government-backed PRONAF and BIP programs (see Chapters Four and Seven) have concentrated on development of tourist facilities, "Las Puertas a México" border crossings, and industrial districts located outside el centro. Nonetheless, the urban core has benefited indirectly in terms of infrastructure improvements and enhanced access as well as through specific projects. The increased role of the government in reshaping the built environment of the core only further accentuates its diversity. The cityscape of el centro is indeed a multilayered palimpsest, a material chronicle, of former land uses. Although it may be the historic heart of the city, preservation efforts have been few, and many historically significant properties have been lost. Yet this willingness to accommodate change, to adjust to new technology and the demands of the marketplace, may itself contribute to the host of reasons why el centro remains a diverse and vital place.

Even though el centro may lack the glitz of the tourist district or the modernity of the new strip developments, it is a vibrant quarter with a boisterous street life that is active from early morning until late night. Its bustling public life is a marked contrast to the North American downtown, which has evolved into a largely financial, legal, and governmental complex with only limited retail and residential functions. It has been widely criticized for its sterility and near-abandonment after normal business hours and on weekends. In el centro, where people live as well as work, the streets and sidewalks are crowded with residents who are drawn to the area's restaurants, entertainment facilities, public spaces, and stores, which stay open well into evening. The presence of many large neon signs and the sounds of music played on radios and stereos in the stores contribute to its lively and evocative nocturnal character. The sidewalks and curbside host a variety of individual businesses, including shoeshine stands, bookstalls, lottery outlets, and especially food and drink vendors. From stationary booths and pushcarts, these vendors ply their fare of charcoaled meats, *mariscos* (seafood), *elotes* (roasted corn on the cob), sliced and peeled fruits, chile peppers and *nopales* (edible cactus pads), candies, soft drinks, fruit juices from large apothecary jars, ice cream, and *raspas* (shaved ice topped with thick fruit syrup) (see Fig. 5.2). Perhaps as well as any single element, these street ven-

FIGURE 5.2 Streetcart vendors, as seen here in Matamoros, are important components in the life and landscape of *el centro*.

dors suggest that many differences between the North American central business district and the Mexican border-city el centro are not only visually apparent but culturally meaningful. They are the products of deeply rooted customs and traditions. This is true also of contrasts that will be drawn subsequently regarding types and spatial distributions of commercial functions in the core. It is unlikely that most of these historically derived patterns will suddenly vanish, even in the face of continued urban growth and transformation.

THE SPATIAL CHARACTER OF EL CENTRO BUSINESSES:
A FOCUS ON REYNOSA

While el centro may differ in many ways from the North American central business district and has a decidedly "Mexican" place personality, the border exerts an undeniably strong influence on the pattern of consumer behavior. This in turn affects the magnitude and types of commercial activities located in el centro.

Competing commercial centers on the U.S. side have stores that are often stocked with comparatively high-quality, reasonably priced goods. This historically has drawn a parade of Mexican shoppers to retail outlets across the border. In general, these transborder consumers have been selective in their purchases. A comprehensive marketing survey conducted in Ciudad Juárez, for example, found that 51 percent of the respondents shopped in El Paso for clothing, 22 percent for appliances, 9 percent for food, and 7 percent for medical goods or services (Palmore et al. 1974: 53). Price was cited by 54 percent as the major reason for shopping in El Paso, while 29 percent were attracted by the quality of merchandise, and 17 percent indicated that product availability was the main factor. Similar results, both in types of purchases and consumer motivations, have been reported in other studies (North 1970; House 1982: 201–204). Although the volume of this trade borderwide is difficult to determine, the results of an in-depth investigation in the 1970s estimated that Mexican consumers spent between $600 million and $740 million in U.S. border communities (Tamayo and Fernández 1983: 107). This figure very likely would have exceeded one billion dollars annually during the 1980s had it not been for peso devaluations (Herzog 1990: 147).

The Mexican government, concerned about this northern flight of capital and the growth of a dependent economic relationship, has introduced various programs and policy initiatives over the past three decades in an attempt to reduce the number of Mexican border-city residents who shop in the United States. In addition to establishing duty-free zones (which were created as early as the 1850s), the efforts have included the following: offering tax and transportation incentives to Mexican companies to send more manufactured goods and consumer durables to the border; building new shopping centers (discussed later in this chapter); creating in the early 1970s the *artículos ganchos* ("hook" articles) program that allowed duty-free importation of many popular foreign products, such as wearing apparel and appliances, for resale in Mexican border cities (Martínez 1986: 143; Herzog 1990: 147). The results of these efforts have been mixed, but the peso devaluations of 1976 and especially since 1982 have seriously eroded the purchasing power of border Mexicans, and the volume of goods bought in the United States has declined. Whether this trend will continue or is only a temporary phenomenon is uncertain. The fact remains that the imports-oriented consumer behavior patterns of border Mexicans has had an impact on the commercial structure of el centro.

It has been suggested that this so-called "border effect" has led to incomplete development of higher-order, central-place functions in the border-city el centro; as a consequence, it is smaller in size than in Mexican cities of the interior that are comparable in population (Baker 1970: 64, 81, 99, 114). This may be a valid contention. However, our concern in this chapter is to assess what types of businesses *are* located in el centro and to determine their distributions. Rather than offering a series of generalizations about the broader patterns, the results of a detailed land-use inventory conducted in Reynosa are presented as illustrative of the spatial character of an el centro's retail and service structure.

Founded in 1749, Reynosa is one of the oldest and largest of the Mexican border cities. The city sprawls inside a municipio of some 350 square miles, and in 1990, its population was approximately 282,000. Located in Tamaulipas on the lower Rio Grande opposite Hidalgo and McAllen, Texas, Reynosa is a major service and petroleum-refining and -distribution center. It links directly to Monterrey, 120 miles to the southwest, and Matamoros, sixty miles downstream (Herrera Pérez 1989). Due to its flat, poorly drained site and early history of flooding that forced abandonment of the original waterside settlement, el centro has been situated about a mile south of the river since 1757. It is a classic plaza-oriented core, laid out in a standard grid format. On the south it is hemmed in by the Anzalduas Canal, which is paralleled on the north side by railroad tracks. Although crossed by bridges and underpasses, the canal still represents a significant divide between the older northern and younger southern sections of the city. Typical of larger border communities, the center is compact and suffers from severe parking and traffic problems. The conversion of its narrow streets to one-ways has done little to alleviate this problem. Where it differs from most of the cities, however, is that its tourist district, La Zona Rosa, is between el centro proper and the border crossing. Consequently, there are few businesses in the core that are oriented toward foreign tourism. This situation presents a more spatially discrete and representative picture of el centro's mainstream (i.e., non-tourist) commercial structure and was the reason we chose Reynosa for the land-use survey.

Based on the density of retail and service establishments, a thirty-five-block-square study area was delimited within the historic and commercial heart of Reynosa (see Fig. 5.3). Taking into account bordering streets, it encompassed a total of 164 block fronts (i.e., one side of a block). In May of 1990, all street-facing, ground-level commercial activities within the area were counted and mapped. The survey was based largely on observation, with only a minimum of interviewing. No attempt was made to gain access to upper floors of buildings or to the interior of city blocks. Where a building served multiple functions, only the dominant activity was recorded, although businesses in residential units were listed. Individual stalls within

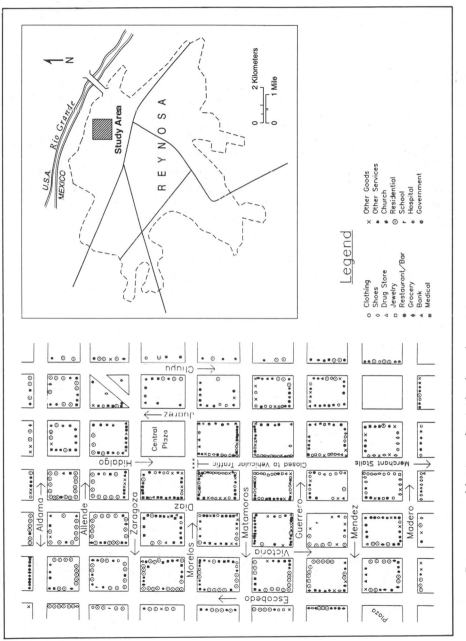

FIGURE 5.3 Reynosa central-business-district land uses by activity.

the central market were not counted; neither were merchant stands along the pedestrian mall on Hidalgo nor numerous street vendors. No effort was made to differentiate by size or function, so tiny retail outlets and large stores were counted equally. Determination of current use was hampered by a lack of signs on some commercial buildings, and in other cases, by signs that may have been out-of-date. Given these methodological limitations, the survey undoubtedly represents an undercount of commercial activities within the study area, but it probably approximates reality.

In total, 666 retail and service establishments were identified; an additional 235 residential units were also recorded, which illustrates the mixed land-use patterns typical of el centro. Although numerous, most of the shops were small and had restricted street frontage. Almost every type of business activity located in the city seemingly was represented in the study area. More than eighty types of businesses were counted, but several—most notably those dealing with motor vehicles and construction materials—were underrepresented in comparison with their number in the greater city. To facilitate analysis, businesses were grouped into ten categories: (1) bank; (2) clothing store; (3) drug store; (4) grocery store; (5) jewelry store; (6) medical office; (7) restaurant or bar; (8) shoe store; (9) other goods; and (10) other services. The numbers and percentages of establishments in each category are displayed in Figure 5.4. The large number of businesses in the other services and other goods categories, which collectively accounted for

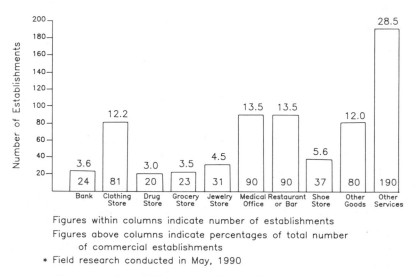

Figures within columns indicate number of establishments
Figures above columns indicate percentages of total number
of commercial establishments
* Field research conducted in May, 1990

FIGURE 5.4 Commercial establishments in Reynosa's *el centro*.

41 percent of the total, reflects the diversity of el centro's commercial trade. Examples of "other services" were barbershops, beauty salons, law offices, photography studios, tailor shops, lodging accommodations, funeral parlors, movie theaters, and other professional, entertainment, and technical services. Representative "other goods" businesses were bakeries, bookstores, appliance dealers, hardware stores, stationary and office supply outlets, record and video stores, furniture stores, gas stations, floral shops, and stores that specialized in religious articles. The diversity within these categories precluded analysis of distribution characteristics by type.

Among the eight specific categories, the number of establishments ranged from a low of twenty for drug stores to a high of ninety for both restaurants or bars and medical offices (dentists and opticians as well as physicians). The distribution patterns varied widely, as some types of establishments were dispersed while others were clustered (see Fig. 5.3). Businesses most likely to cluster included the three categories of wearing apparel and accessories, clothing, shoes, and jewelry stores; together they accounted for more than 22 percent of all establishments. These stores were usually close to Avenida Hidalgo, especially the four blocks south of the plaza. In fact, forty-one of the eighty-one clothing stores (51 percent), twenty-five of the thirty-seven shoe stores (68 percent), and twenty-four of the thirty-one jewelry stores (77 percent) were located on or within one block of Hidalgo. Those types of outlets offer primarily low-cost, mass-appeal convenience goods, including the jewelry stores that generally specialize in lower-value, higher-volume items. As such, they require premium retail locations that draw a high volume of foot traffic. Following the lead of Monterrey, which during a 1970s urban renewal project had pioneered the creation of open-air pedestrian malls within el centro (Crowley 1987), Reynosa created a pedestrian mall in the early 1980s by closing to vehicular traffic the five blocks of Hidalgo south of the plaza. This area, lined with merchants' stalls down its center, is now the busiest pedestrian street in the core (see Fig. 5.5). Banks also tended to cluster, although they were not as concentrated on a single street. Five of the twenty-four faced the central plaza, reflecting a Mexican commercial tradition, and another five were grouped around the intersection of Guerrero and Juárez.

Medical offices and drug stores, which together accounted for 110 establishments, were more dispersed throughout the district. Clearly el centro plays an important role in Reynosa's medical services; their concentration in the core is probably related to el centro's accessibility, especially via public transportation. Medical offices are also clustered in the Zona Rosa tourist district near the border. Although both drug stores and medical of-

FIGURE 5.5 In downtown Reynosa, several blocks of Hidalgo have been closed to vehicular traffic, creating an open-air pedestrian mall.

fices were identified throughout the study area, certain spatial characteristics were nonetheless evident. Interestingly, neither drug stores nor medical offices were particularly concentrated in the immediate vicinity of the two hospitals on the northern edge of the study area. Yet thirteen of the medical offices were situated on a one-block stretch of Avenida Díaz between Zaragoza and Morelos a couple of blocks south of San José Hospital. A number of the medical offices were in residential units, suggesting the small-scale, independent character of many such health-care operations that exist in a society where socialized medicine is common, if not always preferred. Typical of their distribution patterns elsewhere, thirteen of the twenty drug stores, or *farmacias,* occupied corner sites.

The ninety restaurants or bars, which accounted for more than 13 percent of the establishments, were found throughout the study area, with distinct concentrations around the plaza, the central market, and especially along Avenida Hidalgo. Just outside the designated area on the southern margins of el centro another cluster was observed near the train station, illustrating the established association with transportation. The vast majority of businesses in this category were small restaurants and cafes, which cater to el centro workers and shoppers. In fact, few establishments were devoted strictly to the bar business. The largest clusters of cabarets and bars are located in the Zona Rosa tourist district and in the zona de tolerancia ("boys' town") on the extreme northwest edge of the city center.

Finally, there were twenty-three grocery stores (abarrotes), which represented less than 4 percent of the establishments. The limited number probably reflects the size of the resident population in the study area; the positive relationship between the two has been documented in a study of Ciudad Juárez (Palmore et al. 1974: 45–47). Almost all the stores were concentrated in the more residential sectors of the area, especially on the north side. They were mostly low-volume, small, family-run businesses oriented toward their respective neighborhoods; none was large enough to qualify as a *supermercado*. Like the pharmacies, the grocery stores also favored corner locations, with over half (twelve) commanding such sites. Undoubtedly, the number of nonprepared-food retailers would have been higher had the street vendors, especially the merchant stalls, or *tramos,* in the central market, been counted. Indeed, in Reynosa as in many border cities, the role of the mercado central remains important as a food distribution center and a social institution. The need for additional space and more modern facilities, however, has led to extensive renovation of some central markets, as in Ciudad Juárez. In other cities, such as Tijuana, the market has been relocated outside el centro (*San Diego Tribune* 1982a: B1).

THE CENTRAL PLAZA AS PLACE AND SPACE

Perhaps nowhere in the public areas of the border cities is the impress of tradition more evident than in the plazas of el centro, especially the plaza mayor. While the plaza is obviously not a commercial space per se, certain lower-order goods and services are purveyed there. More importantly, of course, the plaza is a conspicuous physical feature in the el centro landscape, and its role symbolically and functionally is intertwined with that of the city center. As a tree-shaded, flower-graced urban oasis, it is a complement to, and separate from, el centro. Its position conceptually as the geographic, political, religious, and commercial hub of the traditional border city was discussed in Chapter Three. Although the plaza may no longer be the uncontested central nexus of public life (if it ever was in at least several of these cities), its status remains important in the system of urban parks and public gathering places. That it is usually maintained as a civic showcase suggests that it continues to serve as a source of community pride. Here as in urban centers throughout the country, a city is tacitly identified with its plaza. This persists as a key perceptual component in residents' collective image of their city, including those who live in outlying suburban barrios (Stea and Wood 1971: 50–54).

Understandably, the plaza is usually less significant in larger cities, given their greater area, fragmentation, and opportunities for private social activities, than in the smaller cities, where residents have a more restricted palette of options. Along this general continuum, however, variations and exceptions exist. Not only does the plaza's relative import vary from place to place, but so do its landscape characteristics and social functions. The popular image of the centrally placed plaza, flanked by the structures of church and state, may not conform to reality. Whereas some studies conducted by geographers on plazas in Latin America have documented morphological and functional variations (Elbow 1975; Hardoy 1975; Gade 1976; Crowley 1977), most have not been comparative in approach. Instead, based on case studies and heavily influenced by the idealized Spanish colonial city model, as codified in the much-touted Laws of the Indies, they have stressed the regularity of plaza design and its singular importance in the social milieu (Nelson 1963; Stanislawski 1950; Takagi 1970; Robertson 1978). Although a great many similarities can be identified, the plaza may not have been, and probably is not now, nearly as standardized as commonly portrayed (Arreola 1992); certainly it is not in the modern Mexican border city. Yet, similarities and differences aside, in many ways it continues to serve as a microcosm of the larger society; as such, its significance in the urban fabric belies its size.

Conforming to the standard plan, most plazas in the border cities were situated originally near the town center. Except for cities such as Matamoros, Reynosa, and Tijuana as well as the smaller communities of Camargo and Sonoita, where the town was first platted some distance from the 1848 demarcation, the plaza was typically located near the ports of entry. This location reflected the small size of these towns and their border orientation. Among those with peripherally located plazas was Camargo, where the plaza was sited on the extreme western edge of the colonial settlement adjacent to the ramparts overlooking the Río San Juan. Mexicali's first plan, which exhibited a modern morphology oriented toward its transportation network rather than a central public space, identified three plazas aligned side-by-side abutting the international boundary (Aguirre Bernal 1983: 348). Not all of the centrally placed plazas have survived to the present, however. Tijuana's city plan of 1889 incorporated a series of broad diagonal streets superimposed on a traditional grid that centered prominently on Plaza Zaragoza (see Fig. 3.1). Yet as early as the 1920s, the direction of growth in the city shifted toward the border, and the plaza was abandoned. In its absence, residents began to use Parque Teniente Guerrero, located six blocks west of Avenida Revolución on the margins of el centro. For all practical purposes, it has functioned since as the city's de facto main plaza (Herzog 1990: 98). Elsewhere, by contrast, close proximity to the ports of entry increased the plaza's vulnerability. In Nogales, for instance, construction of a new border crossing in the 1960s resulted in the loss of its original square, Plaza Trece de Julio (see Fig. 5.6). In 1984, the vestpocket Plaza de Niños Héroes was built as its replacement.

Within el centro, several of the cities have more than one plaza, including some of recent origin and others that are comparatively historic, dating to the nineteenth century. Multiple plazas, often hierarchically organized, were common in the older border towns from the colonial period. For example, an 1890 map of Matamoros (see Fig. 3.10) identified five: Hidalgo (the main plaza), Libertad, Zaragoza, Allende, and Independencia. A 1927 map of Reynosa showed four: Hidalgo (the main plaza), de Mercado, Ocampo, and Juárez (Chatfield 1893; *Reynosa, Nuestro Ciudad* 1990: 118). Now, however, the number of plazas in a city is not always

FIGURE 5.6 Nogales' Plaza Trece de Julio, circa 1920, was destroyed with construction of a new border crossing in the 1960s. Photograph courtesy of Pimeria Alta Historical Society, Nogales, Arizona.

related to its age or size; the pattern is variable. Moreover, the distinction between *plaza* and *parque* has become blurred, and the terms are sometimes used interchangeably on city maps; in Mexicali all the squares are called parques. Where more than one plaza are found, the newer, or historically secondary, plazas are usually subordinate in importance to the plaza mayor. Yet in cities that have several older plazas, residents cannot always correctly identify the historic main plaza, and only infrequently refer to it by the traditional terms of plaza mayor, plaza principal, or *zócalo*. Most commonly, when not referred to simply as "la plaza" or "el parque," it is called by its proper name or occasionally by a localism. One such case is "Plaza de Reloj," a name given Nuevo Laredo's Plaza Hidalgo because it is distinguished by its landmark fifty-foot clock tower (*Laredo News* 1987: 3A). The historic name *plaza de armas* (military plaza) was used originally for the main plazas in Matamoros and Nuevo Laredo, among possible others. In the former city, it was changed in the second half of the nineteenth century to Hidalgo; in the latter, it was renamed Juárez in the 1930s. Plaza de armas is still the formal name in Ciudad Juárez, although most often it is shortened to "The Plaza." Currently, the main plazas in almost half of the eighteen border cities are named after the revered Mexican patriots, Benito Juárez and Miguel Hidalgo; Juárez is especially common in the west and Hidalgo in the east (Table 5.1).

The plazas are almost invariably rectangular, and most encompass a city block, although the size varies considerably and not always in accordance with the size of the contemporary city. The villagelike community of Las Palomas, for example, has a relatively large plaza, as does modest-sized Ojinaga, whereas the main plaza in the metropolis of Mexicali is comparatively small. Regardless of its dimensions, the internal design of the plaza consists most often of a series of circular spaces and a crisscross pattern of walkways radiating from a central focal point, usually a *kiosco* (bandstand). Exceptions include Ojinaga, which has a large paved plaza adorned simply with a fountain, in keeping with the open colonial plaza landscape. This geometric arrangement provides a strong sense of symmetry, and as one researcher has commented, "Even when symmetry does not exist, the illusion does" (Robertson 1978: 33). It is a design that evokes on one hand the feeling of spaciousness, and on the other, a perception of containment.

If the plaza's form conveys a sense of order and of the workings of a central authority, so, too, does its garden-park character, which evolved as a product of the Mexican historical-political process. Prior to the reign of Emperor Maximilian (1864–1867), the Mexican plaza had served variously as a kind of open and austere military parade ground (hence the term plaza

TABLE 5.1 Main Plazas in the Border Cities

City	Name of Plaza	Contains Kiosco	Flanked by Church
Tijuana	Tiente Guerrero *[a]	yes	yes
Tecate	Miguel Hidalgo	yes	no
Mexicali	Héroes de Chapultepec *	yes	yes
San Luis Río Colorado	Benito Juárez	yes	yes
Sonoita	Benito Juárez	yes	no
Nogales	Niños de Héroes[a]	no	yes
Naco	Plaza Pública	yes	no
Agua Prieta	Azueta	yes	yes
Las Palomas	Palomas Plaza	yes	yes
Ciudad Juárcz	Plaza de Armas	no[b]	yes
Ojinaga	Zocalo de la Presidencia	no	yes
Ciudad Acuña	Benjamin Canales	yes	yes
Piedras Negras	Plaza Principal	yes	yes
Nuevo Laredo	Benito Juárez	yes	yes
Miguel Alemán	Miguel Hidalgo	no	yes
Camargo	Miguel Hidalgo	yes	yes
Reynosa	Miguel Hidalgo	yes	yes
Matamoros	Miguel Hidalgo	yes	yes

SOURCE: Field survey.
* Officially known as a *parque*.
[a] Not the original plaza.
[b] Formerly had a kiosco.

de armas) and as an open-air periodic marketplace (Gade 1976: 16–20; Webb 1990: 99–112). Borrowing from ideas that originated in France, Maximilian introduced the garden-park plaza concept to the capital. The plaza's new design emphasized circular spaces and structures, including the kiosco, as well as intersecting pathways and the circular arrangement of flower beds and arboreal groupings. These so-called *rond points* were an integral feature of Renaissance French garden art and landscaping and were intended as either social gathering places or focal points (Spreiregen 1965: 19). In all likelihood the kiosco, which in the nineteenth century was considered a symbol of opulence and urbanity (Robertson 1978: 80), also entered Mexico with the French occupation. As the plaza's centerpiece and visual magnet, it was widely accepted in the border cities and persists in thirteen of the eighteen main plazas (Table 5.1). In addition to trees, shrubs, flowers and lawn, other features of the garden-park plaza included benches (often cast-iron), fountains, monuments, and commemorative elements such as statues, busts, and plaques. The garden-park plaza design spread from Mexico City throughout the country. Although its diffusion is most associated with the Porfiriato (1876–1910), Matamoros provides an example of how rapidly it arrived on the northern border. A photograph taken in May of 1865 shows Matamoros' Plaza de Armas (present Plaza Hidalgo) laid out in the now classic, garden-park format, focusing on a centrally arranged grove of trees (Pierce 1917: 136).

One scholar suggested that the underlying theme of the garden-park plaza was the management of nature. "The plaza describes a nature that has been tamed and arranged according to a reasoned plan; as such, it depicts the triumph of rationality over barbarism" (Richardson 1982: 432). By this interpretation, the garden-park plaza is meant to convey notions of order and control, or at least it was initially. In keeping with similar nineteenth century utopian ideals of a garden in a hostile environment, it also was intended to be a sort of *rus en urb,* or country in the town, to offer an emotional and aesthetic counterpoint to the commerciality and verve of the city center. Despite these philosophical motivations, the plaza was designed first and foremost as a utilitarian space to be used by residents for a variety of purposes.

From its inception, but especially since its transformation to a garden-park, the Mexican plaza has displayed a social character in keeping with the best traditions of the Mediterranean outdoor public meeting place (i.e., the squares, piazzas, and Spanish plazas) from which it sprang. A micro-arena of human interaction and group participation, it has been described as an "open-air drawing room" that plays an "intimate and important part in the national domestic life" (Flandrau 1964: 277). As the setting for formal and informal activities, including daily, periodic, and occasional events, its social uses are varied and complex. Historically it has hosted many of the year's most important religious and secular celebrations and festivals and has served as a convenient venue for political rallies and entertainment ranging from concerts and dances to traveling carnivals. Beyond its role as a place for community-oriented pageantry and diversion, its less-glamorous function as a daily social concourse at the individual and subgroup levels has been equally crucial in the ordinary life of the city.

The curiously romantic tradition of the promenade or *paseo,* in which unattached young men stroll around the plaza in one direction while chaperoned señoritas move in the opposite direction, flirting with each other in passing, is widely known. Although the paseo has largely vanished as social conventions have changed, especially in the large cities (Gade 1976: 20), the plaza is still used daily in many ways. Based on research conducted in Guadalajara's plaza principal complex, Robertson (1978: 173–181) identified eight uses that are sufficiently broad to encompass most activities: (1) socializing; (2) sexual cruising; (3) waiting; (4) resting; (5) attending a formal plaza event; (6) sight-seeing; (7) working; and (8) passing through. He likens the plaza to a "stage" and suggests that there are three categories of "actors" (i.e., users); they are leisure occupants, workers, and passersby. Robertson found that among the leisure occupants (those who visit the plaza to participate in any of the first six uses), *pensionados* (male retirees) represented the largest group of users, followed by males aged seventeen to twenty-nine, although some variation occurred by day of the week—especially Sundays—and by time of use (Robertson 1978: 125). It should not be surprising that passersby constitute a distinct group given the plaza's location in el centro and the fact that it is frequently an important traffic and public transportation hub (Gade 1976: 21–22). The plaza supports not only workers who maintain the premises, such as *jardineros* (gardeners) and *basuradores* (plaza sweepers), it also is a place where *fotógrafos* (photographers), *músicos* (musicians), *boleritos* (mobile shoeshine boys), and all manner of *vendedores ambulantes* (roving vendors) may ply their trades and sell their services and goods. In addition, many plazas have fixed and semipermanent food and drink stands, shoeshine booths, and stalls that offer a variety of items, especially *discos* (records, tapes, and now compact discs), newspapers, magazines, comic books, and the widely popular *novelas* (little novels). Extensive observation suggests that these patterns of plaza use and design are common in border cities, although here as elsewhere in Mexico variations occur among cities as well as among plazas within one city. Nuevo Laredo provides an example of the differences and similarities between plazas found in close proximity.

Along a fourteen-block stretch of Guerrero, Nuevo Laredo's main north-south street that cuts from the port of entry through the heart of el centro, are four plazas of varying age, design, and use (see Figs. 5.7, 5.8, 5.9, 5.10). From north to south, they are Plazas Juárez and Hidalgo on the east side of Guerrero and Plazas México and de la Cultura on the west side. The first three are situated four blocks apart, and de la Cultura is two blocks south of Plaza México. Their respective ages follow this geographic sequence, with Plaza Juárez being the oldest and Plaza de la Cultura the youngest. The former dates to the nineteenth century, when it was known

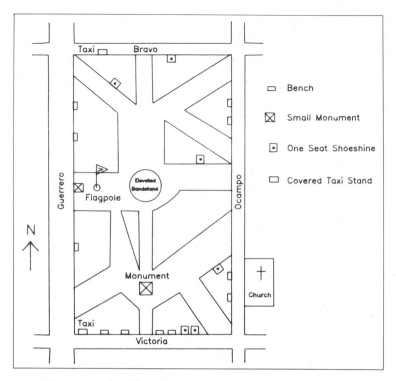

FIGURE 5.7 Nuevo Laredo's Plaza Juárez.

as the Plaza de Armas, while the latter is about twenty years old. Despite their age differences, they share a number of design similarities. Each is rectangular and encompasses a square block, although Plaza Hidalgo is the largest. All focus on a central circular space or structure, including kioscos in Plazas Juárez and Hidalgo, an oval library in Plaza México, and a fountain in Plaza de la Cultura. The interior pathways converge upon these focal points, although Plaza de la Cultura lacks the crisscross pattern of walkways found in the other three. All contain benches, especially along the edges of the perimeter sidewalks, but they are most numerous in Plaza México. Shoeshine stands are another ubiquitous feature, including five-seat, covered stands in Plazas Hidalgo and México, which also had significantly more than the other two plazas. Taxi stands, bus stop waiting areas (often covered), and telephone booths are also found in most of the four plazas. Only Plaza de la Cultura did not have any monuments, but like Plaza Juárez, supported a flagpole. While pushcart vendors are usually found at one or more of each plaza's corners, only Plaza Hidalgo had fixed food and bever-

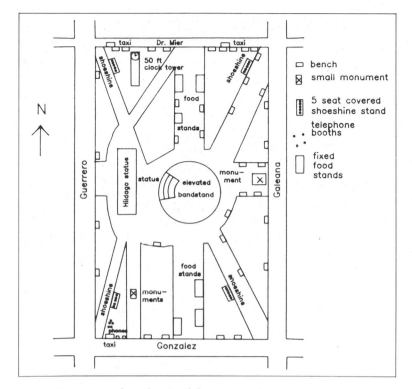

FIGURE 5.8 Nuevo Laredo's Plaza Hidalgo.

age stands. Finally, Plazas Juárez and México front on churches while Plazas Hidalgo and de la Cultura are opposite government buildings. In terms of popularity, at least based on numbers of plaza visitors, Plaza Hidalgo, which was established in the early 1940s, is clearly the people's choice (see Fig. 5.11); it is followed by Plazas México, Juárez, and de la Cultura. True here as in other cities with multiple plazas, the most popular plazas seem to be those with the most shoeshine and food stands; whether residents are attracted to them, or they are drawn to the crowd, is another question. Location, amenities, and tradition are all important factors in plaza use.

While it cannot be easily substantiated, it seems clear that the relative appeal of the plaza is eroding. This appears true especially in larger cities among the middle-class as the process of suburbanization accelerates and as alternative and quasi-public spaces, such as shopping malls, become available. This is not to suggest, however, that the plaza will ever completely lose its important role in the system of urban parks and public gathering places

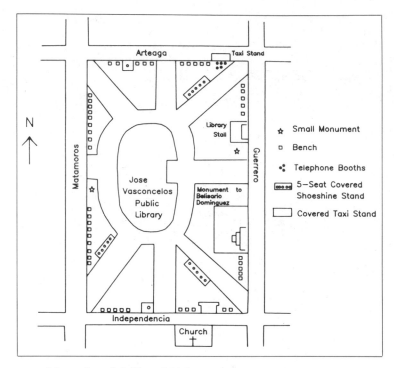

FIGURE 5.9 Nuevo Laredo's Plaza México.

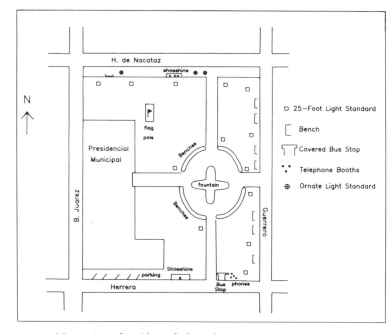

FIGURE 5.10 Nuevo Laredo's Plaza de la Cultura.

FIGURE 5.11   Nuevo Laredo's Plaza Hidalgo, with its central *kiosco*, food stands, and shaded pathways, is the city's most popular plaza.

or its symbolic function as a repository of important memories in the Mexican urban experience.

LANDSCAPE OF THE COMMERCIAL SPINE

The diversity of commercial landscapes in the Mexican border cities has increased greatly since the 1960s, especially over the past decade with the evolution of urban spines. These major arteries, which emanate from el centro but increasingly cut across the city as well, play a crucial role in the transportation system as they link the core to outlying suburbs, hinterland, and intercity highways. In many cases, they are the urban extensions of the intercity highway network. Beyond their transport function, they also are significant business strips. In the early stages of development, the spines were a functional expansion of el centro or were characterized by highway-oriented activities in the rural-urban fringe. Over time they have emerged as more specialized commercial ribbons that complement as well as contrast with the retail and service structure of the urban center. In landscape and spirit, the commercial spine bears little resemblance to el centro. Whereas the built environment and activity patterns of the core emphasize Hispanic traditions and a pedestrian nature, along the auto-oriented spines, North American design and architectural idioms predominate. One stresses the values of the closed city and the other of the open road. This stamp of gringo commercial design is prevalent not only on the spines of the largest cities— Calle Sexta and Avenida Lauro Villar in Matamoros; Avenidas Hidalgo and Morelos in Reynosa; Avenidas México and de la Reforma in Nuevo Laredo; Avenidas 16 de Septiembre and de las Americas–Lincoln in Ciudad Juárez; Boulevards López Mateos and Benito Juárez in Mexicali; and Agua Caliente–Díaz Ordaz Boulevard and Paseo de Los Héroes in Tijuana—but also along the incipient spines of the middle-sized cities, especially San Luis Río Colorado, Nogales, Agua Prieta, Ciudad Acuña, and Piedras Negras.

The evolution and character of the spine signal important spatial and cultural changes taking place in the border cities. These include shifts in consumer tastes; an increasing desire for convenience; the movement of middle- and upper-income groups to more suburban locales; and the building of large, outlying maquiladora industrial parks that accelerated the construction of intracity thoroughfares (see Chapter Seven). The catalysts for these changes, beyond the extraordinary demographic and physical growth of the cities and the inability of their small cores to accommodate such growth, are complex. They range from economic reorientation, emergence of a middle class with a suburban value system, greater disposable income, and increased automobile ownership, especially among middle-income groups, to the pervasive diffusion and influence of American consumer products and habits as well as commercial marketing schemes.

The landscape of the spine typically changes with distance from el centro. As it emerges from the core in the older stretches, it may be rather narrow, with businesses still largely focused on pedestrian traffic. At this point, off-street parking is rare, and stores generally front directly on the sidewalk. It is not unusual to find commercial activities mixed in with older elite homes, occupied or abandoned, as these were favored residential locations toward the end of the pre-automobile era. Some of these structures, as along 16 de Septiembre in Ciudad Juárez, are quite grand. In some of the larger cities, this older in-close section of the spine also occasionally displays commercial elements of the classic 1950s strip, replete with blinking neon lights and idiosyncratic, "extroverted" architectural styles, such as the whimsical sombrero-shaped drive-in restaurant on Tijuana's Agua Caliente Boulevard.

Characteristically, the older spine becomes quite suddenly a new, broad, divided boulevard that is usually curbed and often has a center median that is sometimes landscaped. One of the visually impressive design features of the new spine in the larger cities are *glorietas,* or traffic circles, which add a European flair to the streetscape. Like features of the garden-park plaza, the glorietas are of French inspiration, in Mexico first incorporated into the design of the Paseo de la Reforma in the capital during the brief reign of Maximilian. They are typically located at major intersections on the spine, sometimes also marking its beginning at either or both ends and serving as a symbolic entrance. Enhancing this cosmopolitan effect, monuments have been erected in the middle of the glorietas. This has been done largely under the auspices of PRONAF and the *Partido Revolucionario Institucional* (PRI), the country's major political party. Most of these monuments are massive statues of Mexican heroes, especially Miguel Hidalgo, Benito Juárez, Vicente Guerrero, José Maria Morelos, Ignacio Zaragoza, and Rodolfo Sánchez Taboada. However, there are also bigger-than-life representations of Cuauhtémoc, the last Aztec emperor, Lázaro Cárdenas, and Abraham Lincoln, as well as large pieces of contemporary abstract sculpture (see Fig. 5.12). One scholar of Mexican monuments has written that they are created "to commemorate, praise, perpetuate, glorify, impose, or destroy a set of values and ideologies" (Eder 1989: 61). The placement of this civic statuary has indeed been interpreted by some as an attempt to inculcate a sense of *nacionalismo* (nationalism) (Weisman 1986: 47); Lincoln is honored because of his role in the abolition of slavery in the United States. One observer has opined in respect to Tijuana, which has eleven glorietas with nine monuments, that these statues "were set down upon the city like paperweights upon a map. They are gifts from the capital, meant as reminders" (Rodriguez 1987: 43).

The design of commercial buildings along the newer reaches of the spine reflects its orientation to a driving clientele. These structures, which cater to one-stop shopping trips, are usually free-standing and set back from the street with ample on-site parking. Store signs, which usually show company logos and names and are of backlit plastic rather than flickering neon, are typically perpendicular to the road to attract the attention of passing motorists. Architecturally the newer buildings emphasize the boxy "signature" designs of modern corporate franchises. Increasingly common as well are corner minimalls and clusters of block-front stores, despite considerable open space along the typical spine. While comparisons with the North American strip are obvious and compelling, these spines are by no means as orderly, tidy, and modulated. Nor do they exhibit, at least as yet, the sylvan-like suburban imagery of the "television road," as the contemporary American strip has been labeled (MacDonald 1985: 17–19). Most conspicuous

FIGURE 5.12 This thirty-foot statue of Lincoln stands in a *glorieta* on Tijuana's
    Paseo de los Héroes.

by their absence are trees, flowering shrubs, and annuals. Moreover, commercial property is rarely fenced, and parking lots may or may not be paved.
Overall, the Mexican border-city spine appears as a more open, stark, and
somewhat "unfinished" version of its northern counterpart.

    The spine may also be more complex in terms of land-use patterns, as
it has become a linear growth pole for both commercial as well as noncom-
mercial activities. Most importantly in the latter instance, since at least 1962
and the building of the PRONAF Center in Ciudad Juárez, it has emerged as
the site-of-choice for the relocation and expansion of government centers,

including such large and integrated complexes as the Centro Civico in Mexicali (see Fig. 5.13). Only the concentration of government functions at the newly expanded border crossings has rivaled the spine as a magnet for such development. Commercially the spine features a great variety of establishment types. Some are dependent on passing traffic, others serve the surrounding area, and still others are geared to a citywide clientele. Although generalizations about the character of the Latin American spine have been offered (Griffin and Ford 1980), emphasizing its orientation to a mobile, elite segment of the population, specific land-use studies along this important commercial ribbon are insufficient to draw meaningful conclusions. The findings of one study on secondary urban centers in Guatemala, for example, contradict the general assumptions about the spine's formation and composition (Elbow 1983). To compensate for this lack of information and to complement the previously discussed survey of land uses in el centro, we conducted an inventory of land uses along a two-mile stretch of Reynosa's Avenida Hidalgo.

FIGURE 5.13 The new bullring and statue are part of Mexicali's large and integrated government complex located outside *el centro* on one of the city's commercial spines.

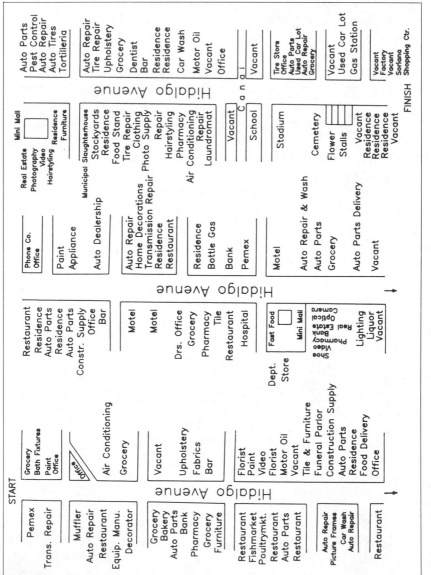

FIGURE 5.14 Land use along Reynosa's Avenida Hidalgo. Transect is 2.1 miles long. Study was conducted in May 1990.

Along with Morelos on the east side of town, Avenida Hidalgo is one of Reynosa's two higher-order spines. It runs from east to west across the center of the city paralleling the Anzalduas Canal, then veers sharply toward the southwest. A broad, four-lane but undivided road, it is the intracity extension of Mexico Highway 40 that connects with Monterrey in the state of Nuevo León. Toward its southern end, it is bordered on both sides by access or frontage roads. It is a busy street that carries a heavy traffic load, including eighteen-wheel trucks, which are slowed somewhat by the presence of several large *topes,* ("speed bumps"). A fleet of vans provides public transportation along the route and into el centro. Although perhaps not as well-landscaped or "beautified" as others, Avenida Hidalgo's basic appearance is representative of spines in the major border cities.

To determine the types and distributions of businesses on Avenida Hidalgo, in May 1990 we surveyed a two-mile transect along the southern section of the avenue. Land uses on both sides of the street were recorded and mapped. Street vendors were not included although several were encountered, including food and beverage vendors and peddlers of motor oil, chrome auto parts, pottery, and furniture; nor were the numerous flower merchants adjacent to the cemetery counted. Uses were not grouped into categories but rather were listed using descriptive terms for each establishment. Residences and vacant land were also recorded. The sequence of land uses is displayed in Figure 5.14, which is divided into three segments but is one continuous street.

Clearly this strip of Hidalgo is in transition, evolving rapidly from extensive rural and highway-oriented activities to more intensive, high-order commercial patterns. New commercial construction is widespread. Institutional uses and spaces were also evident and included a school, stadium, hospital, cemetery, and *rastro municipal* (public slaughterhouse). The latter two have historically been edge-of-the-city uses but are now being encroached upon. There was considerable vacant land, especially toward the southern end of the transect, and a dozen mostly older and marginal residences were scattered along the road. Prominent among the newer commercial developments were two minimalls. One was anchored by a large discount-and-grocery store, and the other, the Soriana regional shopping center, was located at the southernmost end of the study area.

In total, 120 commercial establishments were identified, excluding offices. Auto-oriented businesses, especially those dealing in auto parts, tires, and repair, were overwhelmingly the dominant group, accounting for thirty-four establishments. This probably reflects both the older pattern of highway uses as well as the newer auto-focused character of the spine. In addition to drawing passing motorists, these businesses are patronized by residents from the largely auto-dependent, upper- and middle-income suburbs found in the general vicinity. Moreover, some of these establishments have space requirements that can be met easily given the spine's lower density of use compared to el centro. This might also explain the concentration of construction and building-supply outlets, including paint and tile stores and home decoration and furnishing establishments, all of which require extensive space for showrooms and storage. Food-related businesses were fairly numerous and found with regularity along the strip. Seven grocery stores, two supermercados, ten restaurants (not counting those in the mall and in motels), a bakery, a fish market, and a poultry market were identified. Whereas most of the grocery stores and restaurants were small, family-run, and probably catered to the neighboring residential districts, some were large, upscale establishments or were North American–style convenience outlets. Church's Fried Chicken was the only American chain, fast-food eatery on the strip; however, there were Mexican counterparts. Of the three motels, one (El Virrey) was a large, modern, full-service facility with a restaurant and bar similar to those on highways in the United States.

It is relevant to note the types of businesses that were not particularly prominent, if represented at all. Interestingly, given the location of a large hospital on Hidalgo, the study area had only two medical offices (a physician and a dentist) and four pharmacies. In fact, professional services in general were insignificant, except for technical repair, especially that involving autos. Excluding shops in malls, only two clothing and shoe stores were identified. Moreover, there were but two bars and one liquor store. Atypical of spines examined elsewhere, there were no *yonkes,* or junkyards, at the outer edge of Avenida Hidalgo.

The main commercial attraction is, of course, the Soriana mall. From its extreme southern position just beyond the margins of the built-up area, it exerts a magnetic-like pull for commerce as well as for people. It has been an important force in the intensification and upgrading of land uses along this spine. Like most of the regional shopping centers in the Mexican border cities, it dates from the 1980s and is not yet fully occupied. Prior to the massive peso devaluation in 1982, and despite government efforts to encourage construction of shopping centers to entice Mexican consumers to shop at home instead of in the United States, relatively few such centers were built (Herzog 1990: 147). Since then, however, Mexican investments in shopping centers have increased dramatically. Now regional malls are found in all major cities, and metropolises such as Tijuana and Ciudad Juárez have several.

While the Soriana mall is smaller than many, it is typical in its organization and types of establishments. It is dominated by a single anchor store, which is much more common in Latin America than in the United States (Campbell 1974). Yet it supports a full array of smaller specialty shops, convenience stores, offices, and food and entertainment outlets, including multiplex movie theaters (see Fig. 5.15). While in most respects it appears as a clone of North American shopping centers, there are some subtle differences. Here, as elsewhere in centers along the border, security guards maintain a high profile in the parking lot; there are even guard towers. Inside the mall, traditional Mexican decorative features are incorporated into the design, including such elements as tile, fountains, and wrought-iron benches. (In Ciudad Juárez, one mall had a full-size kiosco, evoking images of the plaza.) For the throngs of Mexican teenagers who, like their contemporaries in the United States, frequent the mall with regularity, it has indeed become a "scene"—the new "plaza" of the new border city.

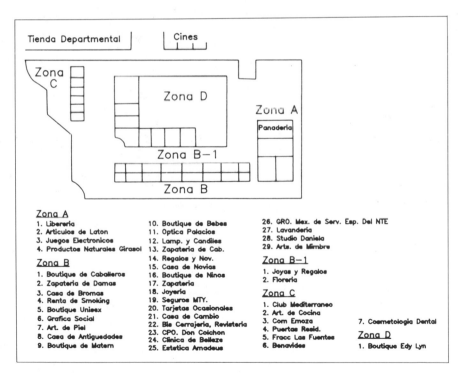

FIGURE 5.15 Reynosa's Soriana Mall: Plan and Directory. Derived from mall directory, May 1990.

6 Residential Townscapes

Dwelling is both process and artefact—the activity of residing and the structure which is the focus of residence (Oliver 1987: 7). In the Mexican border cities, as in any city, dwellings occupy the greatest amount of space. They are estimated to cover 77 percent of the land-use area in Tijuana, for example, and 83 percent in Ciudad Juárez (Hoffman 1983: 212). The density, variety, form, texture, and even color of dwellings and their immediate space give personality to place; Gordon Cullen called this *townscape* (Relph 1987: 238).

Culture is arguably the most significant filter that shapes townscape personality. The residential townscapes in Mexican border cities are complex because they incorporate cross-cultural aspects of Latin American, Mexican, and even North American exterior organization and design. While strolling or driving through the elite districts of the largest cities, one will recognize immediately house styles that echo an elegant past as well as those that boast the latest in North American contemporary fashion. In the same city, frequently within a few miles of this privileged quarter, one can see shanty towns constructed of salvaged materials, the likes of which have not been seen in American cities since the nineteenth century (Ward 1971: 109–117). Between these extremes are neighborhoods of great variation, but which are, nonetheless, fundamentally Mexican in character. In this chapter, our concern is with the outward visual appearance of dwelling spaces, their landscape expression or townscape, and with how this relates to the personality of the border city. A vignette describes an elite residential neighborhood in Nuevo Laredo. First, however, we will consider the nature of housing in Mexico and the border cities.

CONTEMPORARY HOUSING

In the North American city, residential districts are largely defined by congregations of class and frequently designated as either upper-class, middle-class, working-class, or ethnic neighborhoods (Hartshorn 1992: 252). Vast sections of middle-class housing dominate the residential landscapes of our cities, yet they are often criticized as lacking place identity. One author has argued that this placelessness has resulted largely from an overconcern for rational space, or hyperplanning, to satisfy an upwardly mobile middle class (Relph 1987: 87). Elite residential districts as well as ethnic enclaves, on the other hand, often have greater staying power as identifiable communities in the changing urban fabric of the North American city (Burns 1980; Godfrey 1988).

In Mexican border cities as in other Mexican cities, the residential pattern is much more mixed socially, spatially, and architecturally. Residential structure typically appears on maps as a mosaic of districts, each named individually. Thus, while neighborhoods exist informally in North American cities (Keller 1968: 87–92), in Mexican cities, especially the larger ones, they are assigned territorial definition and formal names. In Tijuana, for example, 226 separate residential areas were identified on a recent map of the city (Esparza Torres 1988). At the same time, this orderly segmentation is confounded by a landscape of mixed uses that might include empty lots next to affluent dwellings or shanty housing next to or within middle-income neighborhoods.

Despite this diversity, there remains a logic and spatial order to housing that resembles the pattern, if not landscape, of housing arrangements in other Latin American cities. Thus, housing can be divided into formal and informal sectors (Gilbert and Ward 1985: 5–6). *Formal-sector housing* is what most North Americans would recognize as standard housing, whether it be privately or publicly financed and constructed. To build housing in the formal sector, a party would arrange financing through a bank or mortgage company, purchase land, and hire the necessary professional builders. Old dwellings purchased by private parties are also considered part of the formal housing sector. The size of the private formal housing market in any Mexican city will vary with the wealth of the community. Spatially, however, much of it may include older, privately owned housing that is rented to middle- and lower-income groups, especially in the neighborhoods close to el centro.

In Mexican cities, a privately subdivided residential district is called a *fraccionamiento*. Although these subdivisions may include piped water, sewage, paved streets, land for parks, and other amenities, most are simply private lands sold lot by lot to residents for house construction (Price 1973a: 76; Gildersleeve 1978: 306; Logan 1984: 17–18; Popp 1985: 144). Whereas the term fraccionamiento is commonly used for newer subdivisions in the border cities, the term *colonia* is often used to identify older residential districts. The word can refer to any subdivision within a city, but it typically refers to a particular residential district *(colonia residencial)*. For example, *colonia popular* describes housing that is privately owned or rented but on land that has been surveyed and subdivided by the government (Price 1973a: 75). Colonia can also be used to describe a mature, working-class, residential neighborhood, such as Colonia Libertad in Tijuana, or an affluent district, such as Colonia Bella Vista in Ciudad Juárez. In peripheral squatter settlements composed principally of self-help housing, a colonia might assume the name of the state or town from which most of the residents emigrated, as in Colonia San Luisito for migrants from the state of San Luis Potosí. Colonias of this type also might be referred to in the local government as *asentamientos irregulares* (irregular settlements) (Hopgood 1979: 27; Herzog 1990: 78).

Public housing is the most recent formal housing to appear in the border cities. The national government initiated programs to assist industrial development along the border during the 1960s, and this has spurred government investment in and construction of public housing (Dillman 1970). While state and local governments have tried to participate in these programs, they have been unable to direct development to the degree that the federal government has because they have lacked the necessary resources and political authority. Unlike public housing in the United States, however, in Mexican cities it is not usually intended for the poorest residents. Rather, this housing is often constructed by the government for the emerging middle class, to create jobs and sustain the construction industry, and to reward government supporters working in key industries (Gilbert 1989: 2–3). Three of the largest federally regulated, public-housing programs are Instituto del Fondo Nacional para la Vivienda de los Trabajadores (INFONAVIT), which builds houses for industrial workers; Fondo de la Vivienda para los Trabajadores del Instituto de Seguridad y Servicios Sociales de los Trabajadores del Estado (FOVISSTE), which accommodates public employees; and Instituto Nacional para el Desarrollo de la Comunidad (INDECO), which constructs housing for unaffiliated workers (Herzog 1985b: 32–36). These agencies were established in the 1970s and are financed by a 5 percent tax on all wages paid by the employer (Kelley 1976: 227). In the border cities as in much of Mexico, however, publicly financed housing rarely amounts to more than 10 percent of a city's housing stock, although this may increase with continued industrial growth. Such scarcity coupled with the lack of viable alternatives creates a great demand. In most cities there are more who want this housing than there is housing to accommodate them. Between 1978 and 1982, for example, only 6.7 percent of the government expenditure in Tijuana was allocated to housing, a remarkably small percentage given that city's rapid growth (Herzog 1989: 127).

Beyond formal housing is the so-called *informal-sector housing,* or self-help housing. It typifies much of the housing on the periphery of Mexican border cities as well as housing in disamenity zones, and it may accommodate large numbers of a city's population, frequently at high density. In Tijuana, for example, self-help housing is estimated to shelter 43 percent of the population, but it occupies only 23 percent of the city area (De la Rosa 1985: 45). This housing is self-constructed, often on public land. Most often it is built by the lowest-income residents of the city, utilizing any means and materials available to erect shelter. Although squatter settlements have been stereotyped as the "ghettos" of Mexican cities, their role and function in urban housing is more complex (Ward 1976: 331; Lomnitz 1977: 44–45). A study of migrants to Ciudad Juárez, for example, has shown that during the 1950s, new migrants to the city chiefly sought housing in el centro. After the mid-1960s, new arrivals principally resided in peripheral, self-help housing districts (Ugalde 1974: 14–15; Hoenderos, et al. 1983: 381). By the late 1970s, however, residents of the newer peripheral settlements more often were city residents who had relocated from other districts of Ciudad Juárez than recent migrants to the city (Lloyd 1986: 54). Similarly, in Tijuana, self-help housing areas are populated principally by urban residents who have moved within the city four to five times (Hiernaux 1986: 88–97). Thus, the commonly perceived notion that squatter settlements or self-help residential spaces only attract the newest migrants to a border city is somewhat misleading. The residential histories of recent arrivals suggest varying periods of residence in rental or shared accommodations elsewhere in the city before movement to the periphery.

Although self-help housing may represent the poorest habitation in a physical sense, the sector is increasingly receiving service by government, especially street improvement, electricity, and water. This pattern suggests that these spontaneous developments may eventually be upgraded. In some cities, housing areas that were once squatter settlements are now incorporated into the residential mainstream.

The proliferation of this type of housing in the border cities and throughout urban Mexico has contributed to the recent shift in residential tenure. In 1950, only three cities in Mexico with populations greater than 100,000 (Matamoros included) had a majority of owner-occupied homes. By 1980, almost every large Mexican city, including the border cities of Ciudad Juárez, Tijuana, Mexicali, and Matamoros, had more owners than renters (Gilbert and Varley 1989: 13–15).

DWELLINGS

The dwelling types evident in the border cities today mirror several cultural traditions spanning nearly five centuries of settlement history. The variety of types creates a landscape palimpsest, scribed upon by the immigration of groups with different architectural traditions, by the preference for house styles that reflect cultural status, and by the retention of certain house types because of cultural inertia (West 1974: 130).

For the border cities, dwelling types will be described chronologically from the earliest traditional colonial forms to the modern styles that first appeared in the nineteenth century. In many instances precise historic data on dwellings are absent, so inference from known sources and nearby regions will be substituted to suggest past constructions.

Traditional Dwellings

Several border settlements were founded between the middle seventeenth century and the end of the eighteenth century. It has been said that less is known about Spanish colonial houses in these settlements than about Indian dwellings in the region during the previous thousand years (Bunting 1976: 55). In part this has resulted from the preservation and reconstruction of Indian sites across the region, mostly in the American Southwest, as well as from long neglect of vernacular Spanish colonial architecture in preference for the high-design styles of missions (Sanford 1971). The recent rapid growth of the border cities has also contributed to the destruction of older colonial housing. Architectural historians and cultural geographers have been forced to interpret the built forms of the period and to assemble sufficient evidence to make reasonable inferences about the townscapes of bygone places from a very small sample of surviving structures.

Probably the earliest dwelling type known to the Spanish along the border was the *jacal*. This house type is known throughout Mexico and the American Southwest, and although there are said to be numerous variations, the jacal possesses a fundamental structure and pattern. An Aztec term, jacal is thought to derive from the Nahuatl *xacalli*, *xa* indicating straw, reed, or bamboo and *calli* meaning house (Robinson 1981: 18). The typical jacal was a one-room rectangular structure consisting of four or more posts, often forked at the top, buried in the ground to serve as both wall and roof supports. Between the posts, the spaces of the walls were filled with various kinds of materials including stone, rubble, and adobe brick. Exterior and interior walls were left exposed or covered with a layer of mud, and roofs were either flat, gabled, or hipped (Graham 1988: 1). The scholarly consensus is that the jacal is indigenous to the Americas and is not a Spanish import. It is likely, however, that the Spanish were involved in its diffusion from parts of southern and central Mexico to the northern borderlands. One expert asserts that its origins in the north may be tied to the early pit houses of Southwest Indian peoples (Graham 1988: 2).

References to jacales were common among the early Spanish inspections of the northern border region. Whether as ranch structures (Robinson 1979: 130) or in eighteenth-century towns such as Camargo (Newton 1964: 15) and Laredo (Hinojosa 1983: 17), jacales appear to be the earliest kinds of dwellings erected by settlers. As communities matured, other building types emerged and the jacal became associated with the poorest populations, sometimes becoming stigmatized (Newton 1964: 14). Jacales were still being described along the border in places such as Matamoros and Reynosa until the end of the nineteenth century (Chatfield 1893: 32; Bourke 1894: 601) and at Presidio across from Ojinaga during the 1930s (Lehmer 1939: 183–186). By the 1960s, though, the form was reported to be rapidly disappearing from the region (Graham 1988: 10). In northern Mexico, jacales have been observed principally in rural areas and as outbuildings separate from or attached to newer structures (West 1974: 130). No surviving habitable examples of the traditional jacal have been observed in any of the border cities studied here.

The solid block house, often flat-roofed and constructed of either adobe or stone, became a standard form for town and country dwellings during the Spanish colonial period (Kubler 1948: vol. 1, 188, 207). While the model for this structure can be traced to southern Andalucía and western Extremadura in Spain, the presence of flat-roofed adobe buildings among the sixteenth-century Aztec may indicate a case of cultural convergence in the adoption and spread of this dwelling type in colonial Mexico (West 1974: 111). The block house typically has been described as a post-and-lintel construction, whereby the roof is supported by heavy solid walls, and the walls rest on a foundation of stone or earth (Jackson 1959–60: 27). The earliest of these block houses along the northern border, whether on ranches or in towns, were one-room, rectangular dwellings with a single entrance and usually no windows as a defensive measure against hostile Indians (George 1975: 30).

The Spanish colonial block house was either adobe brick or stone construction. Recent studies of the distribution of adobe housing in northern Mexico show a primary correlation with the Chihuahuan and Sonoran desert areas encompassing border cities such as Ciudad Juárez, Ojinaga, Las Palomas, San Luis Río Colorado, and Sonoita (West 1974: 122; West and Gonzalez 1979: 61–72). A secondary area of adobe use is in the semiarid stretch from eastern Coahuila to northern Tamaulipas that would include the border cities of Ciudad Acuña, Piedras Negras, Nuevo Laredo, Camargo, Reynosa, and Matamoros (Harrington 1945: 11). In both these regions, adobe has been a significant building material for block houses since colonial times (see Fig. 6.1). Historic maps of El Paso del Norte (present Ciudad Juárez) and San Juan Bautista (present Guerrero near Piedras Negras) each label buildings as constructed of adobe *(Todas las obras asi del presidio como de la población son de tierra,* and *Todas estas obras son de adoves)* (Gerald 1966: 38; Eaton 1981: 27).

Neither the Baja California border cities, such as Tijuana, Tecate, or

FIGURE 6.1 The wall-ruins of an adobe structure still standing in *el centro,* Ciudad Juárez.

Mexicali, nor the eastern Sonora towns, such as Nogales, Naco, and Agua Prieta, figured as primary or secondary areas of adobe use, according to one researcher. Although adobe may have been used in these areas, the combination of environmental constraints (too wet or other suitable materials such as stone were available) and cultural preference (resulting from late settlement and the availability of other materials such as fired brick) suggests that it has not been the dominant building material (West 1974: 130).

In northeastern Mexico, coinciding with the border areas between Ciudad Acuña and Matamoros, stone block houses are as common or more common than those of adobe. The presence of sandstone, caliche, and calcareous conglomerate rocks that can be made into a cement mortar makes stone construction possible. Cut stone in this region is termed *sillar;* it is usually chinked with smaller rocks, mud, and cement to fill spaces between the layers of stone, a process known as *rejoneado* (Newton 1964: 35; George 1975: 36). Limestone in this vicinity also made possible the production of stucco that could be applied to building exteriors. Quarries for this purpose near Reynosa were reported to have supplied the building needs of Brownsville in South Texas as well as its cosmopolitan neighbor, Matamoros (Chatfield 1893: 36).

Modern Dwellings

The forms, if not the colonial dwellings and structures themselves, have largely persisted into the modern era, and the preference for certain materials such as adobe and stone continues to be evident in the landscapes of the border towns. However, by the late nineteenth century, exotic building styles and especially the application of different materials brought a new texture to border townscapes. At the end of the nineteenth century, observations by visitors in larger border towns such as Matamoros suggest that brick was being used in some building construction (Chatfield 1893; Bourke 1894). Inspection of Sanborn Fire Insurance maps for Ciudad Juárez in 1893 and 1898 show several brick structures, although most dwellings are shown as adobe as late as 1902 (Sanborn Fire Insurance Co., El Paso, Texas 1893: sheet 22; 1898: sheet 24; 1902: sheet 27). Although brick became visible in the landscapes of border towns at this early date, it appears that in most places, it was used only for major government structures and some commercial buildings.

Fired bricks were usually manufactured locally because of their bulk and weight and because the clay and sand from which they were made were nearly universally available along the border. Brick color varies according to clay-deposit characteristics. It may be reddish in color, suggesting concentrations of ferric oxide, or yellowish—such as those used at Matamoros—which denotes a strong presence of calcium (McKee 1973: 41). As border towns became connected in the 1880s by railroad lines from interior Mexico or across the American Southwest, brick manufacturing became part of an external export economy. Large abandoned brick kilns on the outskirts of Reynosa and Piedras Negras testify to the past importance of this building-material industry. How this technology spread to the border and became institutionalized for building construction is unclear. The sketchy outlines of several known brickyards at D'Hanis and Roma in south Texas may indicate that the industry emerged largely through the efforts of German immigrants in the 1880s (Hodge and Victor 1983: 18; Steely 1986: 9). The presence of Europeans in the lower Rio Grande valley is well known, and they may have contributed to the diffusion of this technology (Jordan 1988; Newton 1973). In border towns such as Camargo, where brick manufacturing became locally significant, the townscape reveals relics of this past in surviving structures (see Fig. 6.2).

Settlements connected by railroads continued to be influenced by out-

FIGURE 6.2 Nineteenth-century gabled and flat-roofed brick dwellings at Camargo are distinctive signatures and clues to the cultural diffusion of building styles along the border.

side building traditions into the early twentieth century. Access to imported saw-lumber at the end of the nineteenth century resulted in modification of the older jacal styles. The thatched roof supported by poles and sticks gradually was replaced by a wooden shingle roof supported by lumber (see Fig. 6.3). Wall cladding was typically board and batten. Corrugated iron began to replace the shingle roof in the twentieth century. This house type, labeled the "one-room-added-on," is hypothesized by one authority as the dominant second-generation folk house along the Texas-Mexico border (Graham 1979: 40–42). As family needs and resources dictated, additional rooms were added, thus marking the house form as distinct from the earlier jacal, which was its parent. Preliminary investigation indicates that this dwelling type may have been common in the region for two to three decades into the present century (Graham 1979: 43).

The Porfiriato and the postrevolutionary era in Mexico (1890–1925) witnessed the introduction of modern European and North American revival styles of architecture (Martín Hernández 1981). Although the northern border towns were distant from the cosmopolitan nucleus of Mexico City, some architectural influence spread from the capital north to mark the

FIGURE 6.3 The "one-room-added-on," an early twentieth-century example of the older *jacal* dwelling style, Ciudad Acuña, Coahuila.

emerging townscapes, chiefly public buildings, of the larger cities. The *aduana,* or customs house, built in Ciudad Juárez in 1889 as well as other official buildings were constructed in the fashionable French Second Empire style (Martínez 1978: n.p.). Perhaps an even more significant influence was that which diffused from the Southwestern United States and shaped the taste of building in the private sector. Most notable was the wide-ranging impact of the Spanish colonial revival on Mexican border cities. This revival has been traced principally to certain architects in Southern California during the 1890s who tried to link this romantic style with the region's Spanish roots (Gebhard 1967: 131). San Diego's Panama California International Exposition in 1915 incorporated an ornate Spanish revival style called Churrigueresque as its architectural theme and thereby spurred a spread of this style of architecture across the Southwest over the next two decades. The exposition has been credited with doing for Spanish colonial revival what the Chicago Exposition of 1893 did for neoclassical architecture all across America (Sanford 1971: 248–253; Gebhard 1967: 136). As the style diffused and became popularized, regional variants evolved. These included the "pueblo," or Santa Fé style familiar in New Mexico, and the "alamo" facade influence in Texas (Newcomb 1937: 37).

In the larger border cities, Spanish colonial revival appears as a style in elegant houses built by the affluent in the early twentieth century (see Fig. 6.4). In Ciudad Juárez, some of these homes are still standing along Avenida 16 de Septiembre; most, however, have been converted from residential to commercial functions as the once fashionable residential street has changed character, especially nearer the urban core. In Tijuana, the Agua Caliente Hotel and Country Club, which also included a casino and spa, was designed by a Southern California architect in the now-classic Spanish colonial–revival style (Newcomb 1937: 119–121).

Additional modern house styles, especially ranch, contemporary, and neoeclectic, began to appear in the border cities after the Second World War. Ranch-style houses likely originated in California during the 1930s. They gained popularity during the 1940s and became one of the dominant house styles built throughout the United States during the 1950s and 1960s. The style is based on the early Spanish colonial style from the American Southwest, modified by Craftsman and Prairie styles that were influential in the early twentieth century (McAlester and McAlester 1984: 479). The low-slung, rambling character of the ranch style may be linked to the widespread adoption of the automobile in post–World War II America and thereby suggests the shift from the compact house on a small lot to the sprawling ranch-style house on a large lot. This fact combined with the exclusiveness of

FIGURE 6.4 A 1920s postcard view of the Bermúdez house, an example of the
Spanish colonial revival style on Avenida 16 de Septiembre in Ciudad Juárez.
From the authors' private collections.

modern housing that is largely restricted to the upper classes in Mexico
meant that the ranch style, like the Spanish colonial revival, had a visible
yet restricted impact on the built environment of the border cities.

The most recent house styles, contemporary and neoeclectic, to appear in border-city residential neighborhoods are similarly reserved for
the most affluent districts. The contemporary styles are derived from the
earlier ranch models and reflect the influence of architect-designed houses
in the United States during the 1950s through the 1970s. In the border
cities they are often flat-roofed, although gabled subtypes common in the
United States are occasionally present. By the late 1960s, fashions in domestic architecture were shifting back to more traditional styles, and the neoeclectic, with its distinctive mansard roof line, became a favorite in both
residential and commercial building. By the 1970s through the 1980s, this
had evolved to a taste for other traditional revival styles: neo-French, with
a strikingly high hipped roof; neo-Tudor, replete with half-timbering; and
neo-Mediterranean, which combined Italian Renaissance and Spanish eclec-

tic styles (McAlester and McAlester 1984: 482, 487). In the border cities, the neo-French style especially appears to have captured the fancy of affluent homeowners in the wealthiest neighborhoods (see Fig. 6.5). Construction, regardless of modern house style, is often concrete block faced with decorative brick or stucco.

HOUSESCAPES

What appears to influence most the form of dwellings and their attendant space is an ideal view held by a people (Rapoport 1969: 47). Built forms, including houses, are symbols in a system of visual communication of that ideal (Preziosi 1979: 5). Once constructed, the permanence of built forms imprints on and influences future generations, even though these generations may not know the reasons for past constructions (Hugill 1984: 21–30). We use the term *housescape*, a house and its immediate landscape, to describe this arrangement (Arreola 1988: 299). Border housescapes are especially characterized by the phenomenon of property enclosure and have distinctive landscape signatures.

FIGURE 6.5 Neo-French influences, such as a mansard roof, are popular in elite neighborhoods of the largest border cities, as in Colonia Jardín in Matamoros.

Enclosure

The most distinctive and widespread practice found in border housescapes is property enclosure, a recognized feature of townscapes throughout Mexico (Nelson 1963). Since the colonial era, courtyard or patio housing has come to signify an ideal form (Arreola 1988: 301–302; Griffin and Ford 1976: 442). In rural New Mexico where Spanish settlement began in the sixteenth century, the gradual enclosure of dwellings to create open space has been described as an "additive" process (Jackson 1959–60: 28–29). The rooms of the additive house are plainly rectangular with a central positioned door, and each wall is a bearing wall, not just a simple partition. The facade of this house appears as a long, low arrangement so that the form is essentially a repetition of nearly identical units, often resulting in an L-shape or U-shape (Bunting 1976: 60–63). In eighteenth-century Spanish Texas, rancho housescapes with courtyards evolved from linear and L-shaped dwelling arrangements (Robinson 1979: 141).

In colonial towns, housescapes—whether for the affluent or common residents—again typified the ideal courtyard form. "The Palace" was an eighteenth-century sillar-and-adobe house built in Cerralvo, Nuevo León, southwest of Miguel Alemán. It occupied half a city block, flush to the street and facing the main plaza of the town. The six-room structure was enclosed on three sides of a courtyard that contained a well and mill stone (Newton 1964: 41, 43, 53). Similarly, at Guerrero, Coahuila, near Piedras Negras, the "Captain's House" is nearly all that remains of the colonial presidio San Juan Bautista (see Fig. 6.6). Its L-shaped structure around an enclosed courtyard measures nearly ninety feet along its west elevation. The walls are sixteen to eighteen inches thick and built of load-bearing rubble stone. Two doorways open onto the street and lead to separate rooms, which give access to the courtyard where a well is located; a centrally positioned kitchen faces the courtyard (Graham et al. 1976: 79–80). Enclosure was typical as well among more common houses. In 1789, most houses in Laredo were jacales, yet more than 90 percent of these modest dwellings were enclosed by fences: nineteen of stone, eighteen of adobe, five of wood, and thirty-seven of rushes from the Rio Grande (Wilkinson 1975: 71).

The preference for enclosed spaces continued through the nineteenth century and well into the twentieth, and fencing became strongly identified with Mexican and Mexican-American housescapes (Robinson 1981: 23; Arreola 1981). Modern architectural styles have continued to emphasize the enclosed pattern so that interior open space is an important aspect of elite houses, middle-income town homes, and even lower-income dwellings in

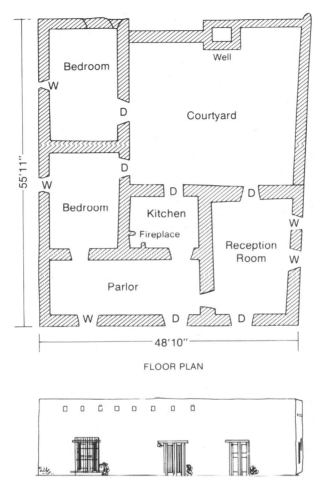

FLOOR PLAN

SOUTH ELEVATION

FIGURE 6.6 The Captain's House in eighteenth-century San Juan Bautista (now Guerrero, Coahuila) was typical of flat-roofed, enclosed courtyard houses. Source: After Graham et al. 1976.

Mexico (Martín Hernández 1981: 99–180). In the border cities today, residential property enclosure is so common that it is rarely questioned and is considered simply part of the house. One study in Tijuana claimed that "virtually every house . . . is fenced" (Griffin and Ford 1976: 443). As if by cultural decree, if you occupy a property, you must enclose the perimeter. This axiom holds whether the house is in the most exclusive district of the city or in the peripheral squatter settlements, whether it was built in the 1880s or 1980s, and whether it stands in Tijuana or Matamoros.

The affluent neighborhoods of the border cities have begun to shift away from the core—the plaza focus of the colonial era—to outlying suburbs that may encompass hillsides or beach sites depending on local environment (Amato 1970: 96–105). This movement has resulted from several forces, including changes in transportation technology and the embracing of North American landscape tastes. Movement away from the congested center, where land use is compact, to peripheral sites has allowed for somewhat larger lots with views, which were not typical of the traditional housescape. Nevertheless, the enclosure principle is still evident in the newer houses of these districts, despite the changing ecology of site. These changes in housescape from most to least enclosed are indicative of an adaptation process from traditional Mexican layout preferences to a modified North American open design. This design adaptation is especially visible in elite neighborhoods in the largest border cities. However, examples cited below affirm that it is also evident in several medium-sized border communities.

In the most traditional style of housescape enclosure, high walls (usually of six feet) surround the property, creating a *fortress* facade when viewed from the street. The entrance to the housescape is a decorative pedestrian gate, and automotive access is hidden behind the street facade. This is a variation of colonial and nineteenth-century enclosed housescapes in which structures fronted directly onto the street and were enclosed by a back or interior courtyard that was walled. In the present housescape, the dwelling is no longer part of the exterior perimeter but is enclosed completely by a separate barricade. The preference for this style of enclosure is not meant to suggest that it is the oldest; the time of construction is not necessarily related to the degree of enclosure.

A modification of the fortress-style enclosure is the *peekaboo,* a transition style. Here the solid wall enclosure includes a series of open iron grates between solid panels (see Fig. 6.7). The peekaboo style maintains the sense of exclusion by its high wall and fence, but it suggests a desire to display the housescape behind the barrier, the first adaptation to the more modern enclosure styles. Again, a pedestrian gate is the entrance from the street and automotive access is on one side or in back.

A third style of housescape enclosure is the *iron and post,* an extremely popular form found in all border towns and throughout Mexico (see Fig. 6.8). Several significant changes can be detected in this style from earlier forms. First, the solid wall enclosure is reduced to a pedestal of usually two to three feet. An iron-grate curtain rests on top of the masonry

FIGURE 6.7 The peekaboo enclosure in Ciudad Acuña.

FIGURE 6.8 The iron-and-post enclosure at Agua Prieta.

pedestal, and the iron fence is anchored to masonry posts. Second, while the height of the enclosure can be up to six feet, as typical in the fortress and peekaboo, the effect of a predominantly see-through curtain reduces the sense of exclusion. This invites the passerby to inspect the view within the enclosure. Elaborate ornamental vegetation often becomes an important landscape signature in this style of enclosed housescape because of its enhanced visibility from the street. Finally, the gate entrance is now both pedestrian and automotive, signaling the willingness to incorporate and display the automobile.

Yet a fourth style of enclosure is a second transitional form that might be termed the *pedestal-post*. This style is a modification of the iron and post in that the enclosure elements of pedestal and post remain, but the iron grate is eliminated. In this style, the enclosure is almost entirely facade and merely buffers the street from the house with little pretense of exclusion. Important, however, is the appearance of the lawn, that nearly ubiquitous signature of American suburban housescapes (Jackson 1987; Hecht 1975), although it may be found in other enclosure forms as well. Also visible in this transition form is the street-front carport or garage, which signals the full embracing of the automobile as part of the housescape.

The housescape enclosure style that is least like the traditional courtyard enclosed space is the *lawn border* (see Fig. 6.9). Not surprisingly, this housescape most resembles North American middle-class suburban tastes, complete with neoeclectic house style, lawn periphery, and the absence of wall or fence. Here the courtyard enclosure has been turned inside-out so that the dwelling itself is the interior refuge. The well-manicured lawn symbolizes the subtle enclosure of the housescape, in the same way that a white cloth draped around the base of a Christmas tree is meant to suggest snow. The lawn border, however, is a minimal space that also creates the illusion of a much larger house. As in the fortress style, the main entrance is solely pedestrian and automotive access is hidden. Large windows on the street face of the house allow inspection of the street from within as well as glimpses of the interior from the street, as with the peekaboo enclosure style.

Middle-income housing, although an admittedly broad category, typically occupies the greatest percentage of housing stock in the border cities. Not surprisingly, therefore, the range of housing conditions and situations is especially diverse. It includes older dwellings from el centro that have filtered down from upper to middle and even lower groups as well as gentrified and infill construction that accommodates the demand for residence near central commercial services. This category also includes much of the

FIGURE 6.9 The lawn-border enclosure in Piedras Negras.

newer housing built in border cities, whether located on the periphery of el centro or distant from this district, and sometimes even more distant than peripheral squatter settlements. This housing can be both privately constructed fraccionamientos as well as government-financed and -built worker housing. Despite the diversity, enclosure remains a persistent feature of middle-income housescapes.

In the typical border city, houses in el centro represent a variety of mature styles and eras of construction. Old colonial masonry buildings, early twentieth-century board-and-batten dwellings, and Spanish colonial–revival styles may stand next to modern housing built anytime between the 1950s and 1980s. Yet, no matter the era of construction or the style of house, all appear to adhere to the dictum of housescape enclosure. In Matamoros, an early nineteenth-century colonial house initially built flush to the street and open to the interior is extended and enclosed when adapted for the automobile. In Reynosa, a Spanish colonial–revival dwelling from the 1940s encloses its front porch with wrought iron as the neighborhood becomes mixed commercial and residential. On a single section of street in Nuevo Laredo, house styles that express a fifty-year span each conform to the front property line, regardless of the extent of setback, and thus create a curtain of enclosed iron and pedestal (see Fig. 6.10).

FIGURE 6.10 Fifty years of house styles enclosed tight to the street in Nuevo
    Laredo's *el centro*.

Outside of el centro, middle-income housing usually conforms to one
of two housescape types: the so-called in situ accretion house, which is often
individually constructed, or the mass-produced worker house built by private or government means. Accretion housing is typically characterized by
an unfinished or "in process" look (Griffin and Ford 1980: 409). Incomplete
second stories or rooms, unpainted cement-block exterior walls or surfaces,
and protrusions of reinforcing bar above the walls are epitome signatures of
the type. Nevertheless, enclosure is given high priority, and side walls or
fences are often combined to frame these houses when viewed from the
street. Mass-produced worker housing is not unlike the tract-home construction typical in much of the United States after World War II. Houses
of similar or identical plan and style are built on tightly delimited lots, usually close to the street line with only a slight setback. Near-uniform enclosure often results within a short time after the site is occupied; frequently it
is a combination of cement-block pedestal, post, and wrought iron (see
Fig. 6.11). Automobile accommodation is restricted to the street because lot
size is usually constrained at the rear as well as front of the property.
    Self-help housing is typically found on the peripheries of border cities

FIGURE 6.11 Fence-enclosed worker housing near a *maquiladora* industrial park in
Nogales.

or next to disamenity zones such as poorly drained areas or steep hillsides
(see Fig. 6.12). Construction styles range from cement block or adobe brick
on occasion to more common salvaged materials of amazing variety (Griffin
and Ford 1976: 447). Like some formal-sector housing, housescapes of this
informal sector display an accretion character because housing is added to
and modified as material availability changes with social and economic opportunity (Valencia 1969: 89–91). Upon historical reflection, the squatter
shanty so common to this housescape in the border cities is in all likelihood
the contemporary version of the colonial jacal described earlier: a simple,
one-room, temporary dwelling that is upgraded when circumstance allows.
Given this economic constraint, which is not uncommon with residents in
peripheral squatter neighborhoods, one might conclude that enclosing a
property would be a low priority in decisions about resource allocation.
Nevertheless, almost immediately upon occupation of a site and erection of
a shanty, property delimitation takes physical form in some kind of fence,
be it of used tires or discarded automobile hoods (Griffin and Ford 1976).
The cultural preference for enclosure is so strong that when squatters in
Tijuana were assisted financially in the construction of new housing after a

FIGURE 6.12 On the southern periphery of Ciudad Juárez, a sharp border is
evident between new worker housing on the right and self-help housing to the
left.

local disaster, the first property improvement after the house was rebuilt
was a fence (Grijalva 1989).

Landscape Signatures

Human geographers and other social scientists have argued that landscape
tastes are signals of group identity (Firey 1945; Duncan 1973; Zelinsky
1973: 73; Salter 1978: 69–83; Curtis and Helgren 1984: 78). In the border
cities, we have seen how enclosed housescapes are important to all social
groups, and we have suggested that the disappearance of the enclosed house
is a bellwether of the changing taste in landscape among certain of the population. Landscape tastes are largely manifested through landscape signatures. One researcher has formulated this idea into an "axiom of cultural
unity and landscape equality," which holds that "nearly all items in human
landscapes reflect culture in some way. There are almost no exceptions. Furthermore, most items in the human landscape are no more and no less important than other items in terms of the clues they provide about culture"

(Lewis 1979: 18). Unfortunately, because ordinary objects in the landscape become so familiar, they tend to be overlooked as clues to group identity.

Unlike traditional affluent groups in Latin America who tended to favor a walled yet elegant pastoral housescape, in the border cities, the nouveau riche of elite neighborhoods want a housescape that can be seen, not hidden from the outside. This preference for ostentation requires a display of symbols and "ornaments" that signal elite status; these can be divided between institutional and personalized elements.

Institutional signatures include patterns for names of subdivisions and streets; infrastructure amenities such as street pavement, lights, curbs, sidewalks, medians, and *topes* (speed bumps); and parks or miniplazas embellished by fountains. Because many of the newer elite residential areas are on the periphery, distant from el centro, they have followed the North American practice of giving environmental or exotic names to the districts, sometimes displaying them on entry signs. In Tijuana, one of the newest posh districts is called Lomas de Chapultepec and is situated in the *lomas* (hills) above the Agua Caliente racetrack and country club, a couple of miles from the city core. The reference to Chapultepec is both a gesture to the Nahautl (Aztec) Indian word for "hill of the grasshopper" and a historic reference to the old elite residential district and park of Mexico City. Chapultepec has been a sacred space in the Valley of Mexico since the thirteenth century and was known as the residence of various Aztec sovereigns, Spanish viceroys, and the nineteenth-century emperor Maximilian.

At Nogales, an elite district, the Jardínes de Kaletea, was constructed in the late 1980s several miles from el centro. The reference to *jardínes* (gardens) is symbolic and frequent in elite neighborhoods throughout Mexico. Combined with the Greek metaphor, the subdivision assumes an exotic air. Galetea, Greek for "milky white," refers to a nymph of classical mythology. The illusion is furthered by the name, Olympia, which was given the median-divided, landscaped, lighted boulevard that is the gateway to the subdivision. The avenue leads uphill to the most prestigious homes.

Personalized signatures refer to the decoration selections of individual homeowners for their exterior housescapes. Choices range from a variety of ornaments, such as fancy gates and Spanish colonial–design motifs, to vibrant exterior color, tropical plantings and lawns, and satellite dishes.

The Madero residential district in Nuevo Laredo is an elite neighborhood that mirrors these elements (see Fig. 6.13). The district is approximately two miles south from el centro, situated between Guerrero, the commercial spine of the city on the west, and the Rio Grande on the east. The glorieta with its signature Juárez Monument where Guerrero breaks to be-

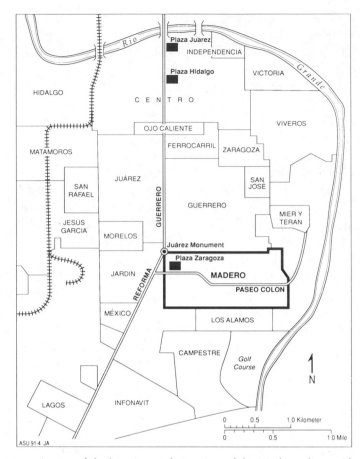

FIGURE 6.13 A map of the location and situation of the Madero elite residential
district in Nuevo Laredo.

come Reforma signals the northwest corner of the district, but access is just
beyond this where Reforma is intersected by Paseo Colón. Median-divided
and interspersed with topes, Paseo Colón is lined with mature trees and is
the principal avenue that bisects the residential quarter. As it exits the neighborhood to the east, this street then leads north and ultimately connects via
a series of back streets to the Juárez-Lincoln Bridge (east of the Guerrero
crossing) that links Nuevo Laredo to Laredo. This illustrates one of the
persistent features, good transit access, of elite districts in the border cities.

Just southwest of the Madero neighborhood where Guerrero breaks
to become Reforma is open land; there is also somewhat of an open-land

buffer between the district and the Rio Grande. To the north and south are the middle-income neighborhoods of Guerrero and Los Alamos, respectively. Beyond Los Alamos is a golf course, one of the signatures of North American suburban townscape. Unlike many subdivisions in the United States, however, the course is segregated from the housing district rather than built around it. Beyond and to the southwest are middle-income districts, including an INFONAVIT worker-housing project. Flanking the Madero district to the west of Reforma are the middle-income neighborhoods of Jardín and México, which buffer the elite quarter from the railroad yards, trucking depot, an industrial park, and the zona de tolerancia.

The core of the area extends about two blocks north of Paseo Colón and is centered on a small plaza, Ignacio Zaragoza, with a modern church on the north side of the square. Houses are moderately spacious on larger-than-average lots and reflect architectural styles of the 1960s and 1970s. Like many elite districts in Mexican cities, the Madero neighborhood is lush with ornamental plantings, especially large shade trees, so from a distance the area appears to have a green canopy. South of Paseo Colón is a more recent addition to the district, with much new construction representing postmodern, neoeclectic house styles.

The street facade of one house that faces Plaza Zaragoza epitomizes the personalized signatures used to project status in the housescapes of this district (see Fig. 6.14). One of the first clues is a fancy, arched, iron gate, an element of many elite enclosed housescapes as described above. This stylized and often ornate entry is arguably a carryover from the magnificent gates that protected the *hacienda* compounds of the colonial era in Mexico (Romero de Terreros 1956: 92). The signature is, perhaps, also related to the *atrio* arch of the open-air church that was common in central Mexico from the conquest (McAndrew 1965: 219–235). In either event, a study of late nineteenth- and early twentieth-century domestic architecture in Mexico City established that arched gateways were distinctive signatures of elite houses (Martín Hernández 1981: 231–235). The mission-style facade, rose window motif, and stucco exterior with masonry molding are all examples of the neo-Mediterranean house style popular in the American Southwest since the 1970s (McAlester and McAlester 1984: 492). Houses nearby are neo-French, another popular style of elite districts along the border. The rich orange stucco of this house reflects a color preference known in Mexico since antiquity. This pre-Columbian inclination toward bright color is a tradition that melded with the Islamic decorative tradition known as *mudéjar* that was introduced to colonial Mexico from Iberia; the preference for these bright hues has persisted in Mexican culture to this day (Arreola 1988:

FIGURE 6.14 An upper-income housescape with personalized signatures such as
     tropical landscaping, wrought iron, and neo-Spanish colonial architecture in
     Nuevo Laredo.

299–315). Ornamental plantings such as palms, which are not native to
this area of the Rio Grande but suggest a tropical ambiance, are combined
with the North American lawn to envelop the housescape in a Mexican
tropical-pastoral setting. Finally, the visible *parabólica* (television satellite
dish)—an element that crowns the roof lines of affluent housing all over
Mexico—is one of the most telling landscape features that characterizes an
elite neighborhood in the border city. One report in 1987 estimated that
there were perhaps 100,000 satellite dishes in Mexico, whereas just five
years earlier there had been almost none (*New York Times* 1987a).

   A few of the elements that are signatures of elite housescapes are also
evident in middle-income housing. These include infrastructure features
such as paved streets, sidewalks, and curbs, and personalized preferences
such as bright exterior color. Ornamental plantings are usually restricted to
more mature middle housing and almost always absent from newer worker-
housing neighborhoods.

   Unlike elite districts with exotic suburban names, middle-housing districts frequently bear national-patriotic names. In Mexicali, these names

TABLE 6.1 Name Types for *Colonias/Fraccionamientos* in Mexicali

Types	Examples	Total N = 144
national-patriotic	Constitución–Héroes de Nacozari	36
environmental-exotic	Los Pinos–Califa	27
geographic	Orizaba	21
saints	Santa Teresa	12
economic	Industrial Alamitos	11
Indian	El Papago	7
other	Universitario	30

SOURCE: Based on Guias Urbanas, *Plano de la Ciudad de Mexicali*, 1986.

were the most frequently counted, representing one quarter of all the colonias and fraccionamientos mapped (Table 6.1). However, when the names for all subdivisions were examined, only one of nine government worker-housing districts boasted a national-patriotic name; most were named after environmental features. This suggests that national-patriotic names for middle-housing districts may have been more common in the past, especially for privately developed fraccionamientos than for recently constructed, government-financed housing. It may also signal a growing status consciousness among middle-income residents and a desire to emulate more affluent subdivisions.

Several features further distinguish worker housing from more mature middle-income housing and other housescapes. Often, worker housing consists of two-storey buildings, tightly organized on small lots to maximize space or intermixed with single-storey structures. There is a pronounced institutional flavor to the streetscape, with common building styles repeated endlessly. Signatures include utility posts near curbside in front of each property, propane tanks (usually positioned on roofs), and television antennae rather than satellite dishes (see Fig. 6.15). These elements appear even when such housing is privately constructed rather than government built and designated for industrial workers. In time, however, housescapes can become personalized by exterior color, and occasionally, by ornamental plantings. Sometimes they resemble accretion houses with construction materials piled on the front property, spilling onto the street.

FIGURE 6.15 New worker housing with institutionalized signatures such as propane gas tanks and utility posts in Reynosa.

One might imagine that distinctive signatures are inconsequential in self-help housing given the poverty that is usually associated with residents in squatter neighborhoods. Nevertheless, signatures persist and can be used to differentiate this housescape from others in the border city. First, self-help neighborhoods commonly lack institutional signatures such as paved streets, curbs, sidewalks, or street lighting. Electricity, however, is almost always available; it represents the first concession that local governments make to peripheral housing districts. Piped water is also increasingly present in more mature self-help neighborhoods. Its absence is apparent by the presence of large forty-gallon water drums that are filled periodically from tanker trucks.

Personalized signatures include the use of bright exterior house color and the frequent use of metal, name-address plates embellished with religious icons as found in several cities (see Fig. 6.16). The display of religious wall shrines, like color, is an ancient heritage. Exterior shrines are usually constructed as a response to a crisis during which an individual promises to erect the shrine as an offering in return for answered prayers (Arreola 1988: 308). It has been established that those who erect shrines often hail from

FIGURE 6.16 This modest yet formal house in a peripheral squatter district of
 Reynosa has access to electricity, is enclosed by a simple wire fence, contains a
 religious name plate above one window, and is painted robin's-egg blue.

rural rather than urban areas. Thus, the presence of this element in self-
help neighborhoods could be interpreted as a celebration of good fortune—
having a house—for a recent rural migrant to the city (Husband 1985:
45, 60).

A second signature of the self-help housescape is a clutter of miscellaneous items, often building materials, on the property. Piles of dirt and
stacks of cement block or lumber are the most common features. Many,
perhaps most, would explain this simply as a function of poverty, equating
it with the shabbiness of some low-income districts of American cities. In all
likelihood, clutter is a product of several factors, chiefly the spatial adjustment of residents in transition between rural and urban settings. In the self-
help housescape, materials accumulate quickly for fear of throwing anything
out that may have value or some future usefulness. This may be the heritage
of a culture of poverty, but it is also the legacy of a rural experience where
space was abundant and things could easily pile up. In the tighter, more
restricted spaces of the city, what was once mere accumulation spread over
a ranch compound becomes clutter in the new landscape.

TABLE 6.2 Frequency of Housescape Characteristics
(Key: C = common; O = occasional; R = rare)

Housing Type	Upper	Middle	Self-Help
ENCLOSURE	C	C	C
PERSONAL SIGNATURES			
exterior color	C	C	C
ornamental plantings	C	O	R
decorative gate	C	O	R
satellite dish	C	O	R
tv antenna	O	C	C
name plates	R	R	C
INSTITUTIONAL SIGNATURES			
paved streets	C	C	R
curbs/sidewalks	C	O	R
exotic names	C	O	R
utility posts	R	C	O
propane tanks	R	C	R

SOURCE: Field observation.

The pattern of housescape elements and their association with housing types in the border cities are plotted on Table 6.2. While some features correlate particularly with one or another housing group, two characteristics figure in all types: enclosure and exterior color. Enclosure was found to be a pervasive condition of housescapes in the border cities from colonial structures through to the present dwellings. The preference for bright exterior color is not nearly as common as enclosure, yet it appears with predictable regularity if not uniformity in all housing neighborhoods, elite, middle, and self-help. Redundancy or patterned repetition is one of the prerequisites for ascribing cultural distinctiveness to the built environment (Rapoport 1982: 149–152). By this measure, enclosure and exterior color stand out as fundamental expressions of the "Mexicanness" of the border-city townscape. Other personal and institutional signatures may be predictable according to economic level or style of housing, but enclosure and exterior color appear to be the most basic cultural features, and thereby the most significant indicators of changing landscape tastes.

7 Landscapes of Industry and Transit

Each working morning in San Diego, American and Japanese businessmen depart by auto south for their offices in maquiladora industrial parks in Tijuana. At the same time, thousands of Mexicans stream north to shop and work in the greater San Diego area (*Christian Science Monitor* 1989). By 1995, it is estimated that between sixty and seventy-five million people will cross this border yearly, up from forty-three million in 1987 (Herzog 1990: 55). This large, complex, cross-traffic pattern is not unusual along the border and illustrates the dynamic flow of commerce, industry, and transit between Mexican and American border cities. The daily passage from the United States of executive and supervisory personnel to industrial parks in Mexico is a telling indication of the mushrooming growth of this economy along the border. The fact that these commuters can now enter and leave Tijuana via a second crossing at Mesa de Otay, near the new industrial parks, symbolizes the increasing accessibility of the Mexican border cities; a third crossing west of the San Ysidro gate has been proposed.

Contrary to the popular view that industrialization is only a recent phenomenon along the border, industrial activities have, in fact, been an aspect of border-city economies and landscapes since the nineteenth century. Although a few cities have supported specialized industrial activities that produced goods for export, most border towns included some small industries to meet the needs of their immediate trade areas. Locations of early industrial activities were typically tied to resource availability, as well as such factors as labor, transportation, market access, and adequate space.

Although new border-city industries must still meet these location criteria, industrial land use in border cities ranks comparatively low to residential and commercial space. In Tijuana, for example, only about 2 percent of the land is devoted to industrial use, approximately half of what is classified as industrial land use in neighboring San Diego (Herzog 1990: 123). Nevertheless, the landscape aesthetics of industrial space have changed with the recent introduction of industrial parks and the role of the federal government in new industries. Moreover, the impact of these new industries can be seen in other landscape transformations, such as worker housing and the incremental growth of new self-help housing on the urban periphery, where squatters who work in maquiladoras frequently reside.

Industry, like tourism, has historically shared a concern with transit. Much of what is produced and the services offered in border cities depend on convenient auto, truck, rail, and pedestrian connections to the American border town as well as to the interiors of Mexico and the United States. The reorientation of border-city economies to maquiladora industries and transborder commerce, combined with the continued growth of tourist activities, has meant the construction of additional bridges and gate crossings for larger cities. In smaller towns, new facilities have replaced older bridges and crossings. The railroad transportation that dominated the commerce of several border cities during the nineteenth century has been supplemented or replaced by significant truck traffic and truck depots in the twentieth century. Additionally, most border cities have at least small airfields that can accommodate private planes. In several of the larger border cities—notably Tijuana and Ciudad Juárez—airports have emerged as the most recent transit nodes, providing passenger service between other large border cities and the interior of Mexico.

In this chapter, our concern turns to the landscapes of industry and transit: where these spaces are situated in the border cities, and how they have changed as the result of growth and recent economic transformation. Nogales, Sonora, will be examined as a case study of these dynamic and economically critical landscapes of production and international movement.

EARLY INDUSTRIES AND LANDSCAPES

Agriculture remains a major economic activity along the border. In 1955, three border cities—Reynosa, Matamoros, and Mexicali—were among twenty-five Mexican cities that each exceeded twenty million dollars of industrial production, chiefly through processing agricultural commodities (Reynolds 1970: 171). (Oil refining would shortly become the leading industrial activity at Reynosa.) Furthermore, two cities founded since the creation of the international boundary, Mexicali and San Luis Río Colorado, owe their raison d'être to agriculture (Chamberlin 1951; Gildersleeve 1978: 75). Dependent on water from the lower Colorado River, each is situated near a hinterland that produces cotton from irrigation as well as wheat and safflower. A third border city, Matamoros, evolved in the twentieth century as the center for irrigated farming on the Mexican side of the lower Rio Grande valley. Sugarcane and cotton were dominant before World War II, but they have yielded to sorghum and corn in the last two decades (Foscue 1934; Kent 1983). Ironically perhaps, in the largest border city, Ciudad Juárez, land is still farmed inside the city limits. This occurs mostly in the southeast sector of the urban area along the Rio Grande, where cotton and alfalfa are cultivated under irrigation, (Schmidt 1973: 47–49) but it also occurs along the Pan American Highway in the south of town. Although this land is in transition to higher-order land uses, agricultural production was still evident in 1992.

Even where a city's immediate livelihood is separated from farming, cultivated land is not far away from places such as Camargo, Miguel Alemán, or Ojinaga, all of which service agricultural hinterlands along the Rio Grande. On the western mountain slopes of the Peninsular Range between Tijuana and Tecate along Mexico Highway 2, olive and grape orchards lend a Mediterranean character to the landscape. Where farming is impractical, and even where it exists, ranching is yet another dimension of agricultural livelihood. At Las Palomas, Agua Prieta, and especially at Piedras Negras and Ciudad Acuña, the *norteño* (the northerner) association with livestock herding and its economy is a fundamental element of the cities. This is evident in the retail services that cater to ranchers and in the near-ubiquitous presence of western wear, especially straw hats and boots. This subcultural trait arguably is most pronounced through the din of *ranchera* (ranch or cowboy) and norteño songs blasting from *disco tiendas* (record/tape stores) that crowd the plazas and commercial avenues of el centro in virtually every border town. This persistence of agriculture and ranching amidst and between the border cities, particularly in light of the norteamericano image of these places as solely urban tourist destinations, is yet another signal of the diversity that exists among these settlements.

The major border cities that service agricultural hinterlands have developed industries for agricultural processing and associated infrastructures. Outside Mexicali, San Luis Río Colorado, and Matamoros, there are elaborate facilities for ginning cotton as well as grain-storage sites, usually accessible to railroad lines or paved highways. In fact, the most intensive highway network along the border is the maze of paved roads that carpet the Colorado River Delta between Mexicali and San Luis Río Colorado; a similar pattern marks the agricultural landscape between Reynosa and Matamoros. These networks resulted from federal road development that complemented agricultural expansion during the post–World War II era. In the 1950s, an everyday scene during the fall harvest was the lineup of trucks transporting cotton across the Brownsville and Matamoros Bridge destined for the port of Brownsville, Texas (Wooldridge and Vezzetti 1982: 177).

Agricultural distributors are still a specialized industry of border cities. Because large quantities of produce grown in Mexico are now marketed in the United States, trucking activity at strategic points along the border has boomed since World War II. Both Reynosa and Nogales are major distribution points for Mexican fruits and vegetables exported to the United States. From Reynosa, goods are trucked across the border to Hidalgo, Texas, where customs brokers and warehouses are situated for transshipment. An even larger facility exists outside Nogales, Arizona, to accommodate Sonoran and Sinaloan produce destined for Southwestern U.S. supermarkets. At ambos Nogales alone, an estimated 2,000–3,000 trucks per week make this crossing during the winter months when product export is highest.

The traditional nonagricultural border industries were typically small-scale, labor-intensive operations that required only limited capital investment and relatively simple technologies. One of the earliest and most widespread of these was brick-making. Because it was based on readily available clay, needed only rudimentary technology, and the demand was constant if not high, many border communities supported this activity. The *ladrilleras* (literally, brick kilns) largely supplied material for local construction, although some, such as those in Camargo, exported in quantity. On Mexican topographic maps, brickyards often are shown on the outskirts of towns. Field observations along the border confirm this still to be the case, except in larger cities where urban sprawl has encroached upon previous peripheral land uses. For large cities, brickyards were usually also located near railroads or highways so that materials could be moved to markets quickly and conveniently. Along Mexico Highway 2 between Miguel Alemán and Matamoros, old brick kilns are conspicuous roadside features. Many of these, however, are abandoned and in ruin. Cement block has largely replaced clay-fired brick in building construction, and the cement and water needed for manufacture are easily acquired. Occasionally, as outside Reynosa, cement-block factories have appeared on these same abandoned sites. In addition to commercial operations, residents on the peripheries of border cities sometimes produce cement blocks in their own yards. This has become practically a cottage industry. It is not unusual to see hand-painted signs along highways that read *se vende block* (cement block for sale). These small operations are also visible in residential locations, especially in squatter settlements where there is demand for this type of building material.

Some border cities have developed specialized industrial economies. At Piedras Negras, its name (black rocks) identifies the rich coal that lies beneath the city along this middle stretch of the Rio Grande in Coahuila. Coal has been mined here and in the nearby Sabinas Basin since the nineteenth century (Griffin and Crowley 1989: 322–323). It fuels the only surviving steel mill along the Mexican side of the border, the Altos Hornos facility on the southeast side of Piedras Negras. It also fuels the largest coal-fired electrical generating plant in Latin America; the plant is south of town along Mexico Highway 57 (House 1982: 88; Weisman 1986: 50; Bernstein 1964: 34). At Reynosa, a Petroleos Mexicanos (PEMEX) refinery dominates the southeast quarter of that city. Established in 1950 to process petroleum and natural gas produced from Mexico's northeast, it is a major employer in the city today (Powell 1956: 77; *Reynosa, Nuestra Ciudad* 1990: 129). Whether the site of a steel mill or refinery, these specialized industrial activities mark the landscapes of some cities and distinguish them economically and socially from any stereotypical image of a border town.

Consider Tecate, a small city in the *sierra* between Tijuana and Mexicali. Although several border cities such as Ciudad Juárez, Tijuana, Reynosa, and Mexicali have had breweries, Tecate is the sole producer of what billboards throughout the American Southwest call "The Gulp of Mexico." Tecate beer, distinctive in its red can with gold-and-black label, is even more popular in northern Mexico, especially the border cities. The town grew from a small ranching center to a significant industrial area by the late 1920s. It was strategically situated in a well-watered valley with rail and road connections to Tijuana and San Diego and with access to Mexicali by railroad on the U.S. side of the border. The brewery, Cerveceria Cuahtémoc, began in 1944 and produces Carta Blanca as well as Tecate beer. The brewery not only dominates the skyline of Tecate (see Fig. 7.1) but until recently was the largest employer in town; it operated three shifts, seven days a week (Price 1973b: 37). Maquiladora employment, however, is beginning to erode this dominance. Nevertheless, large numbers of eateries in el centro and within walking distance of the brewery cater to its labor force and advertise that they are open twenty-four hours.

Other border cities such as Nuevo Laredo have specialized services rather than manufacturing industries. Service industries and manufacturing in the city employ 60 percent of its workers compared to 49 percent in all border cities. Furthermore, Nuevo Laredo is the premier import location for

FIGURE 7.1 The Tecate Brewery is representative of the old industrial landscape
that still marks several border cities.

foreign goods into Mexico along the border, accounting for 49 percent of
all such activity (Trabis 1985: 62–67). One interesting example of this
type of service industry is cardboard recycling in Nuevo Laredo (*Wall Street
Journal* 1987a). Because Laredo, Texas, is a major port of entry for low-cost,
mass-produced consumer goods, especially textiles and electronic equipment from Asia, the downtown merchants receive truckloads of merchandise in cardboard boxes. Once emptied, the boxes pile up in the streets
awaiting the *cartoneros* (carton collectors). About 250 Mexican cartoneros
flatten the boxes and stack them on a *tricicleta* (tricycle) that is a modified
bicycle crossed with a shopping cart that holds the cardboard. After loading the tricicletas, the cartoneros bicycle across the International Bridge to
Nuevo Laredo where the cardboard is redeemable at a downtown recycling
facility.

Mixed traditional industrial activities still are concentrated in the largest border cities such as Ciudad Juárez and Tijuana. Since the nineteenth
century, Ciudad Juárez has maintained flour mills, clothing manufacturers,
breweries, and liquor processors. During the 1930s, one-half of the industrial plants in the city catered to the tourist trade, producing curios and
other items for sale in local shops. By the 1950s, the industrial capacity of

the city doubled with increasing production to meet local demands, not just the tourist trade. These industries included iron and steel smelting; whiskey and beer production; meat packing; oil and lard production; purified-water and soft-drink bottling; construction-material production; shoe, soap, clothing, and leather-goods manufacture; lumber and furniture production; and food processing (Martínez 1978: 24, 61, 98).

RAILROAD SIGNATURES

Historically, industrial activities in the border cities have been located along railroad corridors. These corridors emerged largely during the late nineteenth century when railroad transport was most significant (Coatsworth 1981; Stilgoe 1983). They persist in many cities, however, and even where railroad traffic has declined or changed, the landscape imprint of this industrial legacy remains. This has resulted in several nineteenth-century industrial landscape signatures, most notably the railroad corridor, railroad crossing, and railroad yard with its attendant elements. The presence and size of these railroad landscapes, however, are not always predictable by the size or age of a place; they are mostly a function of the history and individual situation of each border town.

Five of the eighteen border cities are without railroads altogether. Two of these communities, Sonoita and Camargo, date from the Spanish colonial period, and each has been isolated historically from distant development areas. The remaining towns, Las Palomas, San Luis Río Colorado, and Miguel Alemán, were twentieth-century settlements that missed the height of the railroad era. These places grew largely in the post–World War II period, when truck transport was already replacing rail. Not surprisingly, these five border cities lack contemporary industrial distinction.

Border cities that have railroads reflect a varied range of landscape expression associated with this transportation form. Perhaps the most recognizable consequence is the railroad corridor and the land-use segregation it creates. In several border places, the railroad divides the community socially as well as functionally. In Agua Prieta, the Ferrocarril del Pacifico slices the city along its western flank, segregating the older, irregular street pattern on the west from the post-1903 modern grid on the east. Today, the western sector remains a classic disamenity zone built along the low-lying Agua Prieta Arroyo and populated chiefly by low-income residents. At nearby Naco, the same railroad enters the town on the east and splits immediately, one line crossing the international boundary at Naco, Arizona, and one turning southwest toward the mining community of Cananea, Sonora, nestled in the mountains sixty miles distant. These intersecting lines form a "T" on the east side of Naco, separating an older, poorer neighborhood from a newer district west of the railroad junction. Even larger cities, such as Reynosa, Mexicali, and Ciudad Juárez, still have this dividing landscape signature. At Reynosa, the Ferrocarril Nacional cuts clean across the grid east to west paralleling the Canal Anzalduas, which followed construction of the railroad by several decades. In Mexicali, the Ferrocarril Sonora–Baja California that once extended to the international boundary now terminates several miles from the gate crossing to Calexico, California. Yet the landscape imprint of the early corridor is seen in the residential and commercial divisions west and east of this line, with the generally poorer colonias to the west across the Río Nuevo. Finally, in Ciudad Juárez, the railroad corridor historically paralleled Avenida Juárez, and to this day, colonias and commercial districts west of this line are more industrially oriented than those east and north of the divide.

In three border cities, the railroad corridor is peripheral to the grid and main built-up area. At Ojinaga, the Ferrocarril Chihuahua al Pacifico is more than a mile east of the international bridge port of entry and about two to three miles away from el centro. The railroad follows the Arroyo La Zunja to its intersection with the Rio Grande, then crosses the river to connect with the Atchison Topeka and Santa Fe Railroad at Presidio, Texas. In Piedras Negras, the Ferrocarril Nacional crosses the Rio Grande one mile south of the international bridge and divides the principal built-up section of the city from the steel mill and adjoining residential district. Finally, at Ciudad Acuña the Ferrocarril Nacional is about two miles from the port of entry and flanks the city on its south and west, providing access to the newly expanding maquiladora industrial district west of Arroyo Las Vacas; the railroad neither approaches the border nor crosses it.

Of the thirteen border cities with railroads, three (Mexicali, Ciudad Acuña, and Reynosa) have terminal rail lines that do not cross the international boundary. Although Mexicali's railroad did connect to its border neighbor at one time, there is no evidence that railroads at Reynosa or Ciudad Acuña ever linked to the U.S. side. In the case of Ciudad Acuña, the railroad's late arrival in the twentieth century points up the city's longstanding isolation and insular economic orientation (Messmacher 1983: 54–56). Although Reynosa was connected by rail to Matamoros and then Monterrey, Nuevo León, in the late nineteenth century, the city's small size and primarily agricultural orientation meant that it yielded commercial superiority to Nuevo Laredo upriver and Matamoros downstream along the Rio Grande during this time (Margulis and Tuirán 1986: 61–65). When

Reynosa became the center of petroleum refining along the border in the 1950s, this product was largely sent south to Mexico's interior by pipeline rather than via railroad.

Ten of the border cities connect directly to the United States by rail: Tijuana, Tecate, Naco, Nogales, Agua Prieta, Ciudad Juárez, Ojinaga, Piedras Negras, Nuevo Laredo, and Matamoros. In the case of Ciudad Juárez, there are two railroad crossings—both situated near the old pedestrian-automobile bridges—that connect to el centro today (see Fig. 2.14). At Tecate, the railroad crossing does not enter at the American border town of Tecate, California; it is about six miles east of the port of entry, from which it descends to the Imperial Valley and Calexico, across from Mexicali. This was partly because of the difficulty of constructing a rail line down the sheer side of the fault-block Peninsular Range in Baja California below La Rumorosa. It was also a decision on the part of the American capitalists who built the Tijuana and Tecate Railway, a wholly owned subsidiary of the San Diego and Arizona Railway, to service the agriculturally rich Imperial Valley (Hofsommer 1986: 59).

Along the Rio Grande portion of the border, a distinctive element of each rail crossing is the railroad bridge. Typically, these bridges are concrete- or masonry-pillared with a trapezoidal shape and an open, steel-girdered superstructure. Most have survived from the late nineteenth and early twentieth centuries, although with occasional refitting. Because these bridges are usually open, they often have kiosks on either side for customs officials. At Ciudad Juárez, however, the daily flood tide of illegal aliens who enter El Paso has forced the erection of temporary barriers at the middle of these bridges.

Railroad yards are distinctive landscape signatures in all of the largest border cities, yet town size does not appear to be the chief factor determining their visual prominence. For example, Tijuana, Mexicali, Matamoros, and Reynosa each contain railroad facilities and yards, but in each they are small compared to the city's size. In two of these places, as mentioned above, the railroads do not cross the border. These aberrations suggest in part that these towns were peripheral connecting points between the Mexican interior and the United States during the heyday of railroad transport. At Matamoros, despite a late nineteenth-century railroad connection, the crossing's volume of commerce seemed unable to rival that of its Civil War entrepôt days. By the time cotton again became an important export through Matamoros to Brownsville in the post–World War II era, trucks were the favored means of transport. The inconsequential railroad facilities in Tijuana reinforce the geographic fact that this border city is too distant from the industrial heartland of Mexico to merit significant railroad activity. Although Tijuana had a railroad connection to San Diego and Tecate early in the twentieth century, it was not linked by railroad to the interior via Mexicali until 1948. To this day, it does not have an overland connection on the Mexican side of the border beyond Tecate (Price 1973a: 34).

The border cities with the most significant railroad facilities and attendant railroad landscapes are Ciudad Juárez, Nuevo Laredo, and Nogales. Relevantly, these were among the first border cities to be connected by rail to the Mexican interior and to the United States across the boundary; all received railroad service in 1882 (Coatsworth 1981: 162). Consequently, each of these towns has a long history as a railroad node, and each today supports a large railroad yard. These facilities were typically constructed just outside of el centro, but in almost every instance, they have been encroached upon. The rail yards in Ciudad Juárez are approximately one to two miles south of the international bridge (Santa Fe crossing) near the old train station (see Fig. 2.14), whereas those at Nuevo Laredo are about three miles southwest of the old port of entry and west of Avenida Guerrero, the principal commercial spine (see Fig. 6.13). (The Nogales rail yards are described in the case study subsequently.) Each of these railroad yards includes multiple tracks and spur lines; service and shop spaces; and related land uses such as fueling tanks, customs stations, and passenger depots. Conspicuously absent from these landscapes, however, are warehousing facilities typical of such districts in North American cities. This is mostly a result of the nature of border railroad commerce, where the cars are often only temporarily idle until customs clearance is given, and coaches can then proceed across the border or to their ultimate Mexican interior destinations. Thus, railroad yard landscapes are more like transit stations than break-of-bulk points where significant on- and off-loading occurs.

GATES AND BRIDGES

The Mexico-U.S. border officially stretches 1,951.36 miles from the Pacific Ocean to the Gulf of Mexico. The land portion from the Pacific to the Rio Grande is 697.67 miles including 23.72 miles of the Colorado River. The Rio Grande boundary totals 1,253.69 miles (Metz 1989: vi). Yet, neither the Treaty of Guadalupe Hidalgo of 1848, the Gadsden Purchase of 1853, the boundary surveys that followed, nor the re-surveys conducted by Mexico and the United States between 1882 and 1889 have ensured a controlled border.

The jurisdiction over the border on the U.S. side is divided between the U.S. Customs Service (since 1853) and the U.S. Border Patrol (since 1924), whereas on the Mexican side, authority is equally exercised by the Aduana de México (Customs Service) and Inmigración (Immigration) (Whitehead 1963: 122; Myers 1971: 31; Sierra and Martinez Vera 1973). Since 1944, the International Boundary and Water Commission, represented by executives from the United States as well as Mexico, has overseen the allocation of waters along the Rio Grande and the Colorado River (House 1982: 125).

For each of the eighteen Mexican border cities studied, the American paired town is an official U.S. port of entry; thus, it is guarded by the U.S. Customs Service. Because several cities maintain multiple gate crossings, there are twenty-six official points that provide access to the United States from the Mexican border cities (Table 7.1). Four of these crossings restrict access to specific hours; for example, the crossing from Rio Grande City, Texas, to Camargo, Tamaulipas, is open daily from 8 A.M. to midnight only. The majority of gate crossings are open continuously. On the Mexican side, immigration and customs stations similarly monitor access; however, all crossings operate twenty-four hours. Unlike the U.S. gates, entrance to Mexico at these points is not always carefully screened. In part, this results from Mexico's desire to admit tourists and dollars to the border towns; it is also a legacy of the *zona libre* (free zone) status enjoyed by several areas of the Mexican border dating from the nineteenth century (Fernández 1977: 76–81; Martínez 1988: 112–113). However, access to the interior of Mexico is monitored at federal check points on the major highways that lead away from the border cities. At these points, foreigners must present a Mexican tourist visa and relevant documents obtained from Imigración and/or the Aduana that allow foreign registered vehicles to proceed inland.

In anticipation of a North American Free Trade Agreement, Mexico has recently replaced some 3,000 customs agents along the border with agents reportedly called *Los Incorruptibles* (the incorruptibles) (*Arizona Republic* 1991c: A3). This change is being trumpeted as a first step toward establishment of a "clean image" at the Mexican ports of entry. All new agents are younger than the former officials, are high school graduates, and have completed training at the National Academy for Fiscal Agents in Mexico City, including a course in public relations. The new customs officers are paid three times the salary of the older agents—an attempt it is said to discourage the customary mordida, or bribe, that has sometimes been demanded from those who attempt to pass items that would otherwise require high import duties.

The landscape of gate crossings has been especially subject to alter-

TABLE 7.1 Border-City Gates and Access

City	Number of Gates	Access*
Tijuana–San Ysidro–Otay Mesa	2	24 hours
Tecate–Tecate	1	8 A.M.–12 midnight
Mexicali–Calexico	1	24 hours
San Luis Río Colorado– San Luis (Yuma)	1	24 hours
Sonoita–Lukeville	1	8 A.M.–12 midnight
Nogales–Nogales	3	24 hours; 6 A.M.–8 P.M.
Naco–Naco	1	24 hours
Agua Prieta–Douglas	1	24 hours
Las Palomas–Columbus	1	24 hours
Ciudad Juárez–El Paso	4	24 hours
Ojinaga–Presidio	1	24 hours
Ciudad Acuña–Del Rio	1	24 hours
Piedras Negras–Eagle Pass	1	24 hours
Nuevo Laredo–Laredo	2	24 hours
Miguel Alemán–Roma	1	24 hours
Reynosa–Hidalgo (McAllen)	1	24 hours
Camargo–Rio Grande City	1	8 A.M.–12 midnight
Matamoros–Brownsville	2	24 hours

SOURCE: Field surveys 1987–1991.

* Limited access at U.S. gates only; access is 24 hours at Mexican gates.

ations over time. The Mexican government's effort to beautify "Las Puertas a México" as part of the PRONAF developments of the 1960s resulted, in some instances, in radical transformations to the built environment at the ports of entry. Of some $3.3 million originally allocated, however, almost one-third went to one city, Ciudad Juárez; Nogales received 16 percent, Tijuana, only 10 percent, and all other ports less than 10 percent each (Sklair 1989: 29). Through the efforts of Antonio J. Bermúdez, a native of Ciudad Juárez and former director general of PEMEX, the PRONAF complex in that city became the model for other gate and tourist-development projects in border towns. Unfortunately, resources proved inadequate to transform all border towns in the manner of Ciudad Juárez, but Nogales did achieve considerable modification (see case study that follows).

Along the Rio Grande, fifteen bridges, not including railroad crossings, span the international boundary and connect nine Mexican border cities to American border communities. (Technically, there is an additional bridge across the Tijuana River giving access to that city via San Ysidro, but the bridge is entirely within Mexico and does not span the international boundary, although the river does.) Ciudad Juárez and El Paso are linked by four separate bridges, and Nuevo Laredo–Laredo, Matamoros-Brownsville, and Reynosa-Hidalgo are each bound by two bridges (*Excelsior* 1987; *Excelsior* 1988). All other crossings have one bridge apiece (*El Nacional* 1986). In 1990, Los Dos Laredos, Piedras Negras–Eagle Pass, and Matamoros-Brownsville began building additional bridges (*Austin American-Statesman* 1990a; *Austin American-Statesman* 1989c; *San Antonio Light* 1990b).

Until the late nineteenth century, the Rio Grande border cities were accessible only by ferries that crossed the international boundary. The flatboats that plied these waters were called *chalanes* (a scow, lighter, or square boat) and the ferrymen who operated the craft were *chalaneros* (Shanks 1985: 37). Frequently, ferries became fixed features; cables were stretched so the watercraft could be hand-pulled and guided between landings (Chatfield 1893: 24; Thompson 1986: 20).

Modern bridge construction, prompted by railroads that connected the United States with Mexico, first occurred in the 1880s. The Avenida Lerdo–Stanton Street bridge connecting Ciudad Juárez with El Paso was the first bridge built in 1882 (Mangan 1971: 34). Typical of many early bridges, it was privately financed and operated, and levied a toll. In 1892, a second bridge joined the two cities at Avenida Juárez and Santa Fe Street (Price 1989: 6). In 1967, these bridges were reconstructed and renamed. The Stanton Street crossing became the Good Neighbor Bridge, and the Santa Fe came to be called the International Bridge, although in each instance the older names are still recognized. A third bridge in the urban area was added downriver at the Zaragoza-Ysleta crossing during Prohibition. This bridge was reconstructed in 1942 and finally closed in 1990 when a new bridge was erected at the same site (*Arizona Daily Star* 1990). In 1967, the fourth bridge between Ciudad Juárez and El Paso was opened across Cordova Island, east of the Good Neighbor Bridge. This bridge is known locally as the Bridge of the Americas or the Cordova Bridge (Sonnichsen 1980: 70–71; Timmons 1990: 279–282).

Nuevo Laredo and Laredo were first connected in 1889 by a steel-

FIGURE 7.2 An aerial view of the bridge that links Nuevo Laredo (foreground) to Laredo taken August 4, 1928, during the funeral procession for Captain Carranza, a local hero. Photo courtesy of the National Archives.

trestle, pier-supported bridge linking Avenida Guerrero and Convent Street in the respective cities. This structure was destroyed by a tornado in 1905 and rebuilt in 1906, before burning down in 1920. The bridge was again reconstructed in 1922 by the U.S. Army Corps of Engineers, and was said to have been the most elegant bridge along the Rio Grande with graceful, concrete, steel-reinforced arches supporting a paved, four-lane roadbed (see Fig. 7.2). In 1954, this bridge was severely damaged by a flood and not reconstructed until 1957 (Shanks 1985: 37–41). A second international bridge called the Juárez-Lincoln Bridge was completed in 1980 less than a mile east of the first bridge, and the new bridge connected directly to U.S. Interstate 35 on the Laredo side. In 1990, a third bridge was under construction north of the first international bridge (*Laredo Morning Times* 1990).

During the 1910s and 1920s, bridges across the Rio Grande were completed at Matamoros-Brownsville (1910, 1928), Ciudad Acuña–Del Rio (1922, 1929), Reynosa-Hidalgo (1926), and Miguel Alemán–Roma (1929). In the last two decades, newer bridges have replaced the older ones at all of these crossings except Matamoros-Brownsville (Wooldridge and Vezzetti 1982: 96, 144; Jones 1990: 227). At Miguel Alemán–Roma, the original single-span suspension bridge still stands next to the new bridge but is closed to both pedestrian and auto traffic. Piedras Negras–Eagle Pass added a bridge in 1934 (Scarborough 1968: 63).

At Ciudad Acuña–Del Rio and Piedras Negras–Eagle Pass, bridges were initially chartered to private companies and later sold to the American cities in 1954 and 1947, respectively (Jones 1990: 227; International Bridge, n.d.). Along the middle and lower Rio Grande today, eight bridges are publicly owned—five by municipalities, three by counties—and one is privately held, but all ownership (public and private) is by American interests. In the case of almost all bridges, tolls are collected at either the Mexican and/or the American crossing gates. However, passage into the United States is substantially more expensive, especially for autos, and tolls can be three times the amount to cross into Mexico. These higher tolls reflect recent increases that may be related to the need to raise revenues for additional bridge improvements, because for most of the life of the bridges, tolls have been nominal.

The bridge and gate crossings on the Mexican side are typical institutional landscapes. Frequently, they include a kiosk-type structure manned by immigration officials, and larger crossings may have several such booths. Adjacent to the gate is an immigration office where transit documents can be obtained. At some smaller border towns such as Agua Prieta, the old aduana, or customs house, has survived at the border crossing, but in most larger cities, the facility has been relocated to the margins of el centro or to a highway outside of town.

Although the crossing structures and their furnishings are usually modest, they often display national emblems such as the Mexican eagle, either on window decals or mounted on building facades. Reynosa's border entrance displays a replica of an Olmec Indian head, similar to but smaller than the authentic pre-Columbian artifact that graces the entrance to the National Anthropology Museum in Mexico City. At Piedras Negras, the pedestrian walkway that leads to the international bridge has a small glass-enclosed shrine of the Virgin of San Juan de los Lagos, a popular patron saint in northeastern Mexico and South Texas. The newest signature of the border crossing is Paisano (countryman), a logo used for the program instituted by the Mexican federal government to advise border crossers, both Mexican nationals and foreign visitors, "*lo que debes saber al llegar y salir de México*/what you should know when arriving and leaving Mexico." The logo paisano is outfitted in typical norteño western wear, including a straw hat, and he sports the distinctive mustache so common in northern Mexico. The logo is used on bilingual brochures and posters that advertise this program.

Millions of border-crossers pass across these bridges and through these gates each year. In 1980, about 160,000 Mexican commuters regularly crossed into the United States from the nine largest Mexican border cities; nearly one-third of this total came from Ciudad Juárez alone (Herzog 1990: 7). The total number of Mexican commuters across the border is up from just 40,000 in 1967 (North 1970: 112). This, however, represents only a trickle of the total volume of border-crossers as defined by the U.S. Immigration and Naturalization Service, which counts both alien and citizen crossers (U.S. Department of Justice 1988: 134). Furthermore, it is estimated that as many as one million Mexican border residents possess border-crossing cards that allow them to enter the United States and stay as long as seventy-two hours at a time. This permit restricts their mobility to within twenty-five miles of the border and legally prohibits their employment in the United States, but enforcement is difficult (Herzog 1990: 8).

In 1987 (the year of the most recently reported figures), almost 200 million persons crossed legally from Mexico into the United States (Table 7.2). More than 100 million people crossed the border between Mexico and Texas alone, the most for any state. For each border state except New Mexico, the number of border-crossers from Mexico exceeded the number of border-crossers from the United States. Thus, the flow across the border is clearly tilted toward the United States. This situation is apparent

TABLE 7.2 Border-Crossers Admitted by State and Port of Entry, 1987

	Total[a]	Non-U.S. Citizen	U.S. Citizen
TEXAS	104,393,978	64,112,451	40,281,527
El Paso	32,642,901	18,991,667	13,651,234
Laredo	21,393,812	15,193,660	6,200,152
Brownsville	13,393,978	9,131,983	4,597,537
Hidalgo (McAllen)	12,864,278	7,864,338	4,999,940
Eagle Pass	5,491,026	3,704,490	1,786,536
Roma	3,602,827	2,233,691	1,369,136
Del Rio	3,514,214	1,230,551	2,283,663
Rio Grande City	1,468,305	934,132	534,173
Presidio	1,065,373	638,822	426,551
CALIFORNIA	67,202,244	38,974,503	28,227,741
San Ysidro/Otay Mesa	42,953,967	23,136,675	19,817,292
Calexico	14,862,495	11,210,172	3,652,323
Tecate	3,038,732	1,882,121	1,156,611
ARIZONA	24,324,676	15,682,006	8,642,670
Nogales	11,941,084	7,315,617	4,625,467
San Luis	5,874,967	4,615,913	1,259,074
Douglas	4,828,135	2,896,677	1,931,458
Naco	925,393	603,902	321,491
Lukeville	639,309	210,972	428,337
NEW MEXICO	1,031,563	506,365	525,198
Columbus	1,031,563	506,365	525,198
Total	196,952,461	119,275,325	77,677,136

SOURCE: U.S. Department of Justice 1988: 128–129.

[a] Total includes other ports of entry not on the international border.

at any major crossing during the morning rush hour; traffic backs up at the U.S. Customs gate, while traffic in the opposite direction toward Mexico flows easily (see Fig. 7.3).

The three most frequently crossed points by 1987 statistics were Tijuana–San Ysidro–Otay Mesa (forty-two million crossers), Ciudad Juárez–El Paso (thirty-two million crossers), and Nuevo Laredo–Laredo (twenty-one million crossers) (Table 7.2). The traffic congestion at these crossings has prompted the Immigration and Naturalization Service to experiment with a series of express lanes at the busier nonbridge ports (tolls are standard at all bridge crossings). Automobile crossers will pay a fee to use the express lanes to pass more quickly (*Arizona Republic* 1990; *Arizona Republic* 1991a).

Just three ports of entry, Del Rio, Lukeville, and Columbus, had more border-crossers from the United States than from Mexico. Each of these ports faces a Mexican border city—Ciudad Acuña, Sonoita, and Las Palomas, respectively—that is isolated from a major metropolitan area, and

FIGURE 7.3 Ciudad Juárez morning traffic backed up at the Cordova Bridge (Las Americas crossing) waiting to clear U.S. Customs for El Paso.

Sonoita and Las Palomas front U.S. border communities that offer little to tempt Mexican shoppers or workers.

One universal, albeit ephemeral, landscape expression of these border crossings is the cluster of people that crowds the entrance and exit points, which are typically separated. Pedestrians often mill about on the Mexican side, just inside the gate. On the bridges that connect Ciudad Juárez to El Paso, especially the Santa Fe and Cordova crossings, people typically gather at the top of the bridge—technically inside U.S. territory—and pass the time conversing and watching the parade of slow-moving autos. This loitering population is one element of several that characterize almost all crossings. Other elements are strolling or stationed vendors of food and trinkets; foreign visitors waiting to secure immigration visas or papers to drive to the interior; teenage boys who wash windshields for waiting vehicles; taxi drivers leaning against their late-model American cars; immigration officials chatting amongst themselves and slowly waving vehicles through the gate; and lines of trucks parked with motors running, their diesel fumes permeating the air as they wait to cross the bridge to clear U.S. Customs.

Traffic congestion at the largest gates has prompted a call for construction of additional crossings (*El Nacional* 1985). In 1986, the governors of Chihuahua and New Mexico agreed to establish a new crossing near the town of Santa Teresa, New Mexico, a community of 2,000 people located less than a twenty-minute drive from downtown Ciudad Juárez. The Santa Teresa port of entry may become the first binational, master-planned community along the border. Local developers are planning an industrial-park complex modeled after the Irvine Ranch in Southern California (Flynn 1991: 16). This new port of entry on the west side of Ciudad Juárez–El Paso is anticipated by some, chiefly maquiladora businessmen, to bypass much of the congestion at the older crossings. This would give New Mexico a second port of entry in addition to tiny Las Palomas–Columbus, which is about 100 miles west (*El Fronterizo* 1986b; *Diario de Juárez* 1988).

MAQUILADORA INDUSTRIAL PARKS

The anticipated development of a new industrial community on the Chihuahua border near Santa Teresa, New Mexico, is part of a larger pattern of rapid industrialization that has ignited the border region economically. The American news media now frequently report about "U.S. plants south of the border," and "the rise of gringo capitalism," and the Mexican press often touts that maquiladoras are good for the national economy (*Christian Science Monitor* 1985; *Fortune* 1986; *Newsweek* 1987; *New York Times*

1987b; *Business Week* 1988; *Los Angeles Times* 1989; *Washington Post* 1990; *El Fronterizo* 1986a). Most of the interest is centered on the maquiladoras, industrial plants where foreign products, chiefly American but also Japanese, are assembled using inexpensive Mexican labor (*Wall Street Journal* 1987b; *Austin American-Statesman* 1989a; *Wall Street Journal* 1990). The border cities have the highest concentrations of these plants in all of Mexico (Sklair 1989). An important dimension of this new industrial activity is the appearance of an entirely different urban landscape along the border, the industrial park.

Maquiladoras began in 1965 with the Border Industrialization Program (BIP) (Baerresen 1971; Fernández 1977: 134–138). Under BIP, the Mexican federal government established a policy to allow wholly owned subsidiaries of foreign companies to operate in Mexico. Participating firms were given reductions in duties charged for assembled products under items 806.30 and 807.00 of the Tariff Schedule of the United States, whereby only value-added tax based principally on cheap labor and small overhead was apportioned to materials exported and then imported back into the United States (Dillman 1976; Sklair 1989: 9). Proximity to the United States has allowed hundreds of American manufacturing companies to take advantage of Mexico's BIP policy, which ironically was first intended to establish employment opportunities along the border after the United States ended the *bracero* (Mexican agricultural labor) program of 1942 (Sklair 1989: 27). The purported benefits to Mexico were the jobs created in the border cities by foreign manufacturing plants. In its original usage, the Spanish term *maquila* referred to the portion of flour retained by the miller as payment for grinding someone else's grain (House 1982: 216). The wages paid to border-city workers became, in effect, the maquila for the assembly of manufactured goods. Between 1970 and 1980, border manufacturing employment grew 70 percent, whereas in Mexico as a whole, it grew only 40 percent (Haring 1985: 57). In 1990, wage scales in the industry varied across the region, with the more unionized eastern border cities such as Matamoros and Reynosa paying up to one-and-a-half times the hourly wages of those paid in Ciudad Juárez and Tijuana.

In 1986, 93 percent of Mexico's 865 maquiladoras were located in border states, and 71 percent, or 576, of those plants were in the six largest border cities (Stoddard 1987: 19). In 1973, Tijuana, Ciudad Juárez, and Mexicali had 94, 61, and 62 maquiladoras respectively; in 1986, the same cities had 232, 177, and 81, and by 1990, they had 530, 320, and 154 (Dillman 1976: 142; Stoddard 1987: 19; *Twin Plant News* 1990: 84). In November 1990, there were 1,886 maquiladoras in Mexico employing

434,147 workers. Maquiladoras in the border cities totaled 1,564, or 83 percent of all such plants in the country. Only Sonoita and Miguel Alemán—small, isolated, and principally agricultural service cities—lacked these plants. Although the number of border maquiladoras has almost doubled since 1986, the percentage of Mexican maquiladoras that are border plants is down 14 percent according to one source, signaling the growth of this industry away from the border (*Twin Plant News* 1990: 84). Tijuana, Ciudad Juárez, and Mexicali, however, are indisputably the major centers for maquiladora activity; they count almost two-thirds of all border plants, and these plants employ 60 percent of maquiladora laborers on the border (Table 7.3).

As maquiladoras have increased across the border, product lines and worker profiles have changed. In 1969, one-quarter of the maquiladora output was textiles, toys, and other light industrial goods. By 1981, these same

TABLE 7.3 Border-City *Maquiladoras*, 1990

City	Maquilas	Employees	E per M
Tijuana	530	58,590	110
Tecate	86	4,665	54
Mexicali	154	20,576	133
San Luis Río Colorado	12	3,000	250
Nogales	73	21,084	288
Naco	6	1,200	200
Agua Prieta	28	6,160	220
Las Palomas	5	137	27
Ciudad Juárez	320	134,838	421
Ojinaga	1	300	300
Ciudad Acuña	44	14,151	321
Piedras Negras	43	8,130	189
Nuevo Laredo	93	16,162	173
Camargo	4	380	95
Reynosa[a]	71	30,000	422
Matamoros	94	38,268	407
Total	1,564	357,641	225

SOURCES: *Twin Plant News* 1990: 84; Starr County Industrial Foundation, 1990.
[a] Includes Río Bravo.

products accounted for only 12 percent of production, and television and semiconductor assembly accounted for more than 30 percent of the work. Also, in 1969 there were no automobile parts assembly maquiladoras along the border, but today this activity has gained a foothold in Ciudad Juárez and Matamoros. In 1987, motor vehicles and their parts ranked first and fourth respectively among the top ten maquiladora exports, although much of this product is produced outside of the border proper (Scheinman 1990: 25). Further, in 1970 the average number of workers per plant was 120, whereas in 1980 it had risen above 200 per maquiladora (Stoddard 1987: 23–24). By 1990, some 357,000 workers labored in border-city maquiladoras, but the number of employees per plant varied by location. In the eastern cities of Matamoros and Reynosa it averaged over 400, but the western cities of Tijuana and Mexicali averaged less than 150 per plant (Table 7.3).

These changes have significantly affected industrial landscapes in the border cities. Early maquiladoras were usually small operations using converted old buildings and requiring little capital investment in facilities. The trend today is toward large, elaborate installations located on the peripheries of cities. In 1968, Nogales initiated industrial-park development on the border, and by 1973, Ciudad Juárez, Matamoros, and Reynosa followed (Dillman 1976: 141–142). Of 83 industrial parks registered in Mexico in 1987, 52 percent are located in the six northern border states (*El Financiero* 1987). Unlike more traditional industrial activities and spaces, maquiladora industrial parks are usually modeled after North American suburban examples.

After proximity to the parent plant or market and availability of labor, plant managers have consistently rated infrastructure, especially road access and utility service, as the third most important element in the decision to locate a maquiladora (South 1990: 562). Some of the advantages of industrial-park locations on the Mexico border are the same as for locations in the United States and can be summarized as follows. A park allows planning, with uniform setbacks and lot sizes, controlled landscaping and architecture, screening of service areas, and security. With several plants in one location, there is improved access to utilities, paved roads, parking, and off-street loading. Because plants are usually located on the outskirts of towns, land is inexpensive, immediate occupancy can be arranged, and good transportation by highway, rail, and air is frequently available (Hartshorn 1973: 36).

Although most border cities have maquiladoras, not all have industrial parks. The most elaborate complexes are found in the largest cities, especially Ciudad Juárez, Tijuana, and Matamoros. Other towns such as Mexicali, Nogales, Reynosa, Nuevo Laredo, Piedras Negras, and Ciudad Acuña also have industrial parks, but they are fewer and smaller (Haring 1985; Herzog 1990; Messmacher 1983; Trabis 1985; Margulis and Tuirán 1986). In Ciudad Juárez, five industrial-park areas have been identified (George 1986: 134). All are east of the traditional industrial corridor that parallels the railroad and Avenida Juárez. They are strategically situated on the periphery of the city along major highways, and they are either close to the newer border crossings to El Paso or the Ciudad Juárez airport (*The Complete Twin Plant Guide* 1987). In Tijuana, maquiladoras have historically been found along the corridor that parallels the Tijuana River and the railroad and highway extensions out of the city to the southeast (Griffin and Ford 1980: Fig. 11). The new industrial parks, however, are chiefly organized on Mesa de Otay at the eastern end of the urban area, close to a new border crossing and the Tijuana International airport (Herzog 1985b: fig. 1). In 1992, a new toll road opened to connect this industrial district with Tecate to the east. The principal industrial park in Matamoros is south west of the city center on former agricultural land near the major railroad. Not coincidentally, several of the maquiladoras in this park assemble automotive parts that are bulky and require rail as well as truck transport.

Maquiladora parks combine several elements typical of a small town or suburban development found in the United States. Most maintain a grand entrance or gateway. Industrial parks in Ciudad Juárez and Nuevo Laredo, for example, include billboard welcome signs with booster phrases that extol the flashy image of the new industrial spaces. Street plans usually follow a simple grid, and more elaborate parks include tree-lined, median-divided main streets. At a Matamoros industrial park that has auto-parts assembly plants, several streets are named after American industrial states (e.g., Calle Ohio, Calle Michigan).

Most industrial parks contain adequate parking facilities. Inspection of parking lots often reveals that many license plates are from the United States as well as from Mexico. For example, almost all of the cars in several lots at Parque Bermúdez in Ciudad Juárez had Texas license plates. Frequently, supervisory personnel at maquiladoras are American border-town residents who commute daily to their jobs in Mexico, a reverse of the well-documented flow of Mexican domestic and service workers who cross daily into the U.S. border communities. Most workers in the park plants, however, commute by public transportation or private jitney services provided by the factory employers, so passenger stops inside the larger parks and outside of smaller facilities are common.

An important result of the maquiladora presence in border cities is improvement in the transportation infrastructure, especially street paving. Because most products are imported and exported by eighteen-wheeled vehicles, industrial parks require both access and good roadways. Invariably this means that a paved perimeter road is constructed to link the industrial facility with a gate crossing at the international boundary. In Agua Prieta, a Sonoran city of about 40,000, almost the only paved roads outside of el centro and the elite residential neighborhoods are Avenida Sexta and Avenida 20, where the new maquiladoras are situated. These streets connect Mexico Highway 2, the principal perimeter road, with International Street, where maquiladora truck traffic lines up to clear U.S. customs (Ladman 1972). Increasingly common at the more congested, larger, border-city crossings are separate lanes for truck traffic only. At the new Zaragoza crossing opened in 1991 to link Ciudad Juárez with El Paso, the Río Bravo industrial park now has a separate bridge lane designated solely for maquiladora traffic.

The street frontages in the parks range from spare to ornately landscaped, depending on the image a company wishes to project. Many of the larger industrial parks have sidewalks and at least minimal ornamental landscaping. Architecturally, the buildings are large, rectangular, single-storey, factory-type facilities, although front offices that face the street are often decorated, typically in neo-Spanish colonial style (see Fig. 7.4). Some parks have wall- and fence-enclosed facilities with a security gate, while others are open and have a directory listing the names of companies, perhaps with a map of locations. Services also vary with parks. Some include day-care facilities provided by the Mexican government, as well as cafeterias and recreation space, especially basketball and volleyball courts, provided by the employer. The sides and backs of buildings almost universally contain trucking ports and docks, storage spaces, and street access for carriers that travel the short distances between the maquiladoras, the border crossings, and the customs storage areas for some products located on the U.S. side of the border.

In some ways, Mexican border-city maquiladoras mirror aspects of the colonial hacienda, common in parts of north central Mexico from the late sixteenth century through the eighteenth century (Romero de Terreros 1956). Fernández-Kelly (1983) has argued that, sociologically, the large labor pools—chiefly women—employed in border-city maquiladoras represent a new incarnation of the debt peons of the colonial hacienda. Anderson (1990: 7) has said that, economically, the border maquiladoras are in the

FIGURE 7.4 The street facade of a Matamoros *maquiladora* with ornamental landscaping and neo-Spanish colonial architecture.

same enclave position as the foreign-owned extractive industries of the nineteenth century because of their poorly developed links to Mexican suppliers in the interior or on the border. We believe that, physically, the built landscapes of these industrial parks mirror the hacienda compounds of an earlier era. Typically, the large haciendas of the north contained a patio; ore crushers; smelters; a charcoal heap to process silver; dam; irrigation system; flour mill to cultivate and process foodstuffs, chiefly grains; workshops; wagons and loading facilities to carry out the daily chores; housing for the livestock and workers; storage for tools; and even a church for daily ritual (Chevalier 1963: 289).

The "new hacienda" of the Mexican border typically is an industrial-park maquiladora that on the surface projects a Spanish colonial architectural facade with stucco exterior in earth tones. Colonial building motifs decorate this exterior, from mission-revival cornices and Churrigueresque pilasters to rose-window wall insets. The facility may even include a *capilla*, or shrine. Because power is essential to the manufacturing process as well as for interior and exterior lighting, space heating, and cooling, high-voltage electrical lines commonly serve the new maquiladora parks. While the old hacienda was agriculturally self-sufficient, the new haciendas similarly contain cafeterias and eating facilities for workers. The loading docks and truck ports have replaced the wagons and their muleteers of the past, and today workers are likely to commute to the new hacienda in private autos or via mass transit. Not surprisingly, machine space in the form of parking lots, roadways, and driveways is a commanding element of the maquiladora industrial park landscape.

INDUSTRY AND TRANSIT IN NOGALES

Nogales, Sonora, is a community of approximately 107,000 situated in a narrow valley and on surrounding hillsides. Its elevation near 4,000 feet places it in a transition divide between the desert grassland and oak woodland that straddles this segment of the Sonora-Arizona border (Hastings and Turner 1965). It abuts the considerably smaller Nogales, Arizona (population 15,000) at the international boundary. To the south, Mexico Highway 15 and the Ferrocarril al Pacifico connect the city to the state capital at Hermosillo and to the port of Guaymas on the Gulf of California. Both are lower in elevation and are part of the Sonoran desert proper (Dunbier 1968). To the north, U.S. Interstate 19 links ambos Nogales (the two Nogales) to Tucson and Phoenix, Arizona, via U.S. Interstate 10.

Historically, the settlement occupied the valley bottom of this strategic mountain pass. Only since the middle of this century has the city fanned east and west up steep lateral canyons that stretch perpendicular to the town's main street (see Fig. 7.5). The original town focus was platted next to the international boundary by railroad surveyors. This created the skeleton core of today's el centro, although it is significantly modified (Gildersleeve 1978: 279). Since 1882, the railroad that follows the valley floor has been the principal conduit of growth (Zonn 1978: 9–11); later transportation development paralleled this corridor. Today, this linear spine stretches five to six miles south of el centro and contains most of the community's commercial land use, despite expansion of the built-up residential area on the east and especially west.

At ambos Nogales, two gates presently link the border. A pedestrian crossing on International Street connects Calle Elias on the Mexican side with Morley Avenue on the U.S. side. A second gate is one block west on International Street where the railroad lines join from each side at present Avenida López Mateos and Grand Avenue. The fence dividing the two communities was constructed in 1917 by the United States during the height of revolutionary hostilities on the Mexican side (Rochlin and Rochlin 1976:

FIGURE 7.5 Panoramic view of Nogales, Sonora, looking southeast. The Mariposa
   Road crossing is at the lower center and industrial parks are on the right
   periphery.

168) (see Fig. 7.6). With the fence came permanent border structures to
monitor movement across the boundary. Before this there is no record that
the communities were physically separate, and in fact, there is considerable
evidence that the towns were largely symbiotic. For example, the railroad
depot for both towns straddled the international boundary until 1898 when
a buffer zone sixty feet wide was decreed along the border between the
communities (Ready 1980: 18). Small *garitas,* or guarded kiosk-type buildings, appeared first at the Elias-Morley and López Mateos–Grand crossings
and later at Calle Arispe (present Avenida Obregón). In the 1920s and
1930s, these gates were improved with masonry pillars and new buildings
in Spanish colonial–revival style (Ready 1980: 4).

By the mid-1960s, the railroad crossing had been fundamentally al-
tered. The old aduana (customs house), a neoclassical wonder and one of
the most striking buildings ever constructed on the border, as well as the
original town plaza, Trece de Julio on López Mateos (see Fig. 5.6), were

FIGURE 7.6 Westward view of the borderline, fence, and gate crossings at *ambos* Nogales, circa 1940. Photo postcard from the authors' private collections.

removed. A new arched auto-pedestrian gate and immigration building were erected west of the railroad tracks as the focus of PRONAF redevelopment (see Fig. 7.7). Customs was relocated south near the present railroad yards. This effectively closed the Calle Arispe crossing and transformed the old Elias-Morley gate to a solely pedestrian crossing. Further, it shifted both auto and much pedestrian tourist traffic west from the Elias-Morley gate to the new López Mateos–Grand crossing, and indirectly, toward Avenida Obregón (old Calle Arispe), the present tourist strip. The old Elias-Morley gate still operates, especially for Mexican pedestrians who cross to the retail shops in the heart of old Nogales, Arizona, along "La Morley," as it is called throughout northwest Mexico (Weisman 1986: 128).

A third gate crossing was opened in 1974 to the west of el centro and is now referred to as the Mariposa Road crossing (Ready 1980: 15) (see Fig. 7.5). It is served by a new perimeter road, Camino Liberamiento, that feeds into the commercial spine Avenida López Mateos near the southern extent of the city. Originally intended as a truck route to carry the winter produce that crosses the border from the south, the Mariposa Road gate was expanded in the 1980s and is currently used by maquiladora traffic as well as by private autos. In 1991, approximately 3,500 vehicles passed daily through this gate. The new road has pulled urban development west of the older railroad corridor, although development is mostly industrial and residential rather than commercial land use, which has held tight to the old valley bottom.

In late 1991, the Mexican government began renovating the López Mateos gate in anticipation of greater traffic with the passage of a North American Free Trade Agreement. The new construction will bottleneck some 5,600 vehicles that pass this port everyday and put even greater pressure on the Mariposa Road crossing. Nogales residents who make this journey regularly complain bitterly about *la fila* (the line) and the sometimes one- to two-hour wait to cross the border into the United States (*Arizona Republic* 1991d: B1).

During the 1920s, the transshipment of Mexican produce to the United States emerged as a leading industry for Nogales (Rochlin and Rochlin 1976: 168). At this time, Nogales, Sonora, became known as *La Ciudad*

FIGURE 7.7 Northeast view of the main gate crossing at Nogales, Sonora, after the federal PRONAF redevelopment. Copyright © Tarjetas Sonora; photo postcard from the authors' private collections.

Llave para la Gran Región Sur-Oeste de los E.U. de A (the Key City to the Great American Southwest). Its most celebrated citizen, former Mexican president Alvaro Obregón, started an export business. To facilitate commerce, ambos Nogales began public improvement programs that included street paving in the central city sections (Cámaras de Comercio de Nogales 1919: 59, 75, 81). An industrial district was situated along the railroad corridor just south of el centro and included a plant that manufactured ice for railroad refrigerator cars that shipped produce across the border (Gildersleeve 1978: 317). By 1950, however, when a paved highway was completed along the West Coast of Mexico, the transshipment of produce switched from rail to truck. Between 1957 and 1962, Mexican produce shipments to the United States through Nogales by rail declined 36 percent while truck shipments for the same period increased by 46 percent (Stone 1963: 12–13). Refrigerated semitrailer vehicles lined up for inspection at the main gate along Avenida López Mateos were a symbol of Nogales commerce until the opening of the Mariposa gate and the new perimeter road in 1974 (Ready 1980: 84).

When BIP was launched in 1965, industrial production in Nogales was concentrated in food processing and transshipment (Dillman 1983a: 146). In 1968, Nogales built the first industrial park on the border—the 116-acre, master-planned Parque Industrial de Nogales—and it quickly became the model for other border community industrial facilities (Bosse 1973: 18–23). Electronic assembly became the mainstay of the new industrializing effort, accounting for twenty-seven of the city's forty-two plants in 1973 (Dillman 1976: 142). Surveys conducted in that decade suggest that maquiladora workers in Nogales were likely to be better educated, out-of-state migrants, who often resided in housing with potable water, plumbing, and electricity (Seligson and Williams 1981: 64, 50, 51). These same workers were also found to spend more of their wages on U.S. consumer goods, especially in Nogales, Arizona (Ayer and Layton 1974: 109). A recent study revealed that labor availability has become one of the primary constraints to continued maquiladora expansion in the city. Frequently, companies will recruit workers in southern Mexico, transport them north, and house them in employee dormitories (South 1990: 560).

In 1990, Nogales counted seventy-three maquiladoras employing 21,084 workers, approximately 20 percent of the population (Table 7.3). Maquiladora plants are concentrated in two cores on the western and southern peripheries of the city (see Fig. 7.8). Along Camino Liberamiento, approximately equidistant between the Mariposa Road crossing and the intersection of Avenida López Mateos with Mexico Highway 15 to Her-

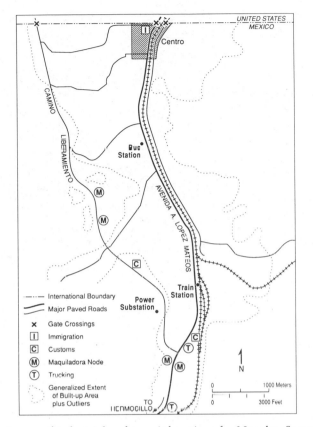

FIGURE 7.8 A map of industrial and transit locations for Nogales, Sonora.

mosillo, is the western core. It includes the Parque Industrial Sanchez (see Fig. 7.9), housing eleven companies, and a second cluster of three maquiladoras. The prominent Grupo Chamberlain facility, perched on top of a hill overlooking the city, is part of the second cluster. This facility employs 1,500 workers who produce garage-door openers and radio control equipment. Nearby, especially on open hillsides west of Camino Liberamiento, are recently constructed squatter settlements that house some of the workers for these maquiladoras (*San Antonio Light* 1990a).

The much larger, southern core of maquiladora industry straddles both sides of the highway south of the confluence of the above-mentioned roads (see Fig. 7.8). Plants here include Apno (a subsidiary of Blackhawk Automotive, Inc.), Circuitos Mexicanos de Nogales (owned by Coleman Products), Rockwell Collins de Nogales (whose parent company is Rock-

FIGURE 7.9 Parque Industrial Sanchez and surrounding hillside squatter
settlements, Nogales.

well International), and several dozen other facilities (*PRISSA 1990–91
Directory*). Large trucking operations that contain parking, services, and
eateries flank this core along the east side of the highway near the railroad
line and yards. An electrical power substation and a new customs facility
are located on the perimeter road to the west of this area.

All truck traffic except for local delivery is routed along Camino Liberamiento to the Mariposa Road crossing, but the railroad still transports
automobiles, assembled in Hermosillo, across the border to American dealers. Maquiladora exports from Nogales are destined for Northeastern, Midwestern, and Western U.S. markets. In fact, Nogales appears to be the
spatial break point along the border from which plants to the east ship
principally to Midwestern and Northeastern U.S. destinations while maquiladoras to the west ship chiefly to Southern California and the West Coast
(South 1990: 556–557). Good interstate highway access on the U.S. side
facilitates this dispersal. Trucks move north from Nogales, Arizona, along
I-19, then either break east toward El Paso on I-10 in Tucson, jog west
toward San Diego on I-8 near Casa Grande, or route north on I-10 through

Phoenix and then west to Los Angeles. Nogales has an airport about five miles beyond the built-up area on Mexico Highway 15 to Hermosillo. Maquiladora executive personnel also use the airport outside Nogales, Arizona, sometimes flying in there and driving across the border to visit operations in Mexico.

That Nogales will figure prominently in any future trade relations between Sonora and Arizona was reaffirmed in January 1992 when the governor of Sonora, Manlio Fabio Beltrones, was invited to address the Arizona state legislature—a political invitation that was last extended to a governor of Sonora in 1937 (*Arizona Republic* 1992). Beltrones called for joint cooperation between the two states, but his speech mostly addressed larger issues of national rather than local scope, especially the pending free-trade agreement between Mexico and the United States. The ultimate success of such joint trade cooperation may be vague at this point, but the present reality at ambos Nogales is rather clear. The Mexican border-city's population is approximately seven times larger than that of its American border-town counterpart, and its industrial production far exceeds that of Nogales, Arizona. Mexicans still cross regularly to the American side to purchase goods that are mostly unavailable in the stores of Nogales, Sonora, while North American executives commute daily to maquiladora industrial parks in the Mexican town. Industry and transit are part of the pattern and process of interaction between the Mexican and American border communities, and the cultural landscape testifies to this important linkage.

8 The Border Cities: Ayer, Hoy, y Mañana

The complex landscapes of some border cities have been evolving for several centuries, but in most for less than one hundred years. One exception notwithstanding, the Mexican border cities are each larger than their American border neighbors. Mexicali, the capital of Baja California, perhaps best epitomizes the pace of change. Founded with the new century in 1903, it will in all likelihood top the one-million population mark by the early twenty-first century. As one writer remarked, few places in the history of the world have grown so large from nothing in one century (Weisman 1986: 167).

Still, the prevailing attitudes held about the Mexican border communities continue to differ on either side of the borderline. Americans may distinguish Tijuana from Ciudad Juárez as places on a map, but each is part of a larger perception held of "the border," one that can evoke caution or even fear, on the one hand, or frolic and adventure on the other. This ambivalence is seen, for example, along the border where Tamaulipas meets Texas. During every college spring break in Texas for the past dozen years, about 150,000 students have crowded the beaches of South Padre Island near Brownsville and across the Rio Grande from Matamoros (Gerlach 1989: 15). Traditionally, students have made periodic runs into Matamoros for cheap beer and general carousing. In 1989, the season's events included the kidnap and ritualistic, macabre murder of one such student by a cult in the city. The story gained national attention and cast a shadow over Matamoros, indicting it as a place to be shunned and reinforcing the images of border towns as wicked, dangerous places (*Austin American-Statesman* 1989b). By the spring of 1990, however, all seemed forgotten. The bars, liquor stores, and curio shops were again crowded with partying students.

Thus, in spite of extraordinary growth and change, the lore and lure of the border have remained consistent since the halcyon days of Prohibition.

Mexicans, too, recognize that the border includes individual cities; collectively, however, the zone is called *la frontera,* which can be translated as "the border" but which literally means "the frontier." In the minds of many Mexicans, certainly in the minds of *los fronterizos* as the border Mexicans are called, la frontera is often equated with prosperity and economic opportunity. This is quite a different vision than the typical American image of the region.

This contrast in viewpoints is illustrated by two vernacular expressions common on either side of the border. In the United States one often hears the expression "Old Mexico" used as a term of affection. The expression is used in the United States generally, and especially in the American border states. Not only is the term heard on television (frequently by weather announcers), it is also visible still on road signs and advertisements that direct North American tourists to the border. The phrase seems to promote a dated, romantic vision of Mexico rather than a recognition of the modern character of the country. It may explain, in part, why one observer recently called Mexico "our distant neighbor" (Riding 1985). From *el otro lado* (the other side), however, one rarely hears such sentimental references to the antiquity or romance of Mexico, unless it appears on a travel poster. Rather, the expression that rings out from radio, television, and the advertising media—the expression that is directed at the everyday Mexican—is *hoy.* Literally, the term means "today," but the intensity and urgency with which it is used suggest the immediate—now, not yesterday. The ever-present lottery ticket vendor on the streets chants, *Para hoy!* (today's [ticket]). A contemporary pop song of the air waves sings about *chicas de hoy* (today's [modern] girls). The peso-to-dollar quote at the hotel, in the restaurant, at the *casa de cambio* (money-exchange house), or on the street is "hoy," (today's [rate]). The impression one is left with is that los fronterizos see themselves and the border cities as active and progressive. Americans, by contrast, still seem to see in the border cities a Mexico *de ayer* (of yesterday), a Mexico seen through gringo eyes, like the donkeys painted to look like zebras for the camera.

This distinction is furthered by the landscapes familiar to each group. Visitors to the border cities for the most part restrict their experiences to the ports of entry and the narrow tourist zones. Thus, they know little of the city beyond the contrived atmosphere of this district. Mexican residents may know the tourist zone, but except for those who live or work within it, the district is not the central focus of their daily experience. The landscapes best known to border Mexicans are those discussed in this essay and familiar to residents of cities throughout Mexico. They include a vibrant commercial core, el centro, and the newly carved commercial spines that emanate from this center; a varied mix of residential neighborhoods, from elite districts to middle- and lower-income colonias to the newly founded squatter settlements on the urban fringe and in disamenity zones; and finally, the old industrial districts and very new industrial quarters of maquiladora parks that employ increasing numbers of border-city residents. These landscapes are the skeletal anatomy of the Mexican border cities. Unfortunately, these areas—the most vital parts of the border communities—remain largely *terra incognita* to the average North American.

Amid these varied perceptions, the border cities remain hybrid cultural landscapes. They display a heritage that is Spanish and Mexican, but they also incorporate and testify to North American landscape tastes. El centro, lower- and middle-income housescapes, and certain specialized industrial landscapes appear to mirror patterns that tie the Mexican border cities to a more traditional landscape expression. Yet, the elite housescapes, automobile commercial strips, and maquiladora industrial spaces seem to embrace a modern North American landscape aesthetic. These landscape changes are emblematic of the fundamental changes occurring in Mexican culture. In Mexico City, the federal government is aware of and sensitive to the political winds that may blow as la frontera aligns itself more closely with North American culture. The federal government has used the landscape of the border cities to give symbolic gesture to national icons. Monumental statues of Cuauhtémoc and Cárdenas, and those regulars of the political pantheon, Juárez and Hidalgo, stand heroically along the new commercial spines. They serve to remind border Mexicans that they are, in fact, Mexicans first, despite the hybridizing nature of la frontera (Rodriguez 1987). There are even those among the border Mexicans themselves who fear that the U.S. and its pervasive ways are an insidious intrusion, be it manifest in the replacement of the taco by the hot dog or in the celebration of American holidays (*El Fronterizo* 1984; *El Universal de Juárez* 1987; *Diario de Juárez* 1987).

At one extreme, this intensity of cultural borrowing and mixing that occurs with seeming bravado in the border zone has led some to declare that a third country, twenty miles wide, ten on each side of the border, is now emerging. In this so-called symbiotic region, both sides are said to be less different from each other than they are from their respective countries. This notion was promoted openly in a 1986 CBS television documentary, "One River, One Country: The U.S.-Mexico Border," written and narrated by Bill

Moyers, although it only discussed the Texas-Mexico portion of the zone. On reflection, one Mexican official called it "an elegant and original, albeit mistaken, concept" (Pastor and Castañeda 1988: 302–303). We share this sentiment.

IMPACT OF FREE-TRADE AGREEMENT

At this writing in early 1992, Mexico and the United States are poised to join with Canada to form a North American Free Trade Agreement. The implementation of this agreement in Mexico would culminate nearly a decade of economic reforms aimed at opening its highly protected domestic market to imports and foreign investments. Reforms have encompassed the restructure of fiscal accounts, liberalization of imports, deregulation of economic activity, and privatization of government-run industries.

Although a trade agreement would likely benefit Mexico's domestic industries by giving them greater access to U.S. and Canadian markets, the impact on the border cities is problematic. The consequence of a free-trade agreement on the maquiladora industry, which is highly concentrated along the border, is of particular concern. One outcome of free trade might be a greater concentration of assembly plants in interior Mexican cities, where labor supply is more secure and urban infrastructure is better developed. This action could lead to more efforts to establish new ports of entry along the border to compete with the already-congested gate crossings in the larger border cities (Cutler 1991: 57). Across from Santa Teresa, New Mexico, west of Ciudad Juárez, and at Columbia, Nuevo León, north of Nuevo Laredo, new ports of entry are presently under construction to meet just such demand. Conversely, however, another impact of a decentralization of maquiladoras away from the border might be a reduction of migrants to the border cities by generating jobs in Mexico's interior, thus stemming the need to venture north (*Los Angeles Times* 1991: H11).

Maquiladoras to interior cities and new ports of entry notwithstanding, the Mexican border cities are not likely to disappear as a result of economic policy changes. After all, maquiladoras already exist in several interior cities, and as this research has demonstrated, new gate crossings have been added to many rapidly growing large and medium-sized border cities. It is important to recognize that the border cities are no longer, if they ever were, one-dimensional urban economies. They have increasingly become self-sustaining demographic and economic entities that generate their own growth inertia, especially the largest cities. Furthermore, it must be realized that a free-trade agreement is a political agenda as well as an economic policy. The shifting winds of national, regional, and local political office in Mexico may bear importantly on any future implementation directed from the federal government. Although the border is an important region economically, border-city Mexicans currently represent only slightly less than 5 percent of all Mexicans. Yet, opposition political parties, especially the conservative Partido Acción Nacional (PAN) are active in the border areas and represent an alternative to the central governing Partido Revolucionario Institucional (PRI).

Despite the very real tilt of cultural influence from the United States and the possible changes that may come with a free-trade agreement, it should not be assumed that Mexican border cities will simply become replicas of North American urban places. Traditional Mexican preferences for landscapes, whether in the plazas and markets of el centro or in enclosed and personalized housescapes, are not likely to disappear from the border cities in the near future. This research has shown that in spite of discernible urban-landscape patterns along the border from east to west, the border region and its cities remain a zone of significant diversity. This variation reflects the individual settlement histories of border places, the range of migrants who brought their traditions to the border cities from many regions of Mexico, and the complexities of environment and economy that characterize the entire borderlands area.

Because cultural diffusion is a process that can work both ways, recent developments along the Mexican border are bringing different conditions, including capital as well as labor, to some of the American border communities (*Los Angeles Times* 1988a). As one astute observer warns, "The Tijuana that Americans grew up with was a city they thought they had created. The Tijuana that has grown up is a city that will re create us" (Rodriguez 1987: 42). In 1991, a five-mile section of the old wire fence that separated Tijuana from San Ysidro near Otay Mesa had been replaced with a steel wall that was ten feet high. Blazed on the Mexican side was graffiti that read, *¿Si el de Berlin cayó, este por qué no?* (If the one in Berlin fell, why not this one?) (*Arizona Republic* 1991b: C3). As the Mexican border cities continue to outgrow their American border neighbors, we may be witness to an even greater movement of people, ideas, and material culture south to north beyond the labor migrations of the past. Cultural ways may prove equally powerful forces as they push across and stimulate changes in land and life on the American side of the borderline, adding to an already rich Mexican-Chicano heritage in the American Southwest. Ironically, however, a recent poll conducted in San Diego found that a majority of respondents believed San Diego and Tijuana were not growing more interdependent, and were, in fact, opposed to closer cross-border ties (*San Diego Union* 1991a: C3). Cooperation, it appears, may be related in part to scale as well as to history of interaction among Mexican and American border towns. It is cultivated where border settlements are small or medium-sized and where there is a history of social connection, but it is strained and difficult to foster in communities that have only recently attempted cooperation and where one or both are of metropolitan stature. Not all changes will come easily.

By the year 2000, it is estimated that 77 percent of Mexico's population will reside in urban areas, and it is likely that the percentage living in cities will be even higher along the border (Population Reference Bureau 1987). If we in the United States are to come to understand and accept Mexico, her people and their ways, we might include in our collective learning agenda a greater familiarity with and sensitivity toward her cities as cultural creations and places. The Mexican border cities of the next century will be that much more alien and difficult to comprehend without an appreciation of their twentieth-century anatomy and personality.

References

Acevedo Cárdenas, Conrado, and David Piñera Ramírez. 1983. Semblanza de Tijuana 1915–1930. In *Panorama Histórico de Baja California*, D. Piñera Ramírez (ed.), 430–442. Mexicali: Centro de Investigaciones Históricas, Universidad Autónoma de Baja California.

Agnew, John A., John Mercer, and David Sopher (eds.). 1984. *The City in Cultural Context*. Boston: Allen and Unwin.

Aguirre Bernal, Celso. 1983. Desarrollo Inicial de Mexicali. In *Panorama Histórico de Baja California*, D. Piñera Ramírez (ed.), 346–349. Mexicali: Centro de Investigaciones Históricas, Universidad Autónoma de Baja California.

Alvarez, Jose Hernández. 1966. A Demographic Profile of the Mexican Immigration to the United States, 1910–1950. *Journal of Inter-American Studies* 8: 471–496.

Alvarez, Robert. 1984. The Border as Social System: The California Case. *New Scholar* 9: 119–133.

Amato, Peter W. 1970. Elitism and Settlement Patterns in the Latin American City. *Journal of the American Institute of Planners* 36: 96–105.

Anderson, Joan B. 1990. Maquiladoras and Border Industrialization: Impact on Economic Development in Mexico. *Journal of Borderlands Studies* 5(1): 5–9.

Applegate, Howard G., and C. Wayne Hanselka. 1974. *La Junta de los Rios Del Norte y Conchos*. Southwestern Studies 41. El Paso: Texas Western Press.

Arguelles, Adalberto J. 1910. *Reseña del Estado del Tamaulipas*. Ciudad Victoria, Tamaulipas: Oficina Tipográfica del Gobierno del Estado.

Arizona Daily Star. 1990. New Bridge Links EL Paso to Zaragoza. December 3: B2.

Arizona Republic. 1990. Fast-Service Fee Weighed for Some Border Entries. December 28: A6.

———. 1991a. Nogales Radio Station in Works to Help Drivers Cross Border. February 25: B3.

————.1991b. Not All the Walls Have Fallen Down. December 8: C1, C3.

————.1991c. Mexico Replaces Customs Agents. December 9: A1, A3.

————.1991d. Traffic-jam Nightmare at Border. December 16: B1.

————.1992. Legislature Hears Governor of Sonora. January 23: B1.

Arreola, Daniel D. 1981. Fences as Landscape Taste: Tucson's Barrios. *Journal of Cultural Geography* 2: 96–105.

————. 1982. Nineteenth-Century Townscapes of Eastern Mexico. *Geographical Review* 72: 1–19.

————. 1988. Mexican American Housescapes. *Geographical Review* 78: 299–315.

————.1992. Plaza Towns of South Texas. *Geographical Review* 82: 52–73.

Asvestas, Steve. 1979. *Nuevo Laredo* (map). Laredo: The Banester Co.

Austin American-Statesman. 1989a. Maquilas Give Texas Business a Shot at Diversity. March 27: 5.

————. 1989b. Tourists Shun Matamoros in Wake of Drug Murders. April 14: A7.

————. 1989c. 7 Bridges to Mexico Approved. August 10: A1, A10.

————. 1989d. Texas Teens Drawn to Mexican Bars. September 10: A1.

————. 1990a. Laredo Bridge Project Begins. March 17: B3.

————. 1990b. Matamoros Labor Boss Steadfast Despite Controversy. May 7: 3.

Ayer, Harry W., and M. Ross Layton. 1974. The Border Industry Program and the Impacts of Expenditures by Mexican Border Industry Employees on a U.S. Border Community: An Empirical Study of Nogales. *Annals of Regional Science* 8: 105–117.

Baerresen, Donald. 1971. *The Border Industrialization Program.* Lexington, M.A.: D. C. Heath.

Baker, Marvin W. 1970. Land Use Transition in Mexican Cities. Unpublished Ph.D. dissertation, Syracuse University.

Banham, Reyner. 1971. *Los Angeles: The Architecture of Four Ecologies.* Hamondsworth: Penguin.

Bannon, John Francis. 1974. *The Spanish Borderlands Frontier 1513–1821.* Albuquerque: University of New Mexico Press.

Barnes, Will C. 1960. *Arizona Place Names.* Revised and enlarged by Byrd H. Granger. Tucson: University of Arizona Press.

Bashford, G. M. 1954. *Tourist Guide to Mexico.* New York: McGraw-Hill.

Beegle, J. Allan, Harold F. Goldsmith, and Charles P. Loomis. 1960. Demographic Characteristics of the United States–Mexican Border. *Rural Sociology* 25: 107–162.

Benedicto, Luis. 1956. *Historia de Nuevo Laredo.* Nuevo Laredo: Clube de Leones.

Bernstein, Marvin D. 1964. *The Mexican Mining Industry, 1890–1950: A Study of* the Interaction of Politics, Economics, and Technology. Albany: State University of New York.

Beyer, G. (ed.). 1967. *The Urban Explosion in Latin America*. Ithaca, NY: Cornell University Press.

Bolton, Herbert Eugene. 1917. The Mission as a Frontier Institution in the Spanish-American Colonies. *American Historical Review* 23: 42–61.

Boorstin, Daniel J. 1961. *The Image: A Guide to Pseudo-Events in America*. New York: Harper and Row.

Bosse, Carl. 1973. Nogales, Sonora: Prosperity from Piccolos, Paper Dresses, Printed Circuits. *Industrial Development* 142: 18–23.

Bourke, John G. 1894. The American Congo. *Scribner's Magazine* 15: 590–610.

Braddy, Haldeen. 1966. *Pershing's Mission in Mexico*. El Paso: Texas Western Press.

Britton, Robert A. 1979. The Image of the Third World in Tourism Marketing. *Annals of Tourism Research* 11: 318–329.

Brown, Jane Cowan. 1972. Patterns of Intra-Urban Settlement in Mexico City: An Examination of the Turner Theory. Unpublished M.A. thesis, Cornell University.

Brownsville Convention and Visitors Bureau, Inc. 1988. *Map of the Cities of Brownsville and Matamoros*. Brownsville: Breeden/McCumber, Inc.

Brownsville Economic Development Council, Inc. 1989. *Directory of Manufacturers and Processors: Brownsville, Texas, U.S.A.*

Bunting, Bainbridge. 1976. *Early Architecture in New Mexico*. Albuquerque: University of New Mexico Press.

Burns, Elizabeth K. 1980. The Enduring Affluent Suburb. *Landscape* 24: 33–41.

Business Week. 1988. The Magnet of Growth in Mexico's North. The Rise of Maquiladoras is Spurring Industrial Bonanza in the Desert. June 6: 48–51.

Byfield, Patsy Jeanne. 1966. *Falcon Dam and the Lost Towns of Zapata*. Austin: Texas Memorial Museum, University of Texas.

Cabral, John. 1991. Down Mexico Way. *Planning* (August): 20–23.

Cahill, Rich. 1987. *Border Towns of the Southwest: Shopping, Dining, Fun and Adventure from Tijuana to Juárez*. Boulder, CO: Pruett Publishing Company.

Cahill, Tim. 1975. Tijuana Confidential. *Rolling Stone* (October 9): 33–37, 68–70.

Cámaras de Comercio de Nogales, Sonora y Nogales, Arizona. 1919. *Folleto de Recuerdos de la Excursión Comercial de Amistad Internacional*. Nogales: Cámaras de Comercio.

Campbell, Ross W. 1974. Stages of Shopping Center Development in Major Latin American Metropolitan Markets. *Land Economics* 50: 66–70.

Canseco Botello, José Raúl. 1981. *Historia de Matamoros*. Matamoros: Los Talleres Tipográficos de Litográfica Jardín.

Caplow, Theodore. 1949. The Social Ecology of Guatemala City. *Social Forces* 28: 113–133.

Cardenas, Leonard. 1963. *The Municipality in Northern Mexico.* Southwestern Studies 1. El Paso: Texas Western College Press.

Cardoso, Lawrence A. 1980. *Mexican Emigration to the United States, 1897–1931: Socioeconomic Patterns.* Tucson: University of Arizona Press.

Carpenter, Frank G. 1927. *Mexico.* Garden City, NY: Doubleday, Page and Company.

Castañeda, Carlos E. 1936–1958. *Our Catholic Heritage in Texas, 1519–1936.* 7 vols. Austin: Von Boeckmann–Jones Company.

Catálogo Nacional de Monumentos Históricos—Inmuebles, Estado de Tamaulipas. 1986. México: Instituto Nacional de Antropología e Historia.

Censo General (II) de La República Mexicana, 1900. 1901. México: Dirección General de Estadística.

Censo General (III) de Población, 1910. 1918. México: Dirección General de Estadística.

Censo General (IV) de Población, 1921. 1926. México: Dirección General de Estadística.

Censo General (V) de Población, 1930. 1933. México: Dirección General de Estadística.

Censo General (VIII) de Población, 1960. 1963. México: Dirección General de Estadística.

Censo General (IX) de Población, 1970. 1973. México: Dirección General de Estadística.

Censo General (X) de Población y Vivienda, 1980. 1983. México: SPP Instituto Nacional de Estadística Geografía e Informática.

Censo General (XI) de Población y Vivienda, 1990. 1990. Resultados Preliminares. México: Instituto Nacional de Estadística Geografía e Informática.

Chamberlin, Eugene Keith. 1951. Mexican Colonization Versus American Interests in Lower California. *Pacific Historical Review* 20: 43–55.

Chatfield, W. H. 1893. *The Twin Cities of the Border and Country of the Rio Grande.* New Orleans: E. P. Brandao.

Chávez, Armando. 1961. *Programa Nacional Fronterizo.* México: PRONAF Press.

Chevalier, Francois. 1963. *Land and Society in Colonial Mexico: The Great Hacienda.* Translated by Alvin Eustis. Berkeley and Los Angeles: University of California Press.

Christian Science Monitor. 1985. U.S. Plants South of Border Offer Help to Mexico's Economic Woes. December 12: 6–7.

———. 1989. Mexico Looks to Asia for Economic Boost. August 8: 1.

Clay, Grady. 1980. *Close-Up: How to Read the American City*. Chicago: University of Chicago Press.

Coatsworth, John H. 1981. *Growth Against Development: The Economic Impact of Railroads in Porfirian Mexico*. DeKalb: Northern Illinois University Press.

Cohen, Erik. 1979. Rethinking the Sociology of Tourism. *Annals of Tourism Research* 11: 18–35.

Cohen, S., and L. Taylor. 1976. *Escape Attempts*. Harmondsworth: Penguin.

Complete Twin Plant Guide 1987 El Paso: Solunet Publications

Conklin, Dean T. 1967. *Tijuana: Génesis y Primeras Noticias*. Tijuana: Asociación Cultural de las Californias.

Conzen, Michael P. 1978. Analytical Approaches to the Urban Landscape. In *Dimensions of Human Geography: Essays on Some Familiar and Neglected Themes*, Karl W. Butzer (ed.), 128–165. Chicago: Department of Geography Research Paper 186, University of Chicago.

Crouch, Dora P., Daniel J. Garr, and Axel I. Mundigo. 1982. *Spanish City Planning in North America*. Cambridge, MA: MIT Press.

Crouch, Dora P., and Alejandro I. Mundigo. 1977. The City Planning Ordinances of the Laws of the Indies Revisited. *Town Planning Review* 48: 247–268.

Crowley, William K. 1977. Plaza Morphology: Examples from Mexico and Guatemala. Paper presented to the Annual Meeting of the Association of American Geographers, Salt Lake City.

———. 1987. La Gran Plaza, Monterry's [sic] Gran Attempt at Urban Renewal. In *Yearbook, Conference of Latin Americanist Geographers* 13, Martha A. Works (ed.), 36–44. Baton Rouge: Department of Geography, Louisiana State University.

Cruz, Gilbert R. 1988. *Let There Be Towns: Spanish Municipal Origins in the American Southwest, 1610–1810*. College Station: Texas A&M University Press.

Cuellar Valdes, Pablo M. 1979. *Historia del Estado de Coahuila*. Saltillo: Universidad Autónoma de Coahuila.

Cumberland, Charles C. 1960. The United States–Mexican Border: A Selective Guide to the Literature of the Region. *Rural Sociology* 25: 1–236.

Curtis, James R. 1981. The Boutiquing of Cannery Row. *Landscape* 25: 44–48.

———. 1985. The Most Famous Fence in the World: Fact and Fiction in Mark Twain's Hannibal. *Landscape* 28: 8–14.

———. 1991. The U.S.-Mexico Border: A Line, or a Zone? In *Regional Geography of the United States and Canada*, Tom L. McKnight, 376–377. Englewood Cliffs, NJ: Prentice-Hall.

Curtis, James R., and Daniel D. Arreola. 1989. Through Gringo Eyes: Tourist Districts in the Mexican Border Cities as Other-directed Places. *North American Culture* 5(2): 19–32.

———. 1991. Zonas de Tolerancia on the Northern Mexican Border. *Geographical Review* 81: 333–346.

Curtis, James R., and David M. Helgren. 1984. Yard Ornaments in the American Landscape: A Survey along the Florida Keys. *Journal of Regional Cultures* 4: 78–92.

Cutler, Blayne. 1991. Welcome to the Borderlands. *American Demographics* (February): 44–49, 57.

Daddysman, James. 1984. *The Matamoros Trade: Confederate Commerce, Diplomacy, and Intrigue.* Newark: University of Delaware Press.

Daily Oklahoman. 1989. Prostitutes Vow to Strip in Protest. August 8: 2.

Dann, Graham M. S. 1977. Anomie, Ego-Enhancement and Tourism. *Annals of Tourism Research* 4: 184–194.

de Blij, Harm, and Peter Muller. 1988. *Geography: Regions and Concepts,* fifth edition. New York: John Wiley and Sons.

Delaney, Robert W. 1955. Matamoros, Port of Texas During the Civil War. *Southwestern Historical Quarterly* 58: 473–487.

De la Rosa, Martín. 1985. *Marginalidad en Tijuana.* Tijuana: Centro de Estudios Fronterizos del Norte de México.

Demaris, Ovid. 1970. *Poso del Mundo: Inside the U.S.-Mexican Border from Tijuana to Matamoros.* Boston: Little, Brown.

Diario de Juárez. 1987. Border Residents Adopt U.S. Ways. July 9. Cited in *U.S.-Mexico Report* 6(8): 10.

———. 1988. New Border Station. March 14. Cited in *U.S.-Mexico Report* 7(4): 18.

Diccionario Porrua de Historia, Biografía y Geografía de México. 1964. 2 vols. Tercera edición. México: Editorial Porrua.

Dillman, Charles Daniel. 1968. The Functions of Brownsville, Texas and Matamoros, Tamaulipas: Twin Cities of the Lower Rio Grande. Unpublished Ph.D. dissertation, University of Michigan.

Dillman, C. Daniel. 1970. Urban Growth Along Mexico's Northern Border and the Mexican National Border Program. *Journal of Developing Areas* 4: 487–508.

———. 1971. Occupance Phases of the Lower Rio Grande of Texas and Tamaulipas. *California Geographer* 12: 30–37.

———. 1976. Maquiladoras in Mexico's Northern Border Communities and the Border Industrialization Program. *Tijdschrift voor Economische en Social Geografie* 67: 138–150.

———. 1983a. Border Industrialization. In *Borderlands Sourcebook,* Ellwyn R. Stoddard, Richard L. Nostrand, and Jonathan P. West (eds.), 144–152. Norman: University of Oklahoma Press.

————. 1983b. Border Urbanization. In *Borderlands Sourcebook,* Ellwyn R. Stoddard, Richard L. Nostrand, and Jonathan P. West (eds.), 237–244. Norman: University of Oklahoma Press.

Domenech, Emmanuel Henri D. 1858. *Missionary Adventures in Texas and Mexico.* London: Longman, Brown, Green, Longman, and Roberts.

Dotson, Floyd, and Lillian O. Dotson. 1954. Ecological Trends in the City of Guadalajara, Mexico. *Social Forces* 32: 367–374.

Dumke, Glenn S. 1948. Douglas, Border Boom Town. *Pacific Historical Review* 17: 283–293.

Dunbar, Gary S. 1974. Geographical Personality. In *Man and Cultural Heritage, Papers in Honor of Fred B. Kniffen,* H. J. Walker and W. G. Haag (eds.), 25–34. *Geoscience and Man* 5. Baton Rouge: Louisiana State University.

Dunbier, Roger. 1968. *The Sonoran Desert: Its Geography, Economy, and People.* Tucson: University of Arizona Press.

Duncan, James S., Jr. 1973. Landscape Taste as a Symbol of Group Identity: A Westchester County Village. *Geographical Review* 63: 334–355.

Eaton, Jack D. 1981. *Guerrero, Coahuila, Mexico: A Guide to the Town and Missions.* San Antonio: Center for Archaeological Research, University of Texas.

Eckbo, Garrett. 1969. The Landscape of Tourism. *Landscape* 18: 29–31.

Eder, Rita. 1989. The Icons of Power and Popular Art. In *Mexican Monuments: Strange Encounters,* Helen Escobedo and Paolo Gori, (eds.), 59–76. New York: Abbeyville Press.

Elbow, Gary S. 1975. The Plaza and the Park: Factors in the Differentiation of Guatemalan Town Squares. *Growth and Change* 6: 14–18.

————. 1983. Determinants of Land Use Change in Guatemalan Secondary Urban Centers. *Professional Geographer* 35: 57–65.

El Financiero. 1987. Industrial Parks Saturated. February 12. Cited in *U.S.-Mexico Report* 6(3): 13.

El Fronterizo. 1984. Hot Dogs vs Tacos. December 5. Cited in *U.S.-Mexico Report* 2(1): 18.

————. 1986a. Maquilas Good for National Economy. April 28. Cited in *U.S.-Mexico Report* 5(5): 23.

————. 1986b. New Border Crossing. June 1. Cited in *U.S.-Mexico Report* 5(7): 1.

El Heraldo. 1985. Industrial Park in Ojinaga. February 19. Cited in *U.S.-Mexico Report* 2(3): 20.

El Nacional. 1985. Bottleneck at Border. November 24. Cited in *U.S.-Mexico Report* 4(12): 22.

————. 1986. Ojinaga-Presidio Bridge Open. April 16. Cited in *U.S.-Mexico Report* 5(5): 9.

El Universal de Juárez. 1987. U.S. Culture Influence. April 9. Cited in *U.S.-Mexico Report* 6(5): 9.

Esparza Torres, Hector F. 1988. *Plano Urbano Tijuana* (map). México: H.F.E.T.

Excelsior. 1987. Reynosa-McAllen Bridge. July 13. Cited in *U.S.-Mexico Report* 6(8): 12.

———. 1988. Matamoros/Brownsville Bridge. July 7. Cited in *U.S.-Mexico Report* 7(8): 3.

Exner, M. J. 1917. Prostitution in Its Relation to the Army on the Mexican Border. *Social Hygiene* 3: 205–220.

Fernández, Raul. 1977. *The United States–Mexico Border: A Politico-Economic Profile.* Notre Dame: University of Notre Dame Press.

Fernández-Kelly, Maria Patricia. 1983. *For We Are Sold, I and My People: Women in Mexico's Frontier.* Albany: State University of New York Press.

Firey, Walter. 1945. Sentiment and Symbolism as Ecological Variables. *American Sociological Review* 10: 140–148.

Flandrau, Charles Macomb. 1964. *Viva México!* Urbana: University of Illinois Press [originally published 1908].

Flores Garcia, Silvia Ragnel. 1987. *Nogales: Un Siglo en la Historia.* Hermosillo: INAH-SEP, Centro Regional del Noroeste.

Flynn, Ken. 1991. On the Horizon: Port of Entry at Santa Teresa, New Mexico. *Border Trax* (February): 14–18.

Fortune. 1986. Business Makes a Run for the Border: U.S. Manufacturers Have a New Way to Fight Low-Priced Imports–Move to Mexico. August 18: 70–77.

Foscue, Edwin J. 1934. Agricultural History of the Lower Rio Grande Valley Region. *Agricultural History* 8: 124–137.

Foster, George M. 1960. *Culture and Conquest: America's Spanish Heritage.* Viking Fund Publications in Anthropology 27. New York: Wenner-Gren Foundation for Anthropological Research Incorporated.

Frieden, Bernard J., and Lynne B. Sagalyn. 1989. *Downtown Inc.: How America Rebuilds Cities.* Cambridge, MA: MIT Press.

Gade, Daniel W. 1976. The Latin American Central Plaza as a Functional Space. In *Latin America: Search for Geographic Explanations,* Proceedings, Conference of Latin Americanist Geographers 5, R. J. Tata (ed.), 16–23.

Gamio, Manuel. 1930. *Mexican Immigration to the United States: A Study of Human Migration and Adjustment.* Chicago: University of Chicago Press.

García Cubas, Antonio. 1889–1891. *Atlas de Geografía y Estadística de México.* 5 vols. México: various publishers.

Garreau, Joel. 1981. *The Nine Nations of North America.* Boston: Houghton Mifflin Company.

Garza Saenz, Ernesto. 1980. *Crónicas de Camargo.* Ciudad Victoria, Tamaulipas: Instituto de Investigaciones Históricas, Universidad Autónoma de Tamaulipas.

Gebhard, David. 1967. The Spanish Colonial Revival in Southern California (1895–1930). *Journal of the Society of Architectural Historians* 26: 131–147.

George, Edward. 1986. Human Resources and Economic Development in Ciudad Juárez. In *The Social Ecology and Economic Development of Ciudad Juárez,* Gay Young (ed.), 121–140. Boulder, CO: Westview Press.

George, Eugene. 1975. *Historic Architecture of Texas: The Falcón Reservoir.* Austin: Texas State Historical Commission.

Gerald, Rex E. 1966. Portrait of a Community: Joseph de Urrutia's Map of El Paso del Norte, 1766. *American West* 3: 38–41.

Gerhard, Peter. 1982. *The North Frontier of New Spain.* Princeton: Princeton University Press.

Gerlach, Jerry. 1989. Spring Break at Padre Island: A New Kind of Tourism. *Focus* 39: 13–16.

Gilbert, Alan (ed.). 1989. *Housing and Land in Urban Mexico.* Monograph Series 31. San Diego: Center for U.S.-Mexican Studies, University of California.

Gilbert, Alan, and Ann Varley. 1989. From Renting to Self-Help Ownership? Residential Tenure in Urban Mexico since 1940. In *Housing and Land in Urban Mexico,* Monograph Series 31, Alan Gilbert (ed.), 13–37. San Diego: Center for U.S.-Mexican Studies, University of California.

Gilbert, Alan, and Peter M. Ward. 1985. *Housing, the State and the Poor: Policy and Practice in Three Latin American Cities.* Cambridge: Cambridge University Press.

Gildersleeve, Charles R. 1975/1976. The Status of Borderlands Studies: Geography. *Social Science Journal* 12/13: 19–28.

———. 1978. The International Border City: Urban Spatial Organization in a Context of Two Cultures along the United States–Mexico Boundary. Unpublished Ph.D. dissertation, University of Nebraska, Lincoln.

Godfrey, Brian J. 1988. *Neighborhoods in Transition: The Making of San Francisco's Ethnic and Nonconformist Communities.* University of California Publications in Geography 27. Berkeley and Los Angeles: University of California Press.

Goldbaum, David. 1971. *Towns of Baja California: A 1918 Report.* Translated with introduction by W. O. Henricks. Glendale, CA: La Siesta Press.

Goldberg, Michael A., and John Mercer. 1986. *The Myth of the North American City: Continentalism Challenged.* Vancouver: University of British Columbia Press.

Gonzalez, Jorge. 1989. Personal communication from the Curator of History at the Nuevo Santander Museum, Laredo, Texas. June 1.

Gormsen, Erdmann. 1981. Die Städte im Spanischen Amerika. *Erdkunde* 35: 290–303.

Graham, Joe. 1979. Folk Housing in South and West Texas: Some Comparisons. In *An Exploration of a Common Legacy: A Conference on Border Architecture,* Marlene Heck (ed.), 38–45. Austin: Texas Historical Commission.

———. 1988. The Jacal in the Big Bend: Its Origin and Evolution. In *Occasional Papers of the Chihuahuan Desert Research Institute* 22, Robert J. Mallouf (ed.), 1–29. Alpine, TX: Chihuahuan Desert Research Institute.

Graham, Roy E., M. Wayne Bell, and Miguel Celorio. 1976. *Texas Border Architecture: Eagle Pass, Texas and Guerrero, Coahuila, Mexico.* Austin: University of Texas School of Architecture.

Grebler, Leo, Joan W. Moore, and Ralph Guzman. 1970. *The Mexican American People: The Nation's Second Largest Minority.* New York: The Free Press.

Griffin, Ernst C., and William K. Crowley. 1989. The People and Economy of Modern Mexico. In Robert C. West and John P. Augelli, *Middle America: Its Lands and Peoples,* third edition, 284–338. Englewood Cliffs, NJ: Prentice Hall.

Griffin, Ernst C., and Larry R. Ford. 1976. Tijuana: Landscape of a Culture Hybrid. *Geographical Review* 66: 435–447.

———. 1980. A Model of Latin American City Structure. *Geographical Review* 70: 397–422.

Grijalva, Rebecca. 1989. Designing for Housing and Community in a Mexican Border Settlement. Paper presented to the Third International and Interdisciplinary Conference on Built Form and Culture Research: Intercultural Processes. Tempe: Arizona State University.

Griswold del Castillo, Richard. 1990. *The Treaty of Guadalupe Hidalgo: A Legacy of Conflict.* Norman: University of Oklahoma Press.

Guerrero, Ricardo. 1968. Prostitution in Tijuana. In *Tijuana '68: Ethnographic Notes on a Mexican Border City,* John A. Price (ed.), Chapter Six. San Diego: San Diego State College.

Guias Urbanas. 1986. *Plano de la Ciudad de Mexicali* (map). Mexicali: Ediciones Corona.

Hadley, Diana. 1987. Border Boom Town—Douglas, Arizona 1900–1920. *Cochise Quarterly* 17: 3–47.

Hansen, Asael T. 1934. The Ecology of a Latin American City. In *Race and Culture Contacts,* E. B. Reuter (ed.), 124–142. New York: McGraw-Hill Book Company.

Hansen, Niles. 1981. *The Border Economy: Regional Development in the Southwest.* Austin: University of Texas Press.

Hardoy, Jorge E. 1972. El Modelo Clasico de la Ciudad Colonial Hispanoamericana. In *Verhandlungen de XXXVIII Internationalen Amerikanisten Kongresses, Vol. 4,* Jorge E. Hardoy, Erwin W. Palm, and Richard P. Schaedel (eds.), 143–181. Stuttgard-Muchen: Verlag.

———. 1975. La Forma de las Ciudades Coloniales en la America Española. In

Estudios sobre La Ciudad Iberoamericana, Francisco De Solano (ed.), 315–344. Madrid: Consejo Superior de Investigaciones Científicas, Instituto Gonzalo Fernandez de Oviedo.

Haring, Henk A. 1985. *Sunbelt Frontier and Border Economy: Manufacturing in El Paso–Ciudad Juárez.* Utrechtse Geografische Studies 35. Utrecht: Department of Geography, University of Utrecht.

Harrington, Edwin Lincoln. 1945. *Adobe as a Construction Material in Texas.* Bulletin 90, Texas Engineering Experiment Station. College Station: Texas A&M University.

Hartshorn, Truman A. 1973. Industrial/Office Parks: A New Look for the City. *Journal of Geography* 72: 33–45.

———. 1992. *Interpreting the City: An Urban Geography,* second edition. New York: John Wiley and Sons.

Hastings, James Rodney, and Raymond M. Turner. 1965. *The Changing Mile: An Ecological Study of Vegetation Change with Time in the Lower Mile of an Arid and Semiarid Region.* Tucson: University of Arizona Press.

Hawkins, Walace. 1947. *El Sal Del Rey.* Austin: Texas State Historical Association.

Hayner, Norman S. 1944. Oaxaca, City of Old Mexico. *Sociology and Social Research* 29: 87–95.

———. 1945. Mexico City: Its Growth and Configuration. *American Journal of Sociology* 50: 295–304.

Hecht, Melvin E. 1975. The Decline of the Grass Lawn Tradition in Tucson. *Landscape* 19: 3–10.

Herrera Carrillo, Pablo. 1976. *Colonización del Valle de Mexicali.* Mexicali: Universidad Autónoma de Baja California.

Herrera Pérez, Octavio. 1989. *Monografía de Reynosa.* Ciudad Victoria, Tamaulipas: Instituto Tamaulipeco de Cultura.

Herzog, Lawrence A. 1985a. Tijuana. *Cities* (November): 297–306.

———. 1985b. The Cross Cultural Dimensions of Urban Land Use Policy on the U.S.–Mexico Border: A San Diego–Tijuana Case Study. *Social Science Journal* 22: 29–46.

———. 1989. Tijuana: State Intervention and Urban Form in a Mexican Border City. In *Housing and Land in Urban Mexico,* Monograph 31, Alan Gilbert (ed.), 109–133. San Diego: Center for U.S.-Mexican Studies, University of California.

———. 1990. *Where North Meets South: Cities, Space, and Politics on the U.S.-Mexico Border.* Austin: Center for Mexican American Studies, University of Texas.

Hiernaux, Daniel. 1986. *Urbanización y Autoconstrucción de Vivienda en Tijuana.* México: Centro de Ecodesarrollo.

Hill, Lawrence Francis. 1926. *José de Escandón and the Founding of Nuevo Santander: A Study in Spanish Colonization.* Columbus: Ohio State University Press.

Hinojosa, Gilberto Miguel. 1983. *A Borderlands Town in Transition: Laredo, 1755–1870.* College Station: Texas A&M University Press.

Hodge, Larry D., and Sally S. Victor. 1983. Steamed Up About Brick. *Texas Highways* (November): 15–21.

Hoenderos, Wouter, Paul Van Lindert, and Otto Verkoren. 1983. Residential Mobility, Occupational Changes and Self-Help Housing in Latin American Cities: First Impressions from a Current Research-Programme. *Tijdschrift voor Economische en Social Geografie* 74: 376–386.

Hoffman, Abraham. 1974. *Unwanted Mexican Americans in the Great Depression: Repatriation Pressures, 1929–1939.* Tucson: University of Arizona Press.

Hoffman, Peter Richard. 1983. The Internal Structure of Mexican Border Cities. Unpublished Ph.D. dissertation. University of California, Los Angeles.

Hofsommer, Don L. 1986. *The Southern Pacific Railroad, 1901–1985.* College Station: Texas A&M University Press.

Hopgood, James F. 1979. *Settlers of Bajavista: Social and Economic Adaptation in a Mexican Squatter Settlement.* Athens, OH: Ohio University for International Studies.

House, John W. 1982. *Frontier on the Rio Grande: A Political Geography of Development and Social Deprivation.* Oxford: Clarendon Press.

Houston, J. M. 1968. The Foundation of Colonial Towns in Hispanic America. In *Urbanization and Its Problems: Essays in Honour of E. W. Gilbert,* R. P. Beckinsale and J. M. Houston (eds.), 352–390. Oxford: Oxford University Press.

Hughes, Anne E. 1914. *The Beginnings of Spanish Settlement in the El Paso District.* University of California Publications in History 1. Berkeley: University of California.

Hugill, Peter. 1984. The Landscape as a Code for Conduct. In *Place: Experience and Symbol,* Miles Richardson (ed.), 21–30. *Geoscience and Man* 24. Baton Rouge: Louisiana State University.

Husband, Eliza. 1985. Geography of a Symbol: The Hispanic Yard Shrines of Tucson, Arizona. Unpublished M.A. thesis, University of Arizona.

International Bridge. n.d. International Bridge, Eagle Pass–Piedras Negras. Typescript, Eagle Pass, Texas, Public Library.

Irigoyen, Ulises. 1943–1945. *Carretera Transpeninsular de la Baja California.* 2 vols. México: Editorial America.

Ives, Ronald L. 1950. The Sonoyta Oasis. *Journal of Geography* 49: 1–12.

Jackson, J. B. 1959–60. First Comes the House. *Landscape* 9: 26–35.

———. 1970. Other-directed Houses. In *Landscapes: Selected Writings of J. B.*

Jackson, Ervin H. Zube (ed.), 55–72. Amherst: University of Massachusetts Press.

———. 1987. The Popular Yard. *Places* 4(3): 26–31.

Jackson, John B. 1962. We Are Taken for a Ride. *Landscape* 11: 20–22.

Jackson, W. A. Douglas. 1985. *The Shaping of Our World: A Human and Cultural Geography.* New York: John Wiley and Sons.

Jakle, John A. 1985. *The Tourist: Travel in Twentieth-Century America.* Lincoln: University of Nebraska Press.

Jones, John M. (ed.). 1990. *La Hacienda.* Del Rio: Whitehead Museum and Val Verde County Historical Commission.

Jones, Richard C. 1982. Undocumented Migration from Mexico: Some Geographical Questions. *Annals of the Association of American Geographers* 72: 77–87.

Jordan, Terry G. 1988. A Gabled Folk House Type of the Mexico-Texas Borderland. In *Yearbook, Conference of Latin Americanist Geographers* 14, T. L. Martinson, A. R. Longwell, and W. M. Denevan (eds.), 2–6. Baton Rouge: Louisiana State University.

Keller, Suzanne. 1968. *The Urban Neighborhood: A Sociological Perspective.* New York: Random House.

Kelley, Joseph B. 1976. In Tijuana, Mexico, Three Programs Are in Use to Solve Problem of Low-Income Housing Needs. *Journal of Housing* 33. 224–227.

Kenamore, Clair. 1917–1918. The Principality of Cantu. *The Bookman* 46: 23–28.

Kent, Robert B. 1983. Agriculture and Ranching. In *Borderlands Sourcebook,* Ellwyn R. Stoddard, Richard L. Nostrand, and Jonathan P. West (eds.), 136–143. Norman: University of Oklahoma Press.

Kino, Eusebio Francisco. 1913–1922. *Las Misiones de Sonora y Arizona.* Publicaciones del Archivo General de la Nación VIII. México: Editorial Cultura.

Kubler, George. 1948. *Mexican Architecture of the Sixteenth Century.* 2 vols. New Haven: Yale University Press.

Ladman, Jerry. 1972. *Economic Impact of the Mexican Border Industrialization Program: Agua Prieta, Sonora.* Tempe: Center for Latin American Studies, Arizona State University.

Langley, Lester D. 1988. *MexAmerica: Two Countries, One Future.* New York: Crown Publishers.

Laredo Morning Times. 1990. Laredoans Air Views on Proposed Bridge. June 12: A1, A8.

Laredo News. 1987. Plaza Hidalgo Has Long History. January 25: 3A.

Lea, John. 1988. *Tourism and Development in the Third World.* London: Routledge.

Lehmer, D. J. 1939. Modern Jacales of Presidio. *El Palacio* 46: 183–186.

León-Portilla, Miguel. 1972. The Norteño Variety of Mexican Culture: An Ethnohistorical Approach. In *Plural Society in the Southwest,* Edward M. Spicer and Raymond H. Thompson (eds.), 77–114. Albuquerque: University of New Mexico Press.

Lewis, Peirce F. 1976. *New Orleans–The Making of an Urban Landscape.* Cambridge, MA: Ballinger Publishing Company.

———. 1979. Axioms for Reading the Landscape. In *The Interpretation of Ordinary Landscapes: Geographical Essays,* D. W. Meinig (ed.), 11–32. New York: Oxford University Press.

Ley, David. 1988. From Urban Structure to Urban Landscape. *Urban Geography* 9: 98–105.

Lloyd, William J. 1986. Land Use Structure and the Availability of Services in Ciudad Juárez. In *The Social Ecology and Economic Development of Ciudad Juárez,* Gay Young (ed.), 47–64. Boulder, CO: Westview Press.

Logan, Kathleen. 1984. *Haciendo Pueblo: The Development of a Guadalajaran Suburb.* University, AL: University of Alabama Press.

Lomnitz, Larissa Adler. 1977. *Networks and Marginality: Life in a Mexican Shantytown.* Translated by Cinna Lomnitz. New York: Academic Press.

López Prieto, Captain Pedro. 1975. *Siege of Camargo.* Translated by Clotilde P. García. Austin: San Felipe Press.

Lorey, David E. (ed.). 1991. *United States–Mexico Border Statistics Since 1900.* Los Angeles: UCLA Latin American Center.

Los Angeles Times. 1987. Tijuana's Children of Despair: Street Urchins Try to Eke Out Living from Tourists. (San Diego County Edition) April 6: J1.

———. 1988a. Mexico's Transplanted Millionaires: Refugees of Peso Devaluations, They Find Haven in La Jolla. October 16: V5.

———. 1988b. Baja Briefly Closes Some Tijuana Bars. (San Diego County Edition) October 28: J2.

———. 1989. Foreign Plants on Rise in Mexico: Number of Maquiladoras Increased 45% in '88. January 10: IV, 2.

———. 1990. A Taste of China South of the Border. May 17: A3, A34.

———. 1991. Border Towns Brace for Influx. October 22: H11.

Lowder, Stella. 1986. *The Geography of Third World Cities.* Totowa, NJ: Barnes and Noble Books.

Luis Valles, Ron. 1985. New Plans for Baja Tourism Launched. *The Forum* (November): 6.

———. 1988. Bustamante Promotes Tijuana Through Bureau. *The Forum* (March): 8.

MacCannell, Dean. 1976. *The Tourist: A New Theory of the Leisure Class.* New York: Schocken Books.

MacDonald, Kent. 1985. The Commercial Strip: From Main Street to Television Road. *Landscape* 28(2): 12–19.

Machado, Manuel A., Jr. 1981. *The North Mexican Cattle Industry, 1910–1975: Ideology, Conflict, and Change.* College Station: Texas A&M University Press.

———. 1982. Booze, Broads, and the Border: Vice and U.S.-Mexico Relations 1910–1930. In *Change and Perspective in Latin America: Proceedings of the 1982 Meeting of the Rocky Mountain Council on Latin American Studies,* C. Richard Bath (ed.), 349–361. El Paso: Center for Inter-American and Border Studies, University of Texas at El Paso.

Mangan, Frank. 1971. *El Paso in Pictures.* El Paso: The Press.

Margulis, Mario, and Rodolfo Tuirán. 1984. Nuevos Patrones Migratorios en La Frontera Norte: La Emigración. *Demografía y Economía* 18: 410–444.

———. 1986. *Desarrollo y Población en la Frontera Norte: El Caso de Reynosa.* México: El Colegio de México.

Martínez, Oscar J. 1977. Chicanos and the Border Cities: An Interpretive Essay. *Pacific Historical Review* 46: 85–106.

———. 1978. *Border Boom Town: Ciudad Juárez Since 1848.* Austin and London: University of Texas Press.

———. 1986. The Foreign Orientation of the Ciudad Juárez Economy. In *The Social Ecology and Economic Development of Ciudad Juárez,* Gay Young (ed.), 141–151. Boulder, CO: Westview Press.

———. 1988. *Troublesome Border.* Tucson: University of Arizona Press.

Martínez, P. L. 1960. *A History of Lower California.* México: Editorial Baja California.

Martinez, Ruben. 1989. Tijuana: Notes from Mexico's New Bohemia. *L.A. Weekly* (July 7–13): 18.

Martín Hernández, Vicente. 1981. *Arquitectura Doméstica de la Ciudad de México (1890–1925).* México: Universidad Nacional Autónoma de México.

Matthews, Harry G. 1977. Radicals and Third World Tourism: A Caribbean Focus. *Annals of Tourism Research* 10: 20–29.

Matthews, Neal. 1987. Gringo Street. *San Diego Reader* (April 23): 14.

McAlester, Virginia, and Lee McAlester. 1984. *A Field Guide to American Houses.* New York: Alfred A. Knopf.

McAndrew, John. 1965. *The Open-Air Churches of Sixteenth-Century Mexico.* Cambridge, MA: Harvard University Press.

McKee, Harley J. 1973. *Introduction to Early American Masonry.* Washington, DC: National Trust for Historic Preservation.

McNamara, Patrick H. 1971. Prostitution Along the U.S.-Mexican Border: A Survey. In *Prostitution and Illicit Drug Traffic on the U.S.-Mexico Border,* Ellwyn

R. Stoddard (ed.), 1–21. Occasional Papers 2. El Paso: Border-State University Consortium for Latin America.

Meade, Adalberto Walter. 1985. *Tecate: Cuarto Municipio*. Mexicali: Universidad Autónoma de Baja California.

Medina Robles, Fernando. 1970. *Mexicali-Calexico: Estudio Descriptivo de su Desarrollo*. Typescript, Special Collections Library, University of Texas, El Paso.

Messmacher, Miguel. 1983. *La Interdependencia en la Frontera Norte de México: Población, Industria, Comercio y Turismo en la Región de Piedras Negras, Coahuila*. México: Centro de Investigaciones y Estudios Superiores en Antropología Social, Cuadernos de la Casa Chata Hidalgo y Matamoros, Tlalpan.

Metz, Leon C. 1989. *Border: The U.S.-Mexico Line*. El Paso: Mangan Books.

Miller, Tom. 1981. *On the Border: Portraits of America's Southwestern Frontier*. New York: Harper and Row.

Monsiváis, Carlos. 1978. The Culture of the Frontier: The Mexican Side. In *Views Across the Border: The United States and Mexico*, Stanley R. Ross (ed.), 50–67. Albuquerque: University of New Mexico Press.

Moorhead, Max L. 1975. *The Presidio: Bastion of the Spanish Borderlands*. Norman: University of Oklahoma Press.

Muller, Thomas, and Thomas J. Espenshade. 1985. *The Fourth Wave: California's Newest Immigrants*. Washington, DC: Urban Institute Press.

Myers, John. 1971. *The Border Wardens*. Englewood Cliffs, NJ: Prentice-Hall.

Myrick, David F. 1975. *Railroads of Arizona, Vol. 1, The Southern Roads*. Berkeley: Howell-North.

Nelson, Howard J. 1963. Townscapes of Mexico: An Example of the Regional Variation of Townscapes. *Economic Geography* 39: 74–83.

Newcomb, Rexford. 1937. *Spanish-Colonial Architecture in the United States*. New York: J. J. Augustin.

Newsweek. 1987. The Rise of Gringo Capitalism: Mexico Lures American Firms to Border Zone. January 5: 40–41.

Newton, Ada Louise. 1964. The History of Architecture along the Rio Grande as Reflected in the Buildings around Rio Grande City 1749–1920. Unpublished M.A. thesis, Texas A&I University.

———. 1973. The Anglo-Irish House of the Rio Grande. *Pioneer America* 5: 33–38.

New York Times. 1987a. Satellite TV Becoming Mexico's Hottest New Dish. October 23: A4.

———. 1987b. Made in Mexico, Good for U.S.A. (Factories on the Border). December 13: F2.

North, David S. 1970. *The Border Crossers: People Who Live in Mexico and Work in the United States*. Washington, DC: TransCentury Corporation.

Nostrand, Richard L. 1970. The Hispanic-American Borderland: Delimitation of an American Culture Region. *Annals of the Association of American Geographers* 60: 638–661.

———. 1983. A Changing Culture Region. In *Borderlands Sourcebook,* Ellwyn R. Stoddard, Richard L. Nostrand, and Jonathan P. West (eds.), 6–15. Norman: University of Oklahoma Press [chapter originally published 1977].

Nuttall, Zelia. 1922. Royal Ordinances Concerning the Laying Out of New Towns. *Hispanic American Historical Review* 5: 249–254.

Officer, James E. 1987. *Hispanic Arizona, 1536–1856.* Tucson: University of Arizona Press.

Ojeda, Mario. 1983. *Mexico: The Northern Border as a National Concern.* El Paso: Center for Inter-American and Border Studies, University of Texas.

Oliver, Paul. 1987. *Dwellings: The House Across the World.* Austin: University of Texas Press.

Owens, Bob. 1982. The Man from the Coco Club. *San Diego Reader* (May 20): 22.

Palmore, Glenn L., Timothy P. Roth, J. Robert Foster, and Dilmus D. James. 1974. *The Ciudad Juárez Plan for Comprehensive Socio-Economic Development: A Model for Northern Mexico Border Cities.* El Paso: Bureau of Business and Economic Research, University of Texas.

Paredes Manzano, Eliseo. 1982. *Breve Reseña Histórica y Estadística de la Matamoros, Tamaulipas.* Matamoros: H. Ayuntamiento.

Pastor, Robert A., and Jorge G. Castañeda. 1988. *Limits to Friendship: The United States and Mexico.* New York: Alfred A. Knopf.

Paz, Octavio. 1961. *The Labyrinth of Solitude.* New York: Grove Press, Inc.

Pearce, Philip L. 1982. *The Social Psychology of Tourist Behavior.* Oxford: Pergamon Press.

Pederson, Leland R. 1990. Borderline and Borderland: A Perspective on Geographic Research in the U.S.-Mexico Boundary Zone. Paper presented to the Annual Meeting of the Association of American Geographers, Toronto.

Pick, James B., Swapan Nag, Glenda Tellis, and Edgar W. Butler. 1987. Geographical Distribution and Variation in Selected Socioeconomic Variables for Municipios in Six Mexican Border States, 1980. *Journal of Borderlands Studies* 2(1): 58–92.

Pierce, Frank C. 1917. *A Brief History of the Lower Rio Grande Valley.* Menasha, WI: George Banta Publishing.

Piñera Ramírez, David, and Jesús Ortiz Figueroa. 1983. Inicios de Tijuana como Asentamiento Urbano. In *Panorama Histórico de Baja California,* D. Piñera Ramírez (ed.), 284–292. Mexicali: Centro de Investigaciones Históricas, Universidad Autónoma de Baja California.

Popp, Kilian. 1985. Land Development in the Private Sector (Fraccionamientos) in the Process of the Expansion of Mexican Cities with Special Reference to the City of Puebla/[State of] Puebla. *Erdkunde* 39: 144–152.

Population Reference Bureau. 1987. Mexico's Population: A Profile. *Interchange* 16(2): np.

Portes, Alejandro, and John Walton. 1976. *Urban Latin America: The Political Condition from Above and Below.* Austin: University of Texas Press.

Pourade, Richard F. 1967. *The Rising Tide.* San Diego: Union-Tribune Publishing Company.

Powell, J. Richard. 1956. *The Mexican Petroleum Industry 1938–1950.* Berkeley and Los Angeles: University of California Press.

Preziosi, Donald. 1979. *The Semiotics of the Built Environment: An Introduction to Architectonic Analysis.* Bloomington, IN: Indiana University Press.

Price, John A. 1973a. *Tijuana: Urbanization in a Border Culture.* Notre Dame: University of Notre Dame Press.

———. 1973b. Tecate: An Industrial City on the Mexican Border. *Urban Anthropology* 2: 35–47.

Price, Thomas J. 1989. *Standoff at the Border: A Failure of Microdiplomacy.* Southwestern Studies 87. El Paso: Texas Western Press.

Prieto, Alejandro. 1873. *Historia, Geografía y Estadística del Estado de Tamaulipas.* México: TIP. Escalerillas, Num. 13.

PRISSA 1990–91 Directory. State of Sonora Maquiladora Directory. Tucson: Promotora de Industrias de Sonora, S.A.

Ramírez López, Jorge. 1983. Tecate. In *Panorama Histórico de Baja California,* D. Piñera Ramírez (ed.), 315–321. Mexicali: Centro de Investigaciones Históricas, Universidad Autónoma de Baja California.

Rapoport, Amos. 1969. *House Form and Culture.* Englewood Cliffs, NJ: Prentice-Hall.

———. 1982. *The Meaning of the Built Environment: A Non-verbal Communication Approach.* Beverly Hills: Sage Publishers.

Ready, Alma (ed.). 1980. *Nogales Arizona 1880–1980 Centennial Anniversary.* Nogales: Pimeria Alta Historical Society.

Reich, Peter L. (ed.). 1984. *Statistical Abstract of the United States–Mexico Borderlands.* Los Angeles: UCLA Latin American Center Publications.

Relph, Edward. 1976. *Place and Placelessness.* London: Pion.

———. 1984. Seeing, Thinking, and Describing Landscapes. In *Environmental Perception and Behavior: An Inventory and Prospect,* Thomas F. Saarinen, David Seamon, and James L. Sell (eds.), 209–223. Chicago: Department of Geography Research Paper 209, University of Chicago.

Relph, Edward C. 1987. *The Modern Urban Landscape.* Baltimore: Johns Hopkins University Press.

Reynolds, Clark. 1970. *The Mexican Economy: Twentieth Century Structure and Growth*. New Haven: Yale University Press.

Reynosa, Nuestra Ciudad: Historia de Cd. Reynosa, Tamaulipas. 1990. México: Ateneo de Reynosa.

Richardson, Miles. 1982. Being-in-the-Market versus Being-in-the-Plaza: Material Culture and the Construction of Social Reality in Spanish America. *American Ethnologist* 9: 421–436.

Riding, Alan. 1985. *Distant Neighbors: A Portrait of the Mexicans*. New York: Alfred A. Knopf.

Robertson, Douglas Lee. 1978. A Behavioral Portrait of the Mexican Plaza. Unpublished Ph.D. dissertation, Syracuse University.

Robinson, Willard B. 1979. Colonial Ranch Architecture in the Spanish-Mexican Tradition. *Southwestern Historical Quarterly* 83: 123–150.

———. 1981. *Gone From Texas: Our Lost Architectural Heritage*. College Station: Texas A&M University Press.

Rochlin, Fred, and Harriet Rochlin. 1976. The Heart of Ambos Nogales: Boundary Monument 122. *Journal of Arizona History* 17: 161–180.

Rodriguez, Richard. 1987. Across the Borders of History: Tijuana and San Diego Exchange Futures. *Harper's Magazine* (March): 42–53.

Roebuck, Julian, and Patrick McNamara. 1973. Ficheras and Free-lancers: Prostitution in a Mexican Border City. *Archives of Sexual Behavior* 2: 231–244.

Rogelio Alvarez, José. 1988. *Enciclopedia de México*. México: Secretaria de Educación Pública.

Romero de Terreros, Manuel. 1956. *Antiguas Haciendas de México*. México: Editorial Patria.

Rowntree, Lester B., and Margaret W. Conkey. 1980. Symbolism and the Cultural Landscape. *Annals of the Association of American Geographers* 70: 459–474.

Sabelberg, Elmar. 1985. The "South-Italian City." *Erdkunde* 39: 19–31.

Salter, Christopher L. 1978. Signatures and Settings: One Approach to Landscape in Literature. In *Dimensions of Human Geography: Essays on Some Familiar and Neglected Themes*, Karl. W. Butzer (ed.), 69–83. Chicago: Department of Geography Research Paper 186, University of Chicago.

San Antonio Light. 1990a. Shantytowns Are Part of Mexican Border Boom. August 19: D1, D4.

———. 1990b. $20 Million Border Bridge Begins. October 19: A12.

Sanborn Fire Insurance Company. 1893, 1898, 1902. *Maps of El Paso, Texas and Ciudad Juárez, Mexico*. New York: Sanborn Company.

San Diego Tribune. 1982a. Famed Hidalgo Market Still Growing With Tijuana. April 14: B1.

———. 1982b. Burro Without Stripes a Rarity on Tijuana Street. August 12: B1.

———. 1986a. Memories of Old Tijuana Burn Brightly for a Native. April 22: E4.

———. 1986b. U.S. Youths Pack Discos and Bars. April 22: E1.

———. 1987. Tijuana Booming as Tourism Makes Strong Comeback. January 5: B1.

———. 1988. Tijuana Chamber Urges End to Extortion of Tourists. February 12: B1.

San Diego Union. 1972. Remodeled Tijuana Jail Now Filled with Visitors. August 6: B1.

———. 1980. A Revolution on Avenida Revolución. July 12: B1.

———. 1987a. Tourism Still Baja's Primary Benefactor. January 26: 12.

———. 1987b. Trés Tijuana. July 5: I1.

———. 1988. Wild in the Streets of Tijuana. November 7: C1.

———. 1989a. People of Tijuana Rediscover City's 100 Years of History. July 9: B1.

———. 1989b. Tourists Find Tijuana More or Less What They Bargained For. July 9: B6.

———. 1991a. Hands Across the Border. November 10: C2.

———. 1991b. Tijuana's Besieged Street Vendors. December 15: B3.

———. 1991c. Fast Food Is Gaining South of the Border. December 15: I1.

Sandomingo, Manuel. 1951. *Historia de Agua Prieta.* Agua Prieta: Tipógrafo Rafael Parra Araiza.

Sandos, James A. 1980. Prostitution and Drugs: The United States Army on the Mexican-American Border, 1916–1917. *Pacific Historical Review* 49: 621–645.

Sanford, Trent Elwood. 1971. *The Architecture of the Southwest.* Westport, CT: Greenwood Press [originally published 1950].

Sargent, Charles S. 1982. The Latin American City. In *Latin America: An Introductory Survey,* Brian W. Blouet and Olwyn M. Blouet (eds.), 201–249. New York: John Wiley and Sons.

Scarborough, Anne Cecil. 1968. *The Pass of the Eagle: The Chaparral Region of Texas.* Austin: San Felipe Press.

Scheinman, Marc N. 1990. Report on the Present Status of Maquiladoras. In *The Maquiladora Industry: Economic Solution or Problem?* Khosrow Fatemi (ed.), 19–31. New York: Praeger.

Schmidt, Robert H. 1973. *A Geographical Survey of Chihuahua.* Southwestern Studies 37. El Paso: Texas Western Press.

Schmidt, Robert H., and William J. Lloyd. 1986. Patterns of Urban Growth in Ciudad Juárez. In *The Social Ecology and Economic Development of Ciudad Juárez,* Gay Young (ed.), 23–45. Boulder, CO: Westview Press.

Scott, Florence Johnson. 1966. *Historical Heritage of the Lower Rio Grande.* Waco: Texian Press [originally published 1937].

Scott, Ian. 1982. *Urban and Spatial Development in Mexico*. Baltimore: Johns Hopkins University Press.

Secretaria de Asentamientos Humanos y Obras Públicas. 1978. *Sonora* (Nogales city map). México.

Secretaria de Desarrollo Urbano y Ecología. 1987. *Plan de Desarrollo Urbano, Nogales*. Gobierno del Estado de Sonora.

Seligson, Mitchell A., and Edward J. Williams. 1981. *Maquiladoras and Migration Workers in the Mexico–United States Border Industrialization Program*. Austin: Mexico–United States Border Research Program, University of Texas.

Shanks, Ann. 1985. *Laredo Reflections*. Laredo, TX: Velia E. Uribe.

Sherrill, David E. 1975. Migration to Colonia Buena Vista. Unpublished M.A. thesis, San Diego State University.

Sierra, Carlos J., and Rogelio Martinez Vera. 1973. *Historia y Legislación Aduanera de México*. México: Dirección General de Prensa, Memoria, Bibliotecas y Publicaciones.

Sklair, Leslie. 1989. *Assembling for Development: The Maquila Industry in Mexico and the United States*. Boston: Unwin Hyman.

Slater, Glenn E. (ed.). 1989. *Let's Go: The Budget Guide to Mexico 1989*. New York: St. Martin's Press.

Socolow, Susan Migden, and Lyman L. Johnson. 1981. Urbanization in Colonial Latin America. *Journal of Urban History* 8: 27–59.

Sonnichsen, C. L. 1980. *Pass of the North: Four Centuries on the Rio Grande*. Vol. II—*1918–1980*. El Paso: Texas Western Press.

South, Robert B. 1990. Transnational "Maquiladora" Location. *Annals of the Association of American Geographers* 80: 549–570.

Spreiregen, Paul D. 1965. *Urban Design: The Architecture of Towns and Cities*. New York: McGraw-Hill.

Stanislawski, Dan. 1947. Early Spanish Town Planning in the New World. *Geographical Review* 37: 94–105.

———. 1950. *The Anatomy of Eleven Towns in Michoacán*. Institute of Latin American Studies 10. Austin: University of Texas Press.

Starr County Industrial Foundation. 1990. *Twin Plants Located Across Starr County, Texas*.

Stea, David, and Denis Wood. 1971. *A Cognitive Atlas: Explorations Into the Psychological Geography of Four Mexican Cities*. Chicago: Environmental Research Group.

Steely, Jim. 1986. Roma: Poetry in Brick and Stone. *Texas Highways* (February): 2–9.

Stevenson, Robert J. 1975. La Zona in Transition: Bordertown Prostitution in Frontier City, Mexico. Unpublished M.A. thesis, State University of New York, Stony Brook.

Stilgoe, John R. 1983. *Metropolitan Corridor: Railroads and the American Scene.* New Haven: Yale University Press.

Stoddard, Ellwyn R. 1975/1976. The Status of Borderlands Studies: An Introduction. *Social Science Journal* 12/13: 3–8.

―――. 1987. *Maquila: Assembly Plants in Northern Mexico.* El Paso: Texas Western Press.

Stoddard, Ellwyn R., Richard L. Nostrand, and Jonathan P. West (eds.). 1983. *Borderlands Sourcebook: A Guide to the Literature on Northern Mexico and the American Southwest.* Norman: University of Oklahoma Press.

Stone, Robert C. 1963. Ambos Nogales: Bicultural Urbanism in a Developing Region. *Arizona Review* 12: 1–29.

Summers, J. N. 1974. *Tijuana.* Ramona, CA: Ballena Press.

Symanski, Richard. 1981. *The Immoral Landscape: Female Prostitution in Western Societies.* Toronto: Butterworths.

Takagi, Hideki. 1970. The Plaza and Its Function in a Mexican Highland Community: Tepeojuma. *Chirigaku Hyoron* 43: 22–31.

Tamayo, Jesús, and José Luis Fernández. 1983. *Zonas Fronterizas (México–Estados Unidos).* México: Centro de Investigación y Docencia Económicas, A.C.

Terry, T. Philip. 1935. *Terry's Guide to Mexico.* Boston: Houghton Mifflin Company.

Thompson, Jerry. 1986. *Laredo: A Pictorial History.* Norfolk, VA: Donning Company.

Timmons, W. H. 1990. *El Paso: A Borderlands History.* El Paso: Texas Western Press.

Trabis, Roland. 1985. *Industrie et Politique à la Frontière Mexique–U.S.A.: le Cas de Nuevo Laredo 1966–1984.* Paris: Centre National de la Recherche Scientifique.

Tuan, Yi-Fu. 1979. *Landscapes of Fear.* New York: Pantheon Books.

Twin Plant News. 1990. Monthly Scoreboard. November: 84–85.

Ugalde, Antonio. 1974. *The Urbanization Process of a Poor Mexican Neighborhood.* Austin: Institute of Latin American Studies, University of Texas.

Unikel, Luis. 1976. *El Desarrollo Urbano de México: Diagnóstico e Implicaciones Futuras.* México: El Colegio de México.

U.S. Department of Justice. 1988. *1987 Statistical Yearbook of the Immigration and Naturalization Service.* Washington, DC: U.S. Government Printing Office.

Valencia, Nestor A. 1969. Twentieth Century Urbanization in Latin America and a Case Study of Ciudad Juárez. Unpublished M.A. thesis, University of Texas at El Paso.

Valk, Barbara G. 1988. *BorderLine: A Bibliography of the United States–Mexico Borderlands*. Los Angeles: UCLA Latin American Center Publications.

Vance, James E., Jr. 1990. *The Continuing City: Urban Morphology in Western Civilization*. Baltimore: Johns Hopkins University Press.

Vandiver, Frank E. 1977. *Black Jack: The Life and Times of John J. Pershing*. 2 vols. College Station: Texas A&M University Press.

Venturi, Robert, Denise Scott Brown, and Steven Izenour. 1977. *Learning from Las Vegas: The Forgotten Symbolism of Architectural Form*. Cambridge, MA: MIT Press.

Verdugo Fimbres, Maria Isabel. 1983. *Frontera en el Desierto: Historia de San Luis Río Colorado*. Hermosillo: INAH-SEP, Centro Regional de Noroeste.

Villarreal Peña, Ismael. 1986. *Seis Villas del Norte*. Ciudad Victoria, Tamaulipas: Instituto de Investigaciones Históricas, Universidad Autónoma de Tamaulipas.

Violich, Francis. 1944. *Cities in Latin America*. New York: Reinhold Publishing Company.

———. 1987. *Urban Planning for Latin America: The Challenge of Metropolitan Growth*. Boston: Oelgeschlager, Gunn, and Hain Publishers.

Wall Street Journal. 1987a. For the Cartoneros, Cycling and Recycling Add Up to a Living. March 10: 1, 18.

———. 1987b. Japanese Companies Increase Presence Near Mexico Border. December 22: 21.

———. 1988. Tijuana Loses Its Ill Repute While Acapulco Gains Penny-Pinching Tourists. October 13: 1.

———. 1990. Mexico's Ugly Duckling—the Maquiladora. October 4: A20.

Ward, David. 1971. *Cities and Immigrants: A Geography of Change in Nineteenth Century America*. New York: Oxford University Press.

Ward, Peter M. 1976. The Squatter Settlement as Slum or Housing Solution: Evidence from Mexico City. *Land Economics* 52: 330–346.

Washington Post. 1990. The Assembly Lines South of the Border: 'Maquiladoras' Thrive on Cheap Labor. July 31: C1, C4.

Webb, Michael. 1990. *The City Square: A Historical Evolution*. New York: Whitney Library of Design.

Weddle, Robert S. 1968. *San Juan Bautista: Gateway to Spanish Texas*. Austin: University of Texas Press.

Weisman, Alan. 1986. *La Frontera: The United States Border with Mexico*. San Diego: Harcourt Brace Jovanovich.

West, John O., and Roberto Gonzalez. 1979. Adobe: Earth, Straw, and Water. In *Built in Texas*, Francis Edward Abernethy (ed.), 60–72. Waco: E-Heart Press.

West, Richard. 1973. Border Towns: What to Do and Where to Do It. *Texas Monthly* 1 (December): 62–73, 109.

West, Robert C. 1974. The Flat-roofed Folk Dwelling in Rural Mexico. In *Man and Cultural Heritage, Papers in Honor of Fred B. Kniffen*, H. J. Walker and W. G. Haag (eds.), 111–132. *Geoscience and Man* 5. Baton Rouge: Louisiana State University.

Whitehead, Don. 1963. *Border Guard: The Story of the United States Customs Service*. New York: McGraw-Hill Book Company.

Wilkie, Richard W. 1973. Urban Growth and the Transformation of the Settlement Landscape of Mexico, 1910–1970. In *Contemporary Mexico: Papers of the IV International Congress of Mexican History*, James W. Wilkie, Michael C. Meyer, and Edna Monzón de Wilkie (eds.), 99–134. Berkeley and Los Angeles: University of California Press.

———. 1984. *Latin American Population and Urbanization Analysis: Maps and Statistics, 1950–1982*. Los Angeles: UCLA Latin American Center Publications.

Wilkinson, J. B. 1975. *Laredo and the Rio Grande Frontier*. Austin: Jenkins Publishing.

Wooldridge, Ruby A., and Robert B. Vezzetti. 1982. *Brownsville: A Pictorial History*. Norfolk, VA: Donning Company.

Work Projects Administration, State of Texas. 1986. *Texas: A Guide to the Lone Star State*. American Guide Series. Austin: Texas Monthly Press [originally published 1940].

Work Projects Administration, Writer's Program. 1940. *Arizona: A Guide to the Youngest State*. New York: Hastings House.

Young, Gay (ed.). 1986. *The Social Ecology and Economic Development of Ciudad Juárez*. Boulder, CO: Westview Press.

Yujnovsky, Oscar. 1975. Urban Structure in Latin America. In *Urbanization in Latin America: Approaches and Issues*, Jorge E. Hardoy (ed.), 191–219. Garden City, NY: Anchor Books.

Zelinsky, Wilbur. 1973. *The Cultural Geography of the United States*. Englewood Cliffs, NJ: Prentice-Hall.

Zonn, Leo E. 1978. The Railroads of Sonora and Sinaloa, Mexico: A Historical Geography. *Social Science Journal* 15: 1–15.

Zoomers, E. B. 1986. From Structural Push to Chain Migration: Notes on the Persistence of Migration to Ciudad Juárez, Mexico. *Tijdschrift voor Economische en Social Geografie* 77: 59–67.

Index

Note: References to figures and tables are in italics.

About the Authors

Daniel D. Arreola received the Ph.D. in geography from the University of California at Los Angeles. He has published extensively in leading geographical journals and in book chapters on topics relating to the cultural geography of Mexico and the American Southwest. Born and raised in Los Angeles, California, he has lived and taught in three of the four states that line the U.S.-Mexico border. He is an Associate Professor in the Department of Geography and in the Hispanic Research Center at Arizona State University.

James R. Curtis holds the Ph.D. in geography from the University of California at Los Angeles. He is coauthor of *The Cuban-American Experience* and has contributed numerous articles and book chapters to the scholarly literature on topics dealing with contemporary urban and cultural themes in both Latin America and the United States. He was raised fifteen miles from the border in San Diego, California. He is an Associate Professor in the Department of Geography at Oklahoma State University.